Oxford
Revision
Guides

AS A Level

Through Diagrams

Alan Gardner
Carl Lyon

Great Clarendon Street, Oxford OX2 6DP

Oxford University Press is a department of the
University of Oxford. It furthers the University's objective
of excellence in research, scholarship, and education by
publishing worldwide in

Oxford New York

Auckland Cape Town Dar es Salaam Hong Kong Karachi
Kuala Lumpur Madrid Melbourne Mexico City Nairobi
New Delhi Shanghai Taipei Toronto

With offices in

Argentina Austria Brazil Chile Czech Republic France Greece
Guatemala Hungary Italy Japan Poland Portugal Singapore
South Korea Switzerland Thailand Turkey Ukraine Vietnam

Oxford is a registered trade mark of Oxford University Press
in the UK and in certain other countries

British Library Cataloguing in Publication Data

Data available

ISBN-13: 978-0-19-918093-6

10 9 8 7 6 5 4 3 2 1

Printed in Great Britain by Bell and Bain Ltd, Glasgow

Paper used in the production of this book is a natural, recyclable product made
from wood grown in sustainable forests. The manufacturing process conforms
to the environmental

Acknowledgements

Many thanks to the staff and students at Greenshaw High School for their
help in the production of this book, and to Afsham and my family for their
support and encouragement

Contents

Contents (cont.)

Contents (cont.)

Relation of contents to current examination specifications

This book has been designed to cover the most of the elements from the AQA, OCR and WJEC specifications which were launched in September 2008. There is also some commonality with the Edexcel specification, although this is not referenced below.

The page and question references below are designed to help structure revision. The topic pages will, however, only make sense within a general framework of knowledge and understanding. In other words, the knowledge gained from the study of one topic will feed into the understanding of other topics. It is best to use this book as just one more resource to help you develop a broad and general understanding of Information and Communication Technology.

Finally, a note of caution: Information and Communication Technology is a field where accelerated change is the norm. By the time this book is published, new developments will have occurred. It is therefore necessary to ensure that you stay current with developments in this area if you are to be wholly successful in its study.

AQA Syllabus
AS INFO1 – Practical Problem Solving in the Digital World

Unit reference	Topic	See pages	Practice questions
1.1	Health and safety in relation to the use of ICT systems	4	94
1.2	Analysis	68–69	133–134
1.3	Design of solutions	42–49, 72	135
1.4	Selection and use of input devices and input media	22–23	14, 22, 26
1.5	Selection and use of storage requirements, media and devices	18, 27	23, 25, 30
1.6	Selection and use of output methods, media and devices	24–26	27–29
1.7	Selection and use of appropriate software	29–45	24, 33–34, 38–46, 48–55, 57, 86
1.8	Implementation of ICT-related solutions	73	136
1.9	Testing of ICT-related solutions	74	138, 145
1.10	Evaluation of ICT-related solutions	75–76	137–138

AS INFO2 – Living in the Digital World

Unit reference	Topic	See pages	Practice questions
2.1	An ICT system and its components	1	1, 2
2.2	Data and information	7–8, 11–15	8–11, 13, 15–16, 56
2.3	People and ICT systems	53, 65–66	61, 75, 87–88, 143–144
2.4	Transfer of data in ICT systems	95, 102, 105–114	64, 67, 69, 70, 72–74, 79–82
2.5	Safety and security of data in ICT systems	54, 87, 134–135, 139	17–18, 62, 71, 101, 106, 130
2.6	Backup and recovery	127–128, 137–138	102–103, 107–109, 111
2.7	What ICT can provide	20–21, 79–85	19–21, 78, 90–93
2.8	Factors affecting the use of ICT	28, 109	4–7
2.9	The consequences of the use of ICT	86–88, 115–118	76, 96–100, 104–105

AS INFO3 – The Use of ICT in the Digital World

Unit reference	Topic	See pages	Practice questions
3.1	Future developments	64, 145–148	47, 85
3.2	Information and systems	5–6, 16–19	3, 12, 15–16, 122
3.3	Managing ICT	77–78, 119	3, 115, 121, 227
3.4	ICT strategy	50, 129, 136	58–59, 110, 117
3.5	ICT policies	125–126, 131–133	89
3.6	Legislation	89–94	95, 112–114
3.7	Developing ICT solutions	13, 56–63, 71	35–37, 81–82
3.8	Developing methods	46–49, 70	146–147
3.9	Techniques and tools for systems development	67, 70, 106–107	72, 132, 134
3.10	Introducing large ICT systems into organisations	51–52, 55,	58–60, 63, 139–142

OCR Syllabus
AS 3.1 Information, systems and applications

Unit reference	Topic	See pages	Practice questions
3.1.1	Information, knowledge and processing	1, 7–12, 14, 15, 19–20, 27–28, 127–128	1, 8–11, 13, 15–21, 25, 107–109
3.1.2	Software and hardware components of an information system	22–28, 59–63	14, 22, 25–30
3.1.3	Characteristics of standard application software and application areas	19–20, 29–45	2, 24, 33, 34, 38–45, 50–52, 86
3.1.4	Spreadsheet concepts	33–34	40, 46
3.1.5	Relational database concepts	39–49	53–55, 57
3.1.6	Application software used for presentation and communication of data	19–20, 31–32, 35–36, 38	2, 24, 48, 49
3.1.7	The role and impact of ICT	4, 9, 79–101, 105–107, 145–148	4–7, 147, 64–74, 78, 90–94, 98–100, 106, 112, 114

AS 3.3 System, Applications and Implications

Unit reference	Topic	See pages	Practice questions
3.3.1	The system cycle	39–49, 56–58, 67–76	53–55, 57, 132, 133–138, 145
3.3.2	Designing computer-based information systems	59–63	83, 84, 122
3.3.3	Networks and communications	95–114	64–74
3.3.4	Applications of ICT	2, 3, 7, 9, 16, 17, 54–55, 76–78, 115–118, 141–144	3, 12, 62, 63, 76, 96, 97, 104, 105, 121, 127, 137, 139–142
3.3.5	Implementing computer-based systems	56–58, 75–76 125	35–37, 131, 137
3.3.6	Implications of ICT	77–78, 106–107, 115–118, 129–133, 139, 140, 145–148	76, 117, 127–130

WJEC Syllabus
AS 4.1 Information systems

Unit reference	Topic	See pages	Practice questions
4.1.1	Data, information and knowledge	7, 8, 10	1, 8–11, 17, 18, 56
4.1.2	The value and importance of information	14	15, 16
4.1.3	Quality of Information	11, 12, 15–17	12, 13, 16
4.1.4	Validation and Verification	20–21	19–21
4.1.5	Capabilities and limitations of ICT	1–3, 29	22, 50
4.1.6	Uses of ICT	18, 22–28, 85, 145–147	4–7, 14, 22–30, 47–52
4.1.7	Presenting Information	13, 19, 20, 30–32, 35–38	13, 24, 33, 34, 38, 39, 41–45, 48–52, 86
4.1.8	Networks	95–102, 105	64–67, 69, 70, 74
4.1.9	Human Computer Interface (HCI)	59–64	83–85
4.1.10	Social Issues	86, 89–94, 115–118	76, 95–100, 104, 105, 112–114
4.1.11	Database systems	39–49	53–55, 57
4.1.12	Modelling	33–34	40, 46

AS 4.3 Use and impact of ICT

Unit reference	Topic	See pages	Practice questions
4.3.1	Networks	95–102, 105	64–67, 69, 70, 74
4.3.2	The Internet	108–114	72, 75, 77, 77–82
4.3.3	Human Computer Interface (HIC)	59–65	83–85
4.3.4	Working with ICT	65–66, 131	87–89, 94
4.3.5	ICT Security Policies	9, 54, 87, 127–128, 132–139	62, 71, 101–103, 106, 107–111
4.3.6	Database systems	50, 53, 55, 103–105	58, 61, 63, 68
4.3.7	Management of change	126, 129, 140	128–130
4.3.8	Management of Information systems	78, 106, 119, 126, 130	115, 116, 118, 127
4.3.9	System Development Life Cycle	56–58, 67–78, 141, 144	35–37, 121, 132–138, 139–142, 145

What is Information Communication Technology?

Information Communication Technology (ICT) is the necessary element required to power information systems. ICT is used to generate, store, organise, process, share and transmit information using electronic devices specifically designed to handle digital data – more commonly known as hardware and software devices. Over the past fifteen years, ICT has penetrated and made an impact in just about every possible element of life imaginable. Weather forecasts, news broadcasts, war reports, shopping,

ICT systems

Many traditional systems are being eroded by ICT systems. Prior to advancements in communication technology, time would have been spent manually recording or collecting data, using a range of tools to transform the collected data into something useful before communicating the findings. This process has been greatly enhanced by the introduction of IT systems which generally perform the same tasks but much faster and to a higher degree of accuracy, and which can be presented in many different formats.

Reporting a missing product from a large delivery at a supermarket would have required filling out forms at the delivery point, detailed checking of incoming stock by staff, taking forms to another person for logging, a phone call to the supplier, further paper work to claim for the missing products and then sending a new order form to apply for the products a second time. All very time consuming! An Information Technology (IT) system would utilise fast data capture methods to check in-coming stock, compare it against what is expected and automatically recognise whether the order has been fulfilled correctly. The system could be programmed to automatically raise the required documentation and re-order the missing products directly from the supplier. This greatly reduces the physical checking by humans, and is far more accurate and efficient in terms of time spent dealing with the whole process of receiving deliveries. The final output could be a computer-generated report which details what was delivered, what is missing and what has been re-ordered. This reduction of detailed information to facts is another key attribute of ICT systems.

A system requires the elements shown in the diagram below to be considered an IT system.

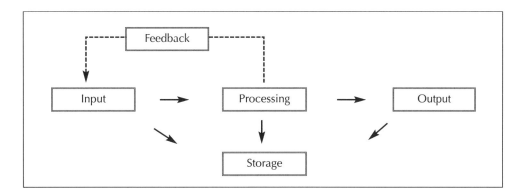

Input

This is the part in the system where data is fed into a computer. This can be done in a number of ways, from the use of the humble keyboard to optical mark readers which read data at high speed.

Processing

At this stage, data is organised into a form required by the user. Types of processing include sorting a list into alphabetical order, changing the colour or size of an image, or comparing input data and responding to it. By reacting to an input a system is said to be reliant on feedback which in turn could affect the next input. For example, a stock list drops by one product. This tells the system (provides input) that one more product is required in the next order.

Output

After processing, users usually want see or hear the results. This can take the form of a word-processed report detailing the requirements of fabrics likely to be used during the next set of fashion shows, an advertisement or a new music track.

Storage

Once information is produced, displayed and altered, it is often desirable to keep a copy. At this stage, the IT system provides the users with the opportunity to store and archive past digital endeavours so that they can be recalled at a later date, used again or altered for another purpose. Storing data should be a regular event to minimise the risk of it being lost.

Capabilities and limitations of computer-based systems

Capabilities

Benefit	Explanation	Application
The facility to undertake repetitive processes	Not only can computers perform some tasks more quickly and more precisely than humans, they can also repeat their operations without becoming 'tired' or 'bored'. This makes them ideal for performing tasks that need to be endlessly repeated.	• Querying a database entails repetitive checking of individual records in order to find a match between the search criteria and the content of the records. This iterative procedure is something that a computer will do much more efficiently than a human.
Increased speed of data processing	The microprocessors found in today's computers can perform thousands of millions of logical operations every second. Many processes that once would have been completed by humans can now be reduced to a series of logical operations and completed in a fraction of the time. The desire to increase speed of processing comes as a result of the increase in code found in newer versions of software.	• The chess-playing computer Deep Blue was able to play – and beat – the world champion because of its ability to process the several million possible move combinations in a very short time. The same principle also applies in flight simulators, which are designed to react to the pilot's actions and then produce different views and scenarios within a split second, every split second.
Increased data storage capacity	As the technology for storing data in digital form has steadily improved, more data can now be stored on media of ever-decreasing size and cost. The first hard drive consisted of fifty 24 inch disks, weighed several tons, and could hold 5Mb of data. The latest IBM hard drive is one inch in diameter and can store 340Mb of data. There are devices which can hold several feature films and fit comfortably in your pocket available to buy for only a few pounds.	• Home users are able to produce films, store music collections and capture digital images with greater ease than ever before. With the opportunity to digitally collect so much data it is no longer just the commercial sector that requires extra storage space.
The facility to locate instances of stored data	One of the prime functions of databases is to facilitate searches for specific pieces of information. Because a search is, in essence, a series of logical steps, this can be performed by the computer very quickly.	• The police use sophisticated in-car data capture methods to read number plates on travelling cars. Any number plates found to match that of one which is not insured or is logged as being wanted by the police will be challenged after the system has alerted the waiting police.
The facility to combine data from different sources	Data such as sound, still and moving images and text are frequently combined to provide alternative outputs. By combining data from different sources new information is formed.	• An obvious use for this can be seen in TV commercials, which often include animations, music, voices and human actors all brought together in one motion picture. Traditional methods of producing reports with images, graphs and text will continue to be prevalent.
The facility to manipulate and transform data	When data is stored in digital format it can be reordered quickly and effectively. This can take place at a simple level, e.g. the editing and formatting facilities of a word-processing application, or at a more complex level, e.g. editing and adding special effects to video files.	• In medicine, scanners such as MRI devices collect data as a series of values representing different magnetic reflections. This data is then transformed into a visual image that can be easily read by a doctor.
Increased accuracy	Computers can perform a variety of processes more consistently and with greater precision and accuracy than humans. This facility, however, is dependent on correctly written programs and accurately inputted data.	• Data logging equipment can be placed in hostile conditions where it is often not safe for humans to work. In such situations the results collected are often precise and can be used to contribute to forecasts and establishing patterns.
Increased speed of data communication	The Internet and all associated developments in communications have been made possible by computer technology. Digital processing enables not just voice but text and images to be communicated with increasing speed and across vast distances.	• The Internet has provided a gateway to millions who use it to talk freely in real time. Voice-over Internet Protocol (VOIP) is simple software which can be downloaded on to most standard laptops or PCs and enables users across the world to talk to each other for no cost. The software tells the user when other users are online and even allows for multiple callers to conference at the same time.

Limitations

Hardware The speed at which a system can perform tasks will depend on its various hardware components – especially those connected with the Central Processing Unit and the computer's primary memory. As the code in the software grows more complex and abundant it places greater memory demands on a system's resources. If the memory and processing components are insufficient, the software will not run as it should.

Software Software – whether it is systems software or application software – is of variable quality. Some software packages can be 'bug-ridden' (i.e. be insufficiently tested and therefore liable to throw up errors) and cause problems; some can be badly designed and inappropriate for the needs of the organisation; and some perfectly good software can become outdated as an organisation's needs change.

Communications Most computer systems are part of a network. The quality of the networking media will affect how quickly and securely data is transmitted. This effect is multiplied when the network is spread across a wide area and/or is based on existing telecommunications media (e.g. the Internet). This is especially the case when memory-heavy files (e.g. video files) need to be transmitted.

Input A computer system is only as good as the data and instructions that are put into it. Although computers have the facility to complete certain tasks at incredible speed, they are still confined to what human operators tell them to do. Also, while they are capable of processing data quickly and accurately, if the initial data is inputted incorrectly, the output will be correspondingly erroneous.

Inflexibility Computers perform certain tasks far more quickly and accurately than humans could ever do, e.g. millions of mathematical calculations in a second. They cannot, however, respond imaginatively and intuitively to a situation as humans can. Nor can they adjust their processes when there is an environmental change they have not been programmed to expect.

Why systems fail

Examples

There have been a number of well-publicised examples of ICT systems failing spectacularly and creating acute problems for the organisation and its clients. For example:

- The system used by the Child Benefit Agency in the UK is a classic example of a system which failed dramatically. It was supposed to keep track of absent fathers and instruct them on what they were to pay for the upkeep of their children. The system could not cope with the thousands of unexpected variables and was eventually scrapped. The original specification was not well thought through and inadequate analysis resulted in the collapse of a hugely unpopular system at the cost of many millions of pounds.
- In 1999 the UK Passport Agency had severe problems processing passport applications. At one stage there were 565 000 applications awaiting processing. A National Audit Office report on this matter concluded that the implementation of a new but inadequately tested computer system was a key causative factor. The cost to the UK taxpayer was £12.6 million.

Causes

Small-scale system failures can be the result of a single problem, e.g. a network crash. Significant system failures result from the combined effects of a number of interdependent causes. The diagram below sets out some of the key factors in system failure:

The nature of computer software

Software design is 'non-linear'. This means that a minor error in a line of code can have a disproportionate effect. A minor typographical error – a misplaced decimal point for example – can affect the way that the whole program behaves. Indeed, the effect of the error grows exponentially as it interacts with the rest of the system. The interdependency of computer systems means that this error can then spread in a viral manner into other systems.

Commercial/political pressures

Organisations can find themselves under pressure to implement a new system more quickly than is advisable. This pressure can be commercial, e.g. the threat of a competitor gaining a market advantage; or political, e.g. to fulfil a promised policy initiative. This pressure can force the pace of system implementation and lead to corners being cut at one or more of the critical stages, i.e. system design, compatibility assessment, testing, etc.

Changes in circumstances during development

Complex systems can take a significant amount of time to develop. Changes that affect the organisation will also be taking place during this period. These changes may be technological (e.g. voice recognition and touch screen control), commercial (e.g. the collapse of certain markets), legislative (new laws to conform to), etc. It is difficult for the system to keep assimilating these changes when it was originally designed without them in mind.

Insufficient testing

Commercial pressure and the sheer quantity of code to be checked often means that systems are pushed onto the market before they have been properly or fully tested. Errors are later found by customers using the software in real conditions. The result on the supplier's reputation will be damaging, not to mention the consequences of the faulty outputs which may have been produced.

SYSTEM FAILURE

Compatibility issues

New systems often have to interact with older (legacy) systems. In some instances inadequate consideration has been given to the compatibility of these two systems. Compatibility problems can occur when a new system has to interact with a system which has been created by a different software provider. A new system can also be incompatible with operating system software. All of these compatibility problems can cause a system to fail.

Lack of user involvement during analysis

There are two problems that may occur here. If, during the analysis/design stage, the developers do not take sufficient account of the needs of the final users, those users are less likely to use the system efficiently. Mistakes are then more likely to occur. This is also the case if users are inadequately prepared for the implementation of the new system. They must therefore be trained sufficiently in its correct use.

Costing issues

When an organisation decides that it needs a new system, it will calculate the likely cost of it. However, during the period of development costs can escalate and, at the same time, the funds that the organisation has available may decline. An example of this is the rise in fuel prices. The simple act of travelling to and from work can have major cost implications for the employees of a firm which may get passed on to the organisation in the form of demands for higher salaries. The organisation then has to choose whether to abandon the project or cut costs in some areas. Cost-cutting can lead to inadequate development of key aspects of the system. This can lead to system failure.

Hardware issues

New software often includes more code. To run this code successfully, or as the user demands, the hardware must be able to process it as expected. Faster processors are released on a regular cycle and it is hardly surprising that developers write software to be run by the latest hardware. Some hardware might only be a few years old but lack the power to incorporate the new system or facilitate the new peripherals which may also be required to work alongside new systems.

User skill level

Failing to ensure that the intended users for a new system are fully prepared to use it is a common mistake. Some organisations take it for granted that staff will be able to learn and use new software with ease or little intervention despite the millions of people who do not use computers systems beyond that of a basic word processor. Users of a system who continuously use it in the wrong way make transferring data difficult at a later date when what they have produced needs to be combined with a that of a user who has undertaken the same task but in a different way. Not only does the equipment need to be compatible but so to does the skill level of those using it.

Eyestrain

Staring continuously at a brightly lit screen all day can lead to eyestrain, the symptoms of which include headaches, blurred vision, dry and irritated eyes. The effects of this are temporary and there is no evidence that computer use causes irreparable damage. None the less, eye strain can cause discomfort and make employees less efficient. It is therefore in an employer's best interests to ensure that working spaces are properly lit and display screens correctly adjusted.

Dependency

The increasing sophistication of communications technology (remote access, the Internet, wireless transmission) has meant that people working with computers can do so from any location and at any time. The consequence of this, combined with the 'addictive' nature of some computer-based work, means that some people find it difficult to 'switch off', continuing their work while they commute and when they are at home. This inability to 'switch off' can lead to stress-related illnesses and other conditions associated with a lack of rest and relaxation.

Stress

There is increasing evidence that working extensively in a computer-based environment can be stressful. While it was originally thought that computers would lighten people's workload, in many instances they have added to it. Computers have raised expectations about what is possible in the workplace and thus increased the demand placed on employees. In some workplaces, e.g. call centres, these expectations are made explicit, i.e. through continuous monitoring and logging of user interactions. Computers, however, remain fallible, breaking down at inopportune moments, 'losing' important documents, refusing to respond as expected, etc. The combination of increased demand and continued fallibility creates the conditions for stress, a psychological condition with physical symptoms.

Repetitive Strain Injury

Repetitive Strain Injury (RSI) refers to a range of conditions affecting the neck, shoulders, arms and hands. RSIs result from forcing particular muscle groups to perform the same actions over and over again, e.g. working at a keyboard all day long. The most common type of computer-related RSI is Carpal Tunnel Syndrome. This is where the nerve that runs through the wrist is affected by the constant pressure of typing. Initially, this leads to wrist pain and numbness in the fingers. In extreme cases, the injury can make it impossible for the sufferer to pick up everyday objects.

ELF radiation

There is some debate about whether ICT workers are at risk from the effects of 'extremely low frequency radiation'. VDUs based on cathode ray tube technology emit non-ionizing electric and magnetic fields at low frequency. Whether or not these emissions have an effect on those exposed to them, is open to debate. There is research that suggests that long-term exposure may be hazardous to the health (especially of pregnant women), but the evidence is far from conclusive and most experts in this field do not believe the danger is significant.

Types of processing

Batch and interactive processing

Many systems are designed to process transactions. The term 'transaction' covers a broad spectrum of events from the borrowing of a library book to the purchase of a house. In general, however, it refers to an event where there is an exchange of goods/services/money between different parties. There are, broadly speaking, two distinct approaches to transaction processing: batch processing and interactive processing.

	BATCH PROCESSING	INTERACTIVE PROCESSING
DEFINITION	• Batch processing involves collecting groups of transactions over a set period of time and processing them all at the same time. The information associated with the transactions may be collected on paper (e.g. invoices) or inputted directly into a computer (e.g. ATM cash withdrawals). • The process that then follows will depend on whether the information is held on paper copy or as computer files. If the 'batch' to be processed is a set of computerised transactions, an automated process will run. This process will use the data held in the transaction file to update information held in various master files. For example, a business may complete a number of computerised transactions during any one day. These transactions are held in a transaction file. During an overnight process, the master files (e.g. clients' accounts) are updated to take into account the day's transactions. • A paper-based version involves some additional stages. For example, a set of invoices would be sorted into batches of 50, control totals calculated for validation purposes and all information relating to the batch written on a batch header form. The information on the sheets would then be keyed in and then validated and corrected where necessary. The inputted information would then be held in a transaction file. This would then be used to update master files.	• This approach is sometimes referred to as 'online transaction processing'. The basic principle behind this approach is that as transactions take place, all associated files are updated. • For example, when a customer makes a booking with an airline the details are entered via a computer screen by an agent. The bookings file is then updated so that double bookings cannot be made. It would clearly be inappropriate to use a batch process for this form of transaction. • Other businesses use the phone to take orders. The agent taking the order speaks to the customer on the phone and takes the details of his order. She has a computer screen in front of her and fills the details in as the customer speaks. The appropriate files are updated immediately. An invoice, delivery order or any similar report can be produced immediately and will be based on up-to-date data. • A distinction may be drawn between systems that are 'real-time' and 'pseudo real-time'. Real-time systems react immediately to changes – an example would be the fly-by-wire system of an aeroplane – whereas pseudo real-time systems seem to react instantly, but there may be a slight delay between the transaction taking place and the updating of files.
ADVANTAGES	• Batch processing is still used in a number of different contexts, e.g. processing wage slips, customer order forms, etc. • It is especially useful for situations where there are predictable blocks of information that need inputting but where there is not an urgent need to update files immediately. • It can make economical use of computer resources by running at a time when other usage is minimal, e.g. overnight, at weekends.	• Online processing is increasingly used for a variety of transaction processing. This has been made possible by the increased processing power of computers and the growing sophistication of communication technology. • Online processing means that files are always up to date and paperwork is kept to a minimum. • These systems are more flexible and responsive to users' needs than are batch-processing systems.
DISADVANTAGES	• The system is not particularly flexible nor responsive to *ad hoc* needs. • Data is not always up to date and, though batch processing is usually completed on data that does not need to be kept absolutely up to date, errors can still occur.	• Online systems require a more complex infrastructure. This means increased capital investment and maintenance costs, as well as reliance on a system that might fail. • Audit trail, and other security checks, are more difficult to perform because updating is happening constantly rather than at set intervals.

Real time processing

This is similar to interactive processing, although it is more reliant on input being entered into the system by sensors, for example, the height, weight and speed of a fighter plane is calculated automatically by readings taken by the sensors and displayed in the cockpit. Small adjustments by the pilot flying the plane are rapidly carried out and new speeds and heights are displayed. In critical time reliant situations it would be inappropriate for the pilot to have to push a submit button each time to make a decision like turning left to avoid an incoming missile. It is the almost immediate reacting to changes which distinguishes between interactive and real time processing. Some would argue that computer processing is so fast now that this distinction is no longer valid.

Data-processing systems

Data-processing systems

- Data-processing systems – also known as transaction processing systems – are designed to deal with the day-to-day processing needs of an organisation, e.g. the sales of goods in a supermarket via Electronic Point of Sale terminals.
- Typically these processing needs will include: payrolls, invoices, stock control and order entry. Data processing involves carrying out routine and repetitive tasks, accurately and at speed. Computers have the ability to complete tasks of this kind much more efficiently than humans do and many of the early computer systems were designed to perform these labour-intensive business tasks.
- Although routine, this type of processing is critical for a large number of businesses, firstly because without automated procedures these necessary tasks would take up many person-hours, and secondly because the data produced forms the basis of higher-level information systems (MIS, DSS, etc.).
- Data-processing systems tend to be 'simple', inflexible systems with little room for manipulation by the end user. They require the data to be inputted in a designated format and will only produce a limited range of specified reports.

Example

The example below is based on a car parts firm. They receive orders during the day. Orders can be placed by fax, by telephone or via the firm's website. Fax orders are keyed by data entry clerks, telephone orders are entered using an on-screen form and website customers have their own on-screen form that can be used to enter order details. The transaction processing system validates the inputted data and creates a new order record in the order file, drawing on data held in the customer file and the stock file.

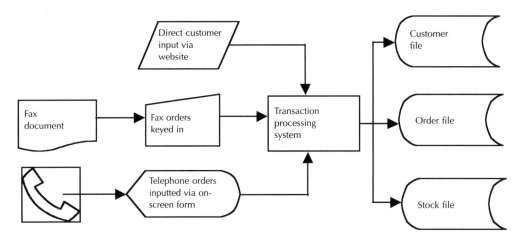

This system can then produce simple operational reports. This will aid the distribution process by providing stock requirements, address labels, customer invoices and, by linking up with a Transport Details file, delivery lists for each of the van drivers.

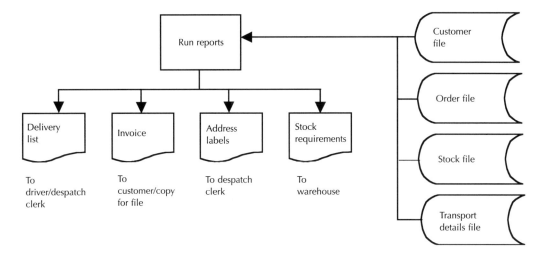

The data held in the various files can now be used by higher-level information systems to produce information for analysis and to aid decision-making.

Data, information and knowledge

DATA	INFORMATION	KNOWLEDGE
Data is merely a character or set of characters with no meaning. It could be a set of letters and numbers combined, but without a label it is difficult to decipher. Data can also take the form of images (moving or still) and sounds. Prior to any processing taking place the data is meaningless and only assumptions can be made as to what they stand for. An examples of data is 9780199150748. By adding to, or organising, this sequence of numbers information is produced.	Information is the result of raw facts and figures being processed. This means data has been fed through a computer system and something meaningful has been output. Information has meaning and makes sense, unlike data. When the example above is recognised by a system and displayed, it transpires that the data is actually an ISBN number for a book. Adding a simple label such as 'ISBN number' before the digits adds meaning. Alternative processing such as multiplying, subtracting from another value, sorting or transferring into a graph, or chart, are other routes of converting meaningless data into information.	Knowledge is knowing what to do with certain known processed facts when they are at the user's disposal. A classic example is the doctor working out treatments to treat various symptoms. By asking questions they are able to eliminate a whole range of medicines known not to be effective until they are left with the most likely best options. Without the prior information about which medicines do what, it would be difficult for the doctor to successfully prescribe the correct medicine. Knowledge is a key factor in aiding decision-making.

The relationship between data, information and knowledge

Information systems collect **data** from various sources, perform processes on it and output it as **information**. This information can then be used by individuals with **knowledge** of the wider context to draw conclusions and make decisions.

For example:

This set of numerical values (i.e. **data**) does not appear to have any meaning:

> 1400,140/80,1500,140/80,1600,120/60

To render the data as information, it must first be given a context. In this instance the context is a medical one. The data represents the blood pressure readings of a hospital patient taken at different times. The patient's doctor wants to know how the patient is doing. Before the data is presented to her as information, it needs to be processed into a recognisable format. In this case it will need to be transformed, sorted and tabulated.

Reading 1: Time: 14.00	Patient's BP = 140/80
Reading 2: Time: 15.00	Patient's BP = 140/80
Reading 3: Time: 16.00	Patient's BP = 120/60

It is now **information** and can be presented to the doctor as a report. The doctor is able to apply her **knowledge** to this information. She has an understanding of the context in which the information appears, i.e. an understanding of the patient's condition and the medical significance of blood pressure readings. She is therefore able to draw conclusions about the patient's state and decide upon an appropriate course of action.

Data, information and knowledge in action

DATA	INFORMATION	KNOWLEDGE
A retail business collects data from Electronic Point of Sale terminals in all its branches. The resulting data consists of sets of values that represent sales of individual products, date and time of sales, branch locations, stock levels, etc. The data is stored in various data files.	The analysts who work for the business wish to ask questions about the data. The data is therefore processed into a form that will be meaningful to them, e.g. a series of charts showing how well each branch has performed relative to its sales targets. The data can now be used purposefully by the analysts. It is now information.	The analysts have developed both a general knowledge of the retail trade and specific knowledge of their own organisation. They can now apply this knowledge to the sales charts in front of them and draw conclusions about the relative performance of each branch. This in turn may help them make decisions, e.g. which branches are due for expansion.

Processed into / Applied to

Types of data

When collected, data is preceded by a question which can be displayed in many formats. The following are the most commonly recognised.

Boolean
Boolean represents the option of selecting one of two values only. Examples include 0 or 1, Yes or No, Male or Female and True or False.

Integer
Integer data displays whole numbers without the option of adding in decimal points. This is suitable for responding to questions such as: 'How many people went to the IT conference?' The answer could be 1440. This makes sense. 1440.0 would also be correct but it would not be necessary to use the decimal point because anything other than zero after the decimal point would not be sensible.

Real
Real data is given as that holding decimal numbers and fractions. Examples include 3.10 and 5.7. The identifier for the data could be a pound sign or other unit of measurement which cannot be shown in this category, but the decimal point does help provide more accuracy than if a simple figure was shown alone.

String
A string is a collection of numbers or letters often used to make up a sentence or other type of data that needs a little more description. A good example of this might be an address or a reference number on a bill. Strings are also able to hold symbols such as £ and @, which would be useful for displaying email addresses or product values.

Date/time
Date of birth and time of delivery, for example, can all be displayed in this format. Many applications allow the user to specify which type of format they want to use, ranging from short versions, such as 27/03/74, to longer versions, such as Thursday, 27th March 1974. Settings between American- and UK-based software need to be checked because occasionally the day and the month are switched around, making the data entered invalid and difficult to verify if the original source document is not present.

Currency
Prices of products, services and other items of monetary value need to be displayed with the correct currency symbol depending on which country is being represented. For example, £, $ and the relatively new € (euro) are all able to purchase the same product, but differing quantities. By specifying the correct symbol suppliers can match the correct quantities for shipping.

Image
Still images show a split second of an event, person, scene or product at a given time. Historians are keen to use images to help construct theories about how something might have been. By adding a date and a location caption this process can be a lot more focused.

Sound
A noise can be any length and can be output at various volumes. Sounds can be used to identify people or convey information about places. Alternatively sound can represent warnings of eminent danger or the signal to start a race.

Without actual context most data is meaningless. By adding labels, dates, times and combining data it becomes more meaningful and useful in terms of providing information and building a knowledge base.

Encryption

What is encryption?

Encryption is the practice of disguising a message so that it cannot be read and understood by any unauthorised persons. It is neither a new practice nor one restricted to the world of ICT. The Roman army used encryption techniques to obscure messages between military commanders, and it has been used throughout time by a variety of people, from merchants who wished to keep their business transactions private, to lovers who wanted their assignations to remain secret. In ICT terms it refers to the deployment of dedicated programs that convert ordinary text (plaintext) into a disguised form (ciphertext) through the use of algorithms (step-by-step instructions for the encryption and decryption of text). The formula that is applied is referred to as the key.

Simple encryption entails substituting one letter for another or transcribing letters so that their relative positions in the overall message are changed. Computer encryption starts with these basic principles but adds additional levels of sophistication. For example, instead of just transforming the letter A into another letter, an encryption program will assign each typographical character a binary value, e.g. 10101011 and then transform each bit (i.e. each 0 or 1) into another value according to a logical formula. The number of bits used in this process is an indication of the level of security offered by the process. Most encryption keys range in size from 56 bits to over 2000 bits.

There are two basic types of keys: symmetric and asymmetric. These are described below.

How encryption works

Symmetric key encryption

The sender inputs a message then applies the encryption program. This uses a key available to the user to transform the plaintext into ciphertext. It is now indecipherable to anybody without the key. The message is now sent.

The recipient also has a copy of the encryption key. When the ciphertext message is received, the encryption key is applied and the message is transformed back to plaintext. Because only the sender and the recipient have a copy of the key, this method is known as 'private key encryption'.

Asymmetric key encryption

The sender encrypts a message using a key that the recipient has sent to all those people who might need to be in communication. This key is not kept secret and so this mode of encryption is referred to as public key encryption. The message is now in ciphertext and can be sent securely.

As well as making her public key available, the recipient has the only copy of a private key. This key is mathematically related to the public key and so is able to decipher text that has been encrypted using this method. This system is generally considered to be the more secure of the two, although the process does take longer.

Encoding and coding

Encoding

Encoding is transferring real world data into a form that can be read and understood by a computer. This is achieved by using input devices which convert hardcopy data into a digital format that can used within a computer system. Scanners, keyboards, cameras and microphones are some of the tools used to achieve this. Once data is encoded it can be processed and manipulated by various software. Images can be cropped and resized, have their contrast adjusted before being electronically transferred elsewhere for further processing. The advantages of working with digital data becomes obvious when tasks previously done manually can be performed quicker and to a higher degree of precision and accuracy.

Coding

Coding data is the simple act of taking a long, often text-based, expression and reducing its character length, for example when the name of a country is entered into a system it is often abbreviated. The United Kingdom becomes UK and The United Arab Emirates becomes UAE. Great care must be taken with coding of data to ensure that no two codes are the same, otherwise it will become confused. To overcome this, each record in a database is identified by a unique reference. By abbreviating data, for example to a couple of letters, data entry speed is greatly increased and there should be fewer errors because fewer key presses are required during data entry.

Value judgements are traditionally difficult to code because they represent opinions. Several people may all agree that karate is the best type of martial art but they may express it differently:

Person	Response	Code
Person 1	Karate is the best martial art for punching techniques	PT
Person 2	Karate is the best for learning self control	LSC
Person 3	Karate is the best for learning self defence	SD
Person 4	Karate is the best for learning rapid attack	RA

All of these responses can be coded, but the more people that are asked, the more variations on the responses there will be, making the coding of the responses almost impossible. Examples such as this demonstrate that care at the design stage of data collection is necessary to avoid making the analysis and processing of data overly difficult and complex. Responses such as M/F for male and female are limiting and fairly obvious. As the number of response options available increases, so too does the problem of analysis, especially if a respondent wants to pick two or three options from a given coded list when they are only supposed to pick one.

When the number of responses is actually known, codes can be assigned. By knowing the number and value of all possible responses, validation within a system can be set up to ensure the data entered is sensible, possible and realistic. Value judgements are difficult to code because the number of responses could be limitless, despite best efforts to cover every eventuality.

Data collection: 1

Different ways in which data may be collected

Data logging devices: e.g. sensors that collect temperature and humidity readings in an art gallery.

Electronic point of sale: e.g. a bar code reader at a supermarket checkout collects data on products sold.

Online: clients/customers send their personal details/order details to an organisation via an online form on a website.

Optical mark readers, e.g. such as those used to scan in the results of examinations.

Optical character readers, e.g. passport application forms.

Manual collection: e.g. a researcher interviews people and records their responses. This data is then keyed into a computer.

Direct/indirect collection of data

Sources of data can be categorised as direct and indirect

Direct   The data is collected to fulfil a specific purpose. For example, when a video store swipes the bar code on a video and links it to the customer who is taking it out, they are collecting data that will inform them of who has taken out what video, when it is due back, whether a fine has been imposed, etc.

Indirect   The data is used to create information that is not directly related to the original purpose of the data collection. For example, the video store data could be used to create customer profiles, e.g. which customers are particularly interested in romantic comedies. This information could be then be used for targeted promotions. Furthermore, because such information has commercial value, it could be sold to another organisation who may use the information for purposes of its own, e.g. a publishing company trying to identify the market for romantic novels. There are some legal restrictions on the use of data for secondary purposes – data subjects have to give their consent to secondary usage – but it is still common commercial practice.

The quality of the data source

The quality of information is dependent on the quality of the data it is derived from. This concept is usefully encapsulated in the phrase 'garbage in – garbage out'. If, for example, when a client fills out their details on a membership form, they make a mistake writing out their address, all subsequent information based on this data will be erroneous. At a very basic level, this will mean that letters are sent to the wrong address. In order to be of value data should be:

- accurate
- up to date
- complete.

There are many reason why this might not be the case:

- If the data has been collected via a data capture form, it might not have been accurately written down. Equally, a correct entry may be inaccurately transcribed by a data entry clerk. Validation routines should pick this up, but these may not be in place.
- An automatic system might have an undetected fault that results in it recording inaccurate data. A sensor, for example, might be logging readings that are erroneous.
- Data might be out of date because changes have not been recorded. If, for example, a person changes address but does not inform their employer, the employer's database will produce information based on non-current data.
- If someone, when filling in an online form, omits a particular piece of data (e.g. a second income), the data will not be complete. This will have a detrimental effect on any information subsequently produced.

Because ICT systems are complex, interdependent and often hide their processes, even minor data inaccuracies can have a catastrophic effect at a later stage. It is therefore important to ensure that the source of the data can be trusted.

Data collection: 2

Desirable features of a data collection system

Data capture refers to a set of procedures whereby raw data is inputted into a computing system prior to being processed. It is a critical phase in any information system. If the data capture is not performed successfully, the quality of the final output will be negatively affected. This principle is summarised in the well-known phrase 'garbage in – garbage out' (GIGO). The following criteria may be used to determine the quality of the data capture system:

Efficient   Capturing data always incurs costs, both financial and in terms of human resources. A successful system will complete the operation in the most cost-effective manner.

Timely   The time taken to complete the data capture, and the intervals at which it is completed, will need to be consistent with the requirement that information systems should deliver their output to the right person at the right time.

Secure   In common with all other phases of an information cycle, the data capture process must ensure that the data it captures is held securely.

Accurate   If the original inputted data is inaccurate, the final output will also be inaccurate. This can lead to managers making business-critical decisions based on false information.

The different stages of data capture

The nature of the original data

The data may be in a variety of formats (text, numerical, verbal, etc.) and may consist of a few items or many thousands of items and may be of variable quality. These factors will all have to be taken into account when undertaking the processes that follow. For example, if the data consists of many items and is in text form, it may be necessary to utilise an OMR/OCR system.

Transcription/translation

Before the data can be inputted it may be necessary to translate it into another format or to transcribe it from one medium into another. For example, verbal responses may need to be transcribed on to an OCR capture form before input. Inevitably the process of transcription/translation has implications for the accuracy of the data. It is a stage in the process where simple errors can occur.

Choice of data capture method

There are a wide range of data capture techniques (bar code scanners, OCR, OMR, magnetic strip, etc.). Each of them have their strengths and weaknesses (see pages 23–4). In choosing a method, one must take into account the nature, volume and quality of the original data. These factors will determine which method is the most efficient in terms of cost and time taken.

Validation

There are several methods of validation that can be performed, either at the point of input or subsequent to it. These are defined by the types of check they perform (e.g. range, length, presence, etc.). Though valuable, validation checks can only determine whether the data is valid, i.e. whether it falls within predefined parameters. They cannot determine whether or not the data is accurate.

Verification

Verification is the process of double-checking the data that has been entered. A standard means of verification is double entry: the data is entered twice and inconsistencies followed up. This method will only identify simple transcription errors. A more time-consuming method involves printing out the inputted data and checking it (or a random sample of it) against the original data source.

Auditing

Audits are systematic checks that ensure the accuracy of organisational data. Their primary purpose is to prevent fraud, but they are also used to determine the effectiveness of a system. The standard approach is to use an 'audit trail' that follows a data sample from its original source to its final output. The process – which is often automated – involves looking for inconsistencies in the data.

Static and dynamic data

Static data is produced and distributed in a state that is not likely to change. Data of this sort is distributed on read-only media such as CD-ROMs. The data is often detailed and informative but can quickly become out of date if it deals with current affairs. This method is best for presenting known facts which cannot change, such as a date of birth or the population of a country at a certain point in history.

Dynamic data is subject to change. For example, a news website will have to be constantly updated as events change. Businesses rely on dynamic data as it endorses a component as being up to date. Details about market trends and prices frequently change, and basing decisions on current data will be more effective than if decisions were taken based on data from several years before. The Internet has made access to dynamic data more available than ever before. Social blogs and commercial websites are just two examples of where data is added to or changed on a regular basis.

Combining data and uses of information

In order to get the most out of any data it is often common for it to be combined with other types. Advertisers and other media-based organisations make huge amounts of money from this practice with the sole aim of getting their information across to consumers in an attractive and understandable format.

When data is combined it is crucial that the resulting information is understood. For example, a travel agent may wish to advertise a new resort in Bulgaria. It is important that good clear images showing the major attractions are selected and display obvious information without the viewer having to guess too much. The use of text with the image is also important. Failing to mention that the image is from a Bulgarian holiday resort could render it useless and lose the customer's interest. If the promotional material was being run through presentation software, sound could be added. Heavy rock music may clash with tranquil pictures and distract from the text, however.

The balance and combination of any data needs sensible planning and research. Often presentations are ruined by including too much text when basic bullet points would have been better. Unclear, cloudy images that have been badly cropped, edited or shot can also reduce the impact of combined data. The volume, tempo and speed of audio can add hugely to the atmosphere provided it has been tested before the final output is released to the consumers.

Recent animations from Hollywood have demonstrated impressive use of combining text, images, moving images and sound to produce films which have captivated the audience and made massive profits as well as generating demand to see more of the characters produced in the digital world. This success is achieved through establishing a clear story line that has been thought through, constructing characters and understanding the needs of the audience. At a simplistic level the same rules apply when combining any data:

- Know what the purpose of combining the data is – what message are you trying to give?
- Collect good quality data from good quality sources.
- Understand what the audience will react to.

Combining data takes place in:
- business documents to convey sales information with text, graphs and charts
- essay's about the war produced by school pupils combine text and images
- estate agents windows that give virtual tours of new properties or estates
- commercial advertisers use cartoons with text over-laid with verbal and musical audio to sell washing up liquid.

Decision-making

After data has been processed and combined it becomes information. There are millions of types of information to be found on the Internet alone. Fundamentally, information is used to aid individuals and organisations in decision-making on a number of different topics at many different levels:

- Senior management use projected and past sales figures to assist with strategic decisions such as whether to go for product diversification, or to close or open new branches or warehouses.
- Consumers use information about products and services to help them decide whether they will buy or use them, or find an alternative.
- Teachers use pupil pass grades and other, sometimes dubious, educational data to help build an academic profile for individual pupils in order to establish realistic and achievable aims and expectations. From this they decide how to tailor support and lessons.
- Teenagers use information to decide which film to watch at the weekend, which MP3 to download and from which site. They use information to construct original essays and make decisions as to what subjects they will study at university or what career path to take after leaving school.

All of the above decisions can easily be taken without any information at all. However, IT should and is exploited to assist with effective decision-making in pursuit of monetary gain, a happier lifestyle, better grades or other personal advantages. The simple act of checking the weather forecast each day provides information from which decisions are taken. If it is raining – stay in bed!

The value of information and data

Good information, i.e. information that is timely, accurate, up-to-date, complete, etc. adds value to organisations in the ways described below:	Producing good quality information incurs costs in terms of money, time and human resources.

To aid decision-making The quality of a decision depends, to a significant degree, on the quality of information that it is based on. Decision-making is an essential feature of the management of an organisation and the more effective the decision-making, the more successful the organisation is likely to be.	**Manpower** If data is collected directly, individuals may have to be paid to produce, send out and collect questionnaires. Companies that want customers to respond to requests for information often have to offer prize incentives (e.g. holidays) to guarantee adequate returns. If the data is collected indirectly, the organisation may have to pay a third party in order to gain access to data in their possession.
To monitor and control Information can help an organisation stay informed about how well it is doing. Information derived from market research and sales figures can help to achieve this. An organisation can also look at the performance of different employees to determine who is the most – or least – effective. This process can help to ensure that the use of resources is cost-effective.	**Data entry** If the data is keyed in, this will take time and operators will have to be paid to do it. There are automated methods of data entry – Optical mark readers (OMR), optical character recognition (OCR), bar code readers, etc. – but they still need to be operated by someone and they need to be purchased in the first place.
To target resources Organisations have limited resources and their efficient use will be a key determinant of success. For example, an organisation should ideally target its advertising and marketing at those customers who are most likely to be interested in its products. Information about customers' buying habits is extremely valuable in this process and can lead to an organisation becoming more profitable.	**Hardware and software** Once the data has been inputted it needs to be processed into information. This requires hardware and software resources. The software may have been purchased 'off-the-shelf' or it may have been a customised development; either way it will have cost money. Large-scale processing can tie up a good deal of an organisation's ICT resources.
To gain competitive advantage Information can tell an organisation how well it is doing in relation to its competitors. Information about, for example, gaps in a particular market can help it take action ahead of its competitors. Identification of strengths and weaknesses will also help to improve its competitive edge.	**Data maintenance** There are costs involved in ensuring data remains accurate and up to date. For example, an organisation might maintain a database of its customers. The database will only remain accurate and up to date if any changes to customers' details are reported and the appropriate records amended. This involves communicating with customers and verifying that their details are correct.

The quality of information

- Organisations and individuals use information to improve the quality of their decision-making. A decision that is made with inadequate or poor-quality information is likely to be a bad decision. This can have negative consequences for the organisation or individual concerned. In some instances these consequences can be disastrous.
- The better the quality of the information, the greater the likelihood of a good decision being made. This is what gives information its value. It can help produce decisions that will add value to the organisation.
- Not all information is of equal value. It is possible to evaluate the quality of information by using the criteria set out below.

The qualities of good information

ACCURATE

Information should be error free and a true reflection of what it represents. Even minor inaccuracies can lead to poor quality decisions being made.

Example A bank keeps records of its customers' accounts. This information must reflect truthfully the transactions that the customer has undertaken. Both the bank and the customer rely on the accuracy of this information to make decisions about future spending plans, loan requests, etc. If there were errors in the information, it might lead to bad decisions being made, e.g. the customer spending money that they don't in fact have.

EXCHANGE

Information should be presented to the people who need it. Giving information to people who have no need of it can contribute to 'information overload'. It can also create confusion and may lead to information that was meant to be confidential being in the wrong hands.

Example A report containing information about possible relocation sites is disseminated throughout an organisation. This creates a climate of anxiety and makes the actual decision-making process more difficult.

SOURCE PRESENTATION

Information should be set out in a clear, accessible format and communicated in a manner that is appropriate for the user. The level of detail included and the language used should reflect the specific needs and expertise of the user.

Example A company's financial managers are investigating the feasibility of a building project. They receive a report from engineers that uses terminology that only other engineers would understand. The decision cannot be made because the relevant information, though present, cannot be understood.

COMPLETE

Information should include all the data which the user needs to make his decision. There should be no significant absences. (Absence of information is just as misleading as inaccurate information.)

Example A company wants to look at its sales performance during a specific period. It therefore needs the figures from all of its branches. If the data relating to the branches in one region was missing, it would lead to the wrong conclusions being drawn. This, in turn, could lead to serious errors in future planning.

Interim report

TIMELY

Information should be made available at the time when it is needed. It must be presented at the appropriate moment in the decision-making process if it is to aid that process.

Example A company is making a decision about where to locate a distribution point. There is relevant information about changes to rail links available. Such information would have to be presented at the right point in the decision-making process. If it were presented too early, its relevance would not be apparent; if it were presented too late, the decision might already have been taken.

RELEVANT

Information should not include data that has no bearing on the user's informational needs. A user receiving more information than they need can lead to 'information overload'. The specific information that the user needs becomes lost amongst data that is not needed.

Example A company manager asks for details of one client's account and receives a report with all clients' details on. The information is not particularly useful to her because she would have to waste time finding the information that was relevant to her needs.

HAS USER CONFIDENCE

Information should have the confidence of the users. If the user believes the underlying data is inaccurate or the original source of the data is not reliable, the information will be useless to them. They won't feel able to make a decision based on such information.

Example A report is presented to an organisation's executive. The underlying data comes from a source which, in the past, has provided inaccurate data. The integrity of the information is questioned by the executive and it is either sent back for verification or else discarded.

UP TO DATE

Information should be accurate at the point when it is presented. It should not be a reflection of an earlier state of affairs.

Example A furniture warehouse stores data on stock levels. Information produced from this data is used to make decisions about re-stocking. Unfortunately this type of data ages quickly, because stock levels can change daily, even hourly. Consequently, the information might be out of date by the time it is presented. This, in turn, might mean that incorrect stock orders are made.

Characteristics of information

Source

When information is generated within an organisation the source is internal. Examples of this type of information are minutes taken at a meeting or a report detailing sales over the past six months. This type of information is used by an organisation to aid its business processes and relates to the current resources and assets held by the organisation. Organisations also rely on external information. This is information that is produced beyond the organisation but still assists with business decision-making. An example of this would be inflation rates published by the government or a price list from a supplier. Internal and external information can be gathered in two ways. The first is known as primary when the information is taken directly from an original source. An example of this is the results of a questionnaire. Alternatively the information could come from a secondary source. This is when the data is gathered from another person, organisation, report or book.

Source			
Internal	External	Primary	Secondary

Nature

Qualitative information is usually presented in text and is opinion based. A large amount of qualitative information can be difficult to analyse quickly using a computer system. Fast analysis of data can be performed on numerical data and this is classified as quantitative. This consists of data presented in numerical form which can be run through a spreadsheet where trends can be identified, and graphs and charts produced to present the findings. Information can be classified as formal and informal. Formal data is that displayed in reports and contracts whilst informal data can result from a simple conversation over the telephone or in the form of a departmental memo.

Nature			
Qualitative	Quantitative	Formal	Informal

Time

Historical information is that which is taken from sources which were produced in the past. For example, company financial reports or a list of previous members of a team. Present data is that which is being used at the current time. For example, price lists detailing what products are being sold for, or a report given in August containing details about a school's most recent exam performance. Future information is based on assumptions on what is likely to happen in the near or distant future. Scientists keenly publish predictions relating to ozone level depletion and what action can be taken to reduce the effects of global warming. Businesses look at what prices are rising and attempt to model future actions based on what the market is telling them.

Time		
Historical	Present	Future

Level

Information is required at several levels within an organisation. The senior management who make the long-term decisions use information at a strategic level. Such information is used to plan for major projects such as future expansion or product development incentives. At a tactical level information is used by middle managers to assist with decisions that enable the business to function over a shorter period of time; usually months or weeks rather than years. Tactical information includes details from staff reviews so that personnel can be organised effectively, or the fuel cost incurred over a period of time so that delivery logistics can be better managed. The final level of information is operational. This information is used on a daily basis by personnel who tend to be involved with physical production or sales in a factory or shop. This could include staff rotas or daily quotas to be fulfilled.

Level		
Strategic	Tactical	Operational

Characteristics of information (continued)

Frequency

Real-time data is that which is constantly updated as circumstances change. For example, the amount of money gained in sales will change each time a new transaction takes place. Scheduled information is provided at a requested time. An example of this is an annual report or a monthly newsletter containing information used for planning purposes. Ad-hoc information is given at the time deemed to be the most relevant. This could be as soon as something new is discovered or as a passing comment when two people meet. The timing of such information is often random and hard to predict, but in a well-managed organisation will be expected.

Frequency		
Real time	Scheduled	Ad-hoc

Use

Information within an organisation is used to plan for future projects, work schedules and other business activities. Without the use of good information an organisation can undertake normal business but is likely to be surpassed by companies that take notice of the information coming from the business community and responding to it. Information is also used to control. This could relate to budgets, staffing requirements or the pace at which an organisation intends to expand. Information relating to who works within an organisation and their skills can all contribute to aspects of control. Decision-making is another important use of information. If an individual or any organisation fails to make decisions, they are likely to find themselves out of business or extremely disadvantaged in a competitive environment.

Use		
Plan	Control	Decision-making

Form

Information can take various output forms and they are not all electronic or digital. Information is best shared between many when it is written. In this form it can be shared globally on websites or in email messages, displayed on notice boards or condensed in reports. The same also applies to visual information, which can be seen, and advances in technology have made aural information, which can be heard, a common using Voice over Internet Protocol (VoIP) and other methods such as Podcasts.

Form		
Written	Visual	Aural

Type

Disaggregated information is information presented with individual data items intact such as a printout of hours worked by each employee in the department. Aggregated information is when only a sample of data is presented in a concise form to make it quicker to read and extract the points that are of particular interest to the reader.

Type	
Disaggregated	Aggregated and sampled

Storing data and file extensions

When data is saved the file extension indicates what software has been used to create it and enables it to be opened again. The file extension dictates the format the data has taken and follows the filename given by the creator.

Data can be stored as:

- Text
- Images
- Moving images
- Sound

Or as a combination of any of the above:

- Text and Images
- Text and sound
- Text, images and sounds
- Text, moving images, still images and sound

Saving the file with the correct file extension will allow it to be opened and viewed or edited on other machines and other software. Some file formats only work on certain operating systems, although software can often be provided which will allow software created on one platform to be opened on another. For a long time files created in Microsoft Windows and for Apple computers were not interchangeable and did not open on each other's systems.

Software developers face the challenge of creating software which can be opened and used on multiple systems. This means that they should be aiming to allow files created in their software to be easily opened in other software products without distorting the original file. By using the most recognised file extension, developers are enabling more users the possibility of interacting with files created in their software.

The following is a list of the most commonly used and accepted file formats.

Portable document file – pdf

Many standard text- and image-based documents created in word processing software can be large and take a long time to download or send by email. By converting the file to a pdf format the file size is greatly reduced, thus making the file transmission and download speed faster and the storage size smaller. Text and images can still be cut from the original document, but additions cannot be made unless the intended editor has the password to allow them to do so.

Graphics formats

- gif – This format is suitable for simple graphics with solid areas of colour and can be stored without loss to the original image by using compression techniques.
- jpeg – This format saves images in a compressed format, again to reduce storage space and transmission rates, and is suited to storing images taken by digital cameras with flowing colours, which are commonly used on web pages.
- png – This format claims to be an improvement on gif as it is a popular cross-platform option for storing files and for image use on the web.

Movie formats

To display movie files there are several popular options. The option chosen is often dictated by the software in which the original movie was produced. The most commonly used and free to download include mpg, avi and mov. The variation largely stems from Microsoft and Apple movie-producing software, although both file types will run on each other's platforms provided the software is installed first.

Text

Any document consisting of just text and numbers can be saved under a variety of file extensions. If there is a need for the file to be opened on many different types of word processor at a later date, the best option for saving the file is txt. This is a standard basic format which simply displays text with no formatting. When saved in this format any formatting that has taken place will be removed. Other options popularly used for saving text and numbers only include dtd, htm, and doc.

Audio

A similar situation as for movie formats exists with audio files. In recent years there has been a lot of competition by those involved with music downloads to capture the market. Audio files can only be opened by certain types of software which can usually be downloaded for free. The most popular way to store audio is in MP3, au, mid and wav formats. The popularity of various MP3 players has made audio download popular and the software producers tend to be behind the sale of audio too. By limiting the devices that can run certain file formats they are trying to encourage loyalty to one music provider.

Presenting and distributing information

Information may be presented in a range of different formats and via different media. A successful information system will ensure that information is presented in the most appropriate format for the intended audience. For example, if the information is in summary form and has to be communicated quickly, a graphical presentation may be the most appropriate format. Factors that will need to be taken into account include:

- The nature and complexity of the original information: some information cannot easily be translated into a different format. The nature of the information determines the output.
- The time available for the recipient to study the information: busy managers sometimes need to have information summarised for them so that they can tell at a glance what the situation is.
- The needs of the recipient of the information: sometimes the recipient will need to understand a situation in detail; at other times they may just need to receive a general impression.
- The 'life-span' of the information – will it soon be supplanted by new information or will it need to be regularly referred to? Some information – a policy statement for example – does not change very often, whereas other information – such as stock market figures – is constantly changing.
- How long the recipient needs to study the situation. If information needs to be referred to over a period of time, then it needs to be presented in a 'permanent' format (e.g. a written report) rather than a temporary one (e.g. a verbal presentation).

After capture, processing and storing, information needs to be presented. The method for presentation will largely depend on what the information is and the needs of the audience.

In business, reports are generally used to convey official and formal information which is designed to be read by the audience. The content of reports will match a clearly defined title and introduction at the start and will include sub-headings that indicate where various details within the report can be found. This allows the reader to skip sections which may not be of interest to them. The report should finish with conclusions and recommendations based on what has been read.

Further presentation methods which can be incorporated into reports include graphs and charts. Often numerical data is best understood when it is transferred into a graphical format. Trends, peaks and troughs can be quickly identified in a spreadsheet and imported into the body of a report, form part of a wall display or a slide-show for a presentation.

Information presented in list/tabulated form is often desirable. By organising the information into a certain order the reader is able to better locate what they are looking for. Such presentation may suit a register of holiday makers on a day trip or the break down of sales figures from a particular department over a given time period. The information can be ordered alphabetically, arranged by days of the week or from biggest to smallest. The method chosen should suit the needs of the audience.

Information can be bound together in presentation software which might include graphs, charts, text, sound and moving images. A skilled presenter will work in harmony with the presentation, which is often delivered as a slide-show through a projector to an audience who are expecting to hear something interesting. Short, sharp facts, a lively presenter, good clear, obvious images and sensible use of sound can bring quite dull content to life. Too much text and a dry delivery defeats the object of mass presentation and the audience often leaves having learnt nothing and feeling drained and bored.

Information can be posted to company websites or other net-based alternatives such as blogs, chatrooms or bulletin boards. In many cases a website is the first port of call for new clients or customers, so the information must be easy to locate and be less than three clicks away. Websites provide the opportunity for millions of people not only to see information but to place orders, and they also generate sales interest.

Information can be distributed verbally in a number of ways. The best known and most natural way is actually talking to someone. This can be in a formally scheduled meeting or interview. A more technological way is by recorded voice, for example, a speech or recording of a conversation that can be digitised and made available as a podcast via a company intranet or website. Another alternative using digital tools is to deliver information as a motion picture stored on DVD or made available for download. In this instance the information could be training material or latest product innovation news.

Information can be attached to or be in the body of emails and sent around the world. Emails are heralding the death of the internal memo as users are finding it easier to send one simple message to several people. Many office workers will leave their email package open while they work on other areas of business. The open email software alerts them when a new message arrives and, provided the computer user is at their desk, they can read and respond to messages quickly.

Many companies find it important that they represent their company image on or around the information they produce. Any formally created company documentation should take into account certain design features. These include ensuring that the style of print used is consistent throughout the range of business stationery used. Business cards, invoices, letter heads, etc. should all look like they come from the same company to promote the company's identity. A particularly good way of achieving this is to produce templates which have fixed data and allow for variable data to be added as and when it is required.

Validation and verification: 1

When inputting data input into a system certain methods are used to ensure that at the point of entry data will only be accepted if it is sensible or realistic. Such methods or techniques are known as validation and verification. The key difference between them is that validation is largely done by a computer system or software at the point of entry while verification is down to the actions of the human.

How do data errors occur?

Data accuracy is critical in all information systems, as even minor inaccuracies can have serious consequences. Most error occur at the data entry stage.

General input error	There are various errors that fall into this category, e.g. customers filling in the details on the data entry form incorrectly, forms being lost or mistakenly entered twice, problems with automatic data collection devices, e.g. a malfunctioning bar code reader.
Transcription error	This is a specific type of error that can occur when a data entry clerk is keying in data, i.e. copying from a data capture form or via telephone instructions. A number of mistakes can occur during this process, e.g. transposing two numbers in a date of birth or mis-spelling a street name.
Processing error	Even if the data has been correctly inputted, errors can occur as it is being processed. For example, the program responsible for the processing could contain a mathematical function that calculates percentage totals. If an error were made (and left undetected) at the program writing stage – a miscalculation would be made every time it was run. The resulting inaccuracies may not be discovered for some time.
Transmission error	At various points in the system the data will need to be transmitted from one location to another. If, for example, a networked system were being used, the data would have to be transmitted from the client terminal to the server. During this process data can be lost or corrupted.

Validation methods

Validation is a means of reducing data errors, especially at the inputting stage. Validation routines ensure that the data being entered conforms to prescribed rules, rejecting it if it does not. Validation may be completed at the point of entry, e.g. by not allowing the operator to enter invalid data into a text box, or subsequent to data entry, e.g. by running a program which returns a list of all invalid entries. There are many different types of validation checks. Some of the most commonly used are set out in the table below.

Type	Description	Example
Presence	A presence check requires that a value must be entered, i.e. there cannot be a null value.	The details of an order are being inputted. The order cannot be processed unless an order number has been included. The validation routine returns an error if the operator tries to leave the input box empty.
Format	The data must conform to a prescribed layout, i.e. a specific pattern of letters and numbers.	An employee code consists of a particular pattern of number and letters, e.g. SY//3480/C. If the operator tries to enter a different arrangement of letters and numbers, an error is returned.
Range	The data must be a value that falls between two predefined values.	The date of birth of a student at a secondary school must be between 01/09/83 and 31/08/95. Any date that falls outside this range is rejected.
Data type	The data must be of a specified type, i.e. numerical, text, Boolean, image, etc.	The data entered for a 'number in stock' item must be numerical. If the operator entered any value that was non-numerical, e.g. a text item, it would be rejected.
Fixed value	The data must conform to one of the values in a predefined list.	The only entries that can be made for the 'gender' item on a form are Male and Female. Any attempt to enter anything other than these values will result in an error message.
Lookup	Data is matched to a value already entered and automatically added to complete other request fields.	By using a lookup value a postcode can be added and the rest of the address is added into the remaining blank address fields. Often the house name or number will still need to be added. Alternatively membership numbers can be used to match with contact details.

Check digits

This is a particular type of validation check that is used to check for transcription errors in long, numerical identifiers, e.g. the ISBN number on the back of this book. The check works by performing a mathematical calculation on the code number and returning an error if there is a discrepancy between the expected and actual outcome. The most commonly used test is called 'modulus 11'. In this system each number in the code is multiplied by a number (10 for the first number, 9 for the second and so on). The multiplied numbers are summed and the total divided by 11. The remainder from the division is then subtracted from 11. This is the check digit. If the remainder is 10, this is written as X, to restrict the outcome to one digit.

Validation and verification: 2

Checking for transmission errors

One form of checking that is used to detect errors that might occur during the transmission of data is the 'check digit' system. It works by using the binary digits that are used to transmit data. For example:

1   The letter 'A' is represented by the ASCII code 1000001.
2   When this combination of digits is transmitted a parity bit is added to the end of the sequence. The parity bit is either a 0 or 1, depending on whether the sum of the bits is an even or an odd number.
3   In an even-parity system, the total of all the bits (including the parity bit) must be an even number. In the case of the letter A, the bits already add up to an even number so a 0 will be added.
4   If they didn't add up to an even number (e.g. a 'C' which is 1000011), then a 1 would be added.
5   This then provides a means of checking whether that particular byte of data has been correctly transmitted.

This is by no means a flawless system. If, for example, there were two errors in the transmission they would cancel each other and the data would be accepted as correct.

Another, similar, system that is used is the 'checksum' system. When data is transmitted in packets a checksum – i.e. a total of the numeric value of the transmitted bytes – is included in the transmission. This can then act as a checking value at the point of reception.

Validity and accuracy

Just because data has been accepted as valid – i.e. it has passed through a system's validation routines – it does not mean that it is accurate. To be valid, data has to be reasonable and fall within a system's accepted parameters; to be accurate it has to be a truthful representation of an original source.

Example   *A customer completes a data capture form with 05/07/68 as their date of birth. The operator who enters this makes a transcription error: instead of 05/07/68 being entered, 07/05/68 is keyed in. This entry passes through all the system's validation routines – because, though erroneous, it is in the correct format for a date of birth – and is duly processed. The data is valid but inaccurate.*

Validation then is no absolute guarantee of accuracy. In order to increase the level of data accuracy verification routines must be used.

Verification

Verification refers to routines that might be used to establish the accuracy of inputted data. These routines include:

• proofreading the screen entries against the original document;
• reading back details to a customer whose data had been inputted via telephone;
• sending printouts of inputted data to the data source (e.g. a customer) and asking them to confirm the accuracy of the data.

One – rather time-consuming – method of verification, involving double inputting of data is shown below.

ERRORS	
Record 1:	Name field
Record 35:	DOB field
Record 42:	Town field
Record 56:	DOB field
Record 69:	PostCode field
Record 75:	PostCode field
Record 92:	DOB field
Record 105:	HomeTel field

The first data entry clerk enters the data, copying from the source document.

The second data entry clerk repeats the routine, copying from the same document.

The verification program compares the two sets of data and identifies discrepancies that require further checking.

Input devices: 1

	HOW IT WORKS	EXAMPLES OF APPLICATIONS	STRENGTHS AND LIMITATIONS
Bar code reader	• Uses a laser to read the light reflected from an arrangement of lines (or bars) of different widths. • The lines represent a number which represents information about the product. This information is stored in a database.	• Product sales in the retail trade • Loan systems in libraries • Package tracking in delivery firms • Stock management in warehouses • Some identification cards	✓ Bar code readers are fast and accurate when dealing with product identification. ✓ The data can be scanned in a fraction of the time it would take to key it in. ✗ They are limited to 'fixed' data, i.e. details cannot be changed.
Digital camera	• The pattern of light associated with the image is stored digitally rather than on film. • The image, now stored in a standardised format, can be imported into a range of different applications and modified to suit the user's needs.	• Everyday personal use, e.g. weddings, holidays, etc. • For engineers to communicate to clients the progress of a project • For estate agents to update websites using digitally captured images • Speed cameras and number plate recognition	✓ The image can be used flexibly in a wide range of applications. ✓ It can be modified using specially designed applications. ✓ It can be attached as a file to an e-mail. ✗ Image files can be 'memory-heavy'. ✗ Quality of output will depend on quality of printer and paper.
Keyboard	• The keyboard translates key selections into digital format text/number values. • It also contains a number of 'function' keys which allow the user to send instructions to the computers, e.g. 'delete', 'scroll down'.	• To enter data that must be copied from a document or audio source • To input text directly into the computer • To send instructions and commands to computer-based control systems	✓ Keyboards remain the most common method of inputting text-based data. ✗ Transcription errors are common. ✗ Data entry is time-consuming and dependent on typing skills. ✗ They can contribute to repetitive strain injury if overused.
Concept keyboard	• Works in a similar way to a normal traditional keyboard but whole words or images are pressed instead of single letters. • Words or images are often enough to clearly identify what each button does.	• Restaurants use images of drinks or meals on the till to speed up data entry. • Children make use of concept keyboards to select animals from the screen to hear the noises they make.	✓ Restricts data that can be entered to available selection only. ✓ Intuitive, which allows novice users to quickly understand the meaning of each button ✓ Transcription errors reduced. ✗ When used at high speed or with little care the wrong image or word can be selected affecting the final outcome. ✗ Can only be used on the system it is designed for.
Magnetic ink character recognition (MICR)	• The data is printed in the form of specially designed characters. The ink used to print these characters contains a magnetic substance. • This can then be read by an appropriately sensitive input device. Software then translates the patterns into text/numerical values.	• Banks use this approach to process cheques. Cheques are designed to have key data (branch details, account number) printed in magnetic ink across the bottom. This can then be read in using the input device and the data processed by the bank's computers.	✓ For the processing of cheques, MICR is quick and highly efficient. ✓ Unlike bar codes, humans as well as machines can make sense of the data. ✓ It is resistant to forgery. ✗ It only has limited applications and, with the decline of cheques as a means of payment, its use is in decline.
Mouse	• The mouse is a flexible input device which allows the user to communicate a wide range of commands to the computer. • The mouse ball sends positional information to the computer which is then translated into the movements of a pointer on the screen. • Other information is sent via clicking of buttons.	• For the user to communicate with a graphical user interface • To select icons and, through them, activate commands • To issue commands to the computer directly (e.g. 'scroll down') • To allow the user to select from a range of menu items and activate specified commands	✓ With the advent of graphical user interfaces, a means of pointing to various places on the screen became necessary. The mouse fulfils this function well. ✓ There are constant developments in the functionality of these devices and their use is likely to continue for some time. ✗ Some users dislike having to shift constantly from keyboard to mouse and will tend therefore to use keyboard short-cuts. ✗ Hand-to-eye coordination is an issue for some users.

Input devices: 2

	HOW IT WORKS	EXAMPLES OF APPLICATIONS	STRENGTHS AND LIMITATIONS
Optical character recognition (OCR)	• A scanner device reads the reflected light from characters on a page. These may have been typed or hand-written. • The scanner creates an image of the character. Software then tries to match it against a 'library' of similar character shapes. • When a match is found, it inputs the appropriate character.	• This method is used to input large blocks of text held in 'hard copy' format. • It is also used to input data captured on forms. Often these forms require the person filling it in to write each character in a box. This is because OCR systems need to be able to read each character individually. An example of this is the passport application form.	✓ This method can speed up an otherwise lengthy process of keying in. ✗ It often misreads letters, and documents captured in this way almost always have to be proof-read afterwards. ✗ For capturing hand-written text, the cursive style must be clear and the document must be 'clean', i.e. not contain any marks or smudges that could be interpreted as characters.
Optical mark recognition (OMR)	• This method works on the same principle as OCR but, instead of trying to interpret characters, OMR systems read marks made at specified points on a specially designed form. • These marks equate to pre-set values and, once read, can be sent for processing.	• The most popular application of this method is the filling in of National Lottery forms. • It is also used for examination papers where multiple choice questions are used and for submitting grades to examination boards. • School registers.	✓ Avoids need for file transfer. ✓ This can be an extremely quick way of entering large amounts of data. ✗ The input forms necessarily limit the range of permissible responses. ✗ Incorrect marking of the sheet will lead to the data being rejected.
Sensors	• Sensors are devices which read changes in the environment around them. • There is a wide range of sensors which can detect changes in: light, air pressure, temperature, humidity, speed, etc.	• Sensors are frequently used in control systems. They can be used to measure the temperature of a room. This input can then be used to trigger a control system which adjusts the heating. • Other examples include: humidity sensors in an art gallery and movement sensors in a security system.	✓ Sensors are a necessary element of any control system and can also be used for data logging. ✓ Data can be captured cheaply and with little human effort. ✗ They are limited in the type of data they can collect. ✗ They can 'misread' environmental changes, e.g. a car alarm activated by a strong gust of wind.
Touch screens	• Values are associated with different positions on a VDU via a 'grid' of infrared beams across the front of the screen. • When the user touches a particular part of the screen, the associated value is sent to be processed.	• Touch screens are used by museums and galleries to communicate information. • They can also be used by small children and people whose disabilities might prevent them from using other input devices. • They are increasingly common in places where customers place orders, e.g. fast food outlets.	✓ They are user-friendly. Even people who might be intimidated by computers feel comfortable using these devices. ✗ They are limited as input devices because only a limited number of values can be displayed at any one time.
Voice recognition systems	• The data is inputted in audio form, either directly, via a microphone, or indirectly, via an audio tape. • Software analyses the inputted sound and matches it against a library of sounds. • When a match is found the value is sent for processing.	• A voice recognition system allows users to dictate text straight into the computer. The resulting text can then be edited using standard word-processing applications. • It has also been used in control systems, e.g. instructions to robots in the manufacturing industry. • It is sometimes used in security systems.	✓ A user can speak much more quickly than even the most skilled of typists can type. ✗ Interpreting human language is a complex process because meaning can be ambiguous. Software cannot, as yet, interpret meaning. ✗ The human voice is not uniform: we speak in different styles and different accents. Voice recognition software has to be 'trained' to recognise the voice patterns of individual users. This can take a long time.
Graphics pad and light pen	• The light pen is moved over the graphics pad which translates the pen movements into a digital form and displays the results of the movements on a monitor. The light pen can also perform similar functions to the mouse with regards to selecting tools and applications.	• Used by animators to manipulate and create character movements and to add colour and body and facial expressions. • Used by architects and interior designers to create blue prints of buildings or produce models of potential internal design features.	✓ Allows for more flexibility when used on design work. ✓ Artists are able to quickly produce exactly what they want, as if using a pencil, and have it directly transferred into a computer system. ✗ Can take up a lot of desk space when used with other peripherals. ✗ Not suitable for inputting text data, as technology to read hand writing is still developing to a level that is satisfactory for experienced users.

Printers: 1

Different types of printers

TYPE	HOW THEY WORK	COMMENT
Dot matrix	1 A printhead, consisting of a number of pins, moves back and forth on a cartridge. 2 Each pin – there are usually 9 or 24 – is mounted on a spring. On the head of the pin is a magnet. Above each pinhead is a small electromagnet. 3 The printer's microprocessor analyses the information from the computer and translates the instructions into a series of electrical impulses. 4 These signals are sent to the electromagnets, the effect of which is to push selected pins down towards where the paper is being fed through. 5 Between the printhead is an ink ribbon. The 'firing' pin heads therefore impress a series of ink dots on to the page. 6 These dots constitute the text/graphic being printed.	Dot matrix – or impact – printers were amongst the first on the market for home and small office use. They are relatively cheap and fairly reliable. However, the print quality is poor and they are only suitable for producing draft material where print quality is not an issue. They are also the slowest and noisiest of the printers. As the price of ink-jet printers has decreased, dot matrix printers have virtually disappeared from the market.
Ink-jet	1 A controller receives information from the computer about what needs to be printed. This is translated into a series of instructions that are sent to the various elements of the printer. 2 The printhead, which moves back and forth across the pages, contains a series of nozzles. The number of nozzles will affect the print quality. A black and white printer might have 50, a colour printer up to 600. 3 Above the printhead is an ink cartridge, either a single one with black ink or a set of 3–6 different coloured ones for colour printing. Each nozzle takes ink from the cartridge, and heats it to produce a small bubble of ink. The bubble pushes a droplet of ink out of the nozzle and on to the paper.	Ink-jet printers are relatively cheap, reliable and can produce good quality prints. The quality of ink-jet printing has improved steadily over the past few years. The newer, colour versions are, at the moment, good, economical alternatives to expensive colour laser printers. They are slower than laser printers and they cope less well with bulk printing, but they are still cost-effective solutions for homes and small offices.
Laser	1 The printer's processors prepare the received data and then send a series of instructions to the printhead. 2 The printhead contains a laser which emits a beam of light. A spinning multi-faced mirror directs the beams in a horizontal line across a rotating drum. 3 The drum is covered with a zinc-oxide-based film whose electrical properties change when it is hit by light. 4 The laser is switched on and off in a designated pattern, thus creating an equivalent pattern of positively or negatively charged dots on the drum. 5 On its rotation the charged area of the drum then picks up black powder from a toner cartridge, the black powder being attracted by the electrical charge. 6 The arrangement of toner is then deposited on to the paper as it passes by the drum. The paper passes through a 'fusing system'. This uses heat and pressure to bind the toner to the paper. 7 The drum then passes a thin wire, the corona wire, which emits a strong positive charge. The drum is thus prepared to receive another pattern of charged dots via the laser.	Laser printers are fast, reliable devices that can produce high-quality output. They have come down in price over the past few years and are therefore within the range of small businesses and home workers. They are quiet and can handle bulk printing. They are more expensive than ink-jets and the differential is more pronounced where colour printing is concerned. The replacement of toner cartridges is a regular, costly expense that needs to be taken into account.

Printers: 2

Other printer functions

The popular use of digital photography has prompted the birth of new types of printers. Smart cards taken from digital cameras can be loaded into printers which display each image and allow the user to edit and select individual images for printing. Such printers can provide images of the same quality as those previously achieved by professional developers. Also available are printers with built-in scanners, photocopiers, the ability to print double-sided (duplex) and fax facilities. Such devices are relatively cheap, the ink cartridges being the main expense.

Blue tooth technology allows for wireless links to be established between printers and computer systems as well as digital cameras and some mobile phones with built-in cameras. By taking advantage of faster processing and intuitive graphical user interfaces and software, novice home users are becoming more adept at handling their own printing requirements.

Selecting a printer

When selecting a printer the following criteria may be used:	
Quality of output	Different printers create outputs of differing quality. If it is important to have a product that is clearly defined and professional looking, then a printer capable of producing such output will be needed. The quality of output is related to the printer's 'resolution'. This is measured in dots per inch (dpi).
Bulk printing capacity	Some printers, e.g. those used for domestic purposes, will only be required to produce one or two documents at a time. Others, based in large offices, may need to produce multiple runs more or less constantly.
Cost	Cost is always a criterion when selecting a hardware device. Printers can now be purchased quite cheaply, but such printers will not be able to produce professional standard output, nor will they be able to manage long, 'memory-heavy' print runs.
Speed	In a business where time is a critical factor, it will be important for the printer to be able to process incoming data and produce the output quickly and efficiently.

How a printer communicates with the CPU

When a software application produces a document for printing, it must be able to communicate instructions to the printer in a format that the printer understands. This is achieved via a printer 'driver', a piece of software that acts as a communication interface between computer and printer.

The instructions to the printer can be transmitted in a variety of ways. If the printer is located close to the computer, the parallel port is usually used. Transmission may also take place via a network connection, or in some offices, via wireless transmission.

If the printer is connected to a network, it will be necessary to have a queuing system so that the printer isn't swamped with requests. This is achieved via a technique called 'spooling': data is saved to a disc location where it is stored and placed in a 'job queue' until the printer is free. At this stage some jobs may be prioritised.

A CPU can process data much faster than a printer. So that the CPU doesn't have to 'wait' for the printer, a technique called buffering is used. Data needed for the print job is sent to a 'buffer' memory until the printer is ready to process it. This memory store may be located in the printer or in the computer.

A printer has to translate instructions from the computer into commands that can be sent to its different working parts. Many printers use a technique called 'Page Description Language', a code that specifies what the printer will need to do to create the appropriate marks on the page.

Most printers have the capacity to send 'feedback' messages to the computer, e.g. to indicate when the paper supply has run out. The message is sent back to the driver which, in turn, generates an on-screen error message to inform the user of the problem.

Equipment

Monitors

The monitor allows processed data to be viewed on a screen. This is a visual device which, prior to the explosion of the Internet and home use, was only used to display text and numbers in a fairly standard format. Monitors were large heavy devices which dominated working space. The footprint of monitors has dramatically reduced in weight and depth giving the user more space to work. Modern monitors are available in a variety of sizes from 15 inches to as much as 100 inches and are usually selected based on the needs of the user. Most monitors purchased are now flat screen, lightweight and plug directly into the CPU. The pursuit of crystal clear images has been greatly boosted by the advent of LCD TFT screens, which replaced the more cumbersome cathode ray tube boxes. Many stand-alone monitors, as well as those attached to laptops, are just as good as home theatre systems with high-definition capabilities. Indeed many home users now use their computer monitor as an alternative television set with no deterioration in picture quality.

Projectors

Projectors are used to increase the view of what would normally be shown on a computer monitor. They are ideal for conveying information to large audiences and in recent years the prices have dropped. Projectors are becoming a viable alternative to rear projection TV screens as home users attach laptops to projectors and enjoy home cinema-style viewing. Interactive white boards used to need a projector to work alongside them but new technology means that this double act is no longer necessary. The future for projector units looks likely to be a reduction in size, to that of a sugar cube some claim, which could see them built into mobile devices such as cameras and phones.

Speakers and headphones

Data that is to be heard is played through speakers or headphones. Headphones are designed for a single user whilst speakers are generally designed to share sound with an audience or more than one person. Music, recorded voice and sound effects are all presented through one or either of these devices. There is a very broad selection of speakers which tend to show larger price tags as the clarity and volume improve and increase. Speakers are used to enhance presentations which may also include video and animation. Apple has made great strides in popularising audio to millions through MP3 players and the ability to download podcasts that may contain news, sport or even a radio play. Headphones have changed dramatically over several decades. Originally they covered the user's head, but it is not uncommon for small earphones to be used which fit directly in the ear. As with all technology the best decision on the kit required is often made when the task it is to perform is clear and fully identified. Those with hearing problems can take advantage of headphones which amplify the sound from a system to a level that can be better heard on a personal level.

Storage devices

Secondary storage devices are needed to store and transfer software and data files. There are many such devices on the market and this is an area of fast-changing technology. There is a constant drive to increase the capacity of storage media while maintaining security of storage and keeping costs low. One reason for this is because applications are becoming more complex and users increasingly wish to store memory-heavy items such as sound/video files. In addition to capacity, the following criteria should be taken into account when choosing a storage medium: speed of transfer, speed of access, reusability, cost, portability, ease of use and vulnerability to corruption.

Compact disc

Description: CDs are polycarbonate discs with a fine coating of aluminium. They have data written on to them by a powerful laser that 'burns' a pattern of 'pits' on to the surface. Another laser then reads this pattern and converts it into a sequence of binary digits. Some CDs can only have data read from them (ROM) but, increasingly, writable and rewritable CDs are being used.

Evaluation: CDs have high storage capacity, are relatively cheap and fairly robust. They are often used for storing application software that will be sold to users, e.g. computer games. Writable and rewritable CDs are increasingly being used to store user-created data.

Hard drive (Internal and external)

Description: Hard drives usually consist of a series of metal discs, mounted on a spindle. They each have a read/write head which accesses the magnetically stored data. The discs rotate continuously while the computer is in operation.

Evaluation: The standard means of storing data in a PC, hard drives provide good capacity, are relatively robust and offer fast access times. They can, however, crash and so back-up systems are required. In a network this usually takes the form of a RAID system (see page 129 for more information about this).

Digital tape

Description: Digital Audio Tape works by storing data on Mylar film coated with iron oxide. Sections of the tape are magnetised to represent bits. The tape is held in a plastic cassette and played through a device which may be externally or internally located. Digital Linear Tape is a more expensive, more advanced version of this technology. It has greater capacity and faster access time.

Evaluation: Tape storage uses 'sequential access' which means that access to data can be slow (the whole tape must be played, up to the point where the required data is stored). However, tape has a high storage capacity and is cheap. It is therefore a popular back-up medium.

Zip drive

Description: Plastic container encases a single hard drive of the same diameter as a floppy disc. This stores data in the same way that a standard hard drive does. Zip drive cassettes are either used with a drive located in the computer or via a hand-held device which is plugged into the parallel port. They can store between 100 and 250Mb of data.

Evaluation: Good capacity, portability and reasonably fast transfer rates make zip drives a good alternative to floppy discs for the transfer of data. Unfortunately, many PCs do not have built-in zip drives and using the hand-held devices can be cumbersome. They are good for individual back-up but are rarely used for network back-up systems.

Memory/flash cards

Description: Memory or flash cards have gradually reduced in size and increased in storage capacity up to the point where they fit comfortably into mobile phones. They are also used for storing digital images in cameras, handheld and portable laptops, MP3 players and video game consoles.

Evaluation: They are a popular option for storage because of their size and robustness. A big issue with memory cards is the range of formats available. This has led to computer system developers having to provide a variety of extra slots in their machines to read the cards and consumers often make the wrong purchase when they need to buy replacements.

DVD

Description: The Digital Versatile Disk has the same look and feel as CDs but stores around 4.7Gb because of the smaller pits burnt into the DVD. DVDs are used to transfer and view movie footage and there are currently several formats available.

Evaluation: Most modern computers are equipped to play DVDs in the same drive used to play CDs. DVDs allow the user to skip sections of content and have recently undergone a change to satisfy high definition (HD) requirements. The introduction of smaller flash cards and USB memory sticks could mean that within a generation this type of storage will be superseded by smaller options.

USB Memory sticks

Description: The USB stick/key device is an incredibly popular storage device, with plug and play capabilities. The capacity has gradually increased while the price has fallen over a relatively short period of time. USBs store data in digital form on a microchip which is housed inside a robust case, usually no bigger than half matchbox size. The are able to store most file types and range from 16Mb to 4Gb, although this is increasing all the time.

Evaluation: USB devices can be plugged into just about any recent computer system because the USB port is becoming an accepted standard for plug and play technology.

The portability and ease of use of USB devices makes them attractive to most users who are not keen on spending time downloading drivers and organising multiple storage levels and accounts.

The type of storage selected is based on what it is designed to store in terms of size, format and value to an organisation or individual. Often important data is stored more than once and kept in a secure location away from the main source. Storage options have changed significantly, largely as a result of the increased functionality offered by portable devices such as MP3 players and mobile phones. The need to store images, music, contacts, business files and motion pictures continues to prompt new developments.

Specialist equipment

Famously Professor Stephen Hawking utilises technology to enable him to communicate with those around him. The technology, driven by the use of muscles in one of his cheeks, is enough for him to select words from a screen and slowly construct sentences which are broadcast through speakers with a digitised voice. It also powers and steers his wheel chair. For other users, who have certain physical restrictions, there is a host of technology designed to give them equal access to, and the ability to interact with, computer systems.

Puff suck switch

This device is used by people with restricted movement who need to interact with a computer system. The puff suck switch works by the person blowing or sucking a tube which is attached to an electronic interface box that translates the blow or suck into a predefined digital instruction. The resistant level expected by the interface can be adjusted to suit the user. Such a device may appear to be fairly limited, but for an experienced user it can be customised to perform a whole range of tasks including icon selection, website navigation and document production.

Braille printer and keyboards

Braille keyboards, for those with limited or no sight, are very much like standard Qwerty keyboards in terms of the layout of where each key is positioned. The addition of Braille, raised patterns on each key, distinguishes these keyboards from other types. There are claims that those who do not suffer with vision impairment can still benefit from braille keyboards, as some manufacturers claim that data entry, after learning the patterns, can be twice as fast as any professional typists can achieve.

Foot mouse

The foot mouse allows the user complete control over the screen cursor without having to take hands away from the keyboard. The foot mouse is also ideal for those who have difficulty using a traditional mouse and keyboard. There is a broad range of foot mice and the selection of which product to use is based on the user requirements. Some people use a foot mouse to avoid RSI, whilst others use it to increase productivity by reducing the number of times hands need to leave the keyboard area.

Eye typer

Eye typer technology is driven by eye movements and is for those with severe movement restrictions. The eye typer comes with a keyboard and a communication device which displays typical keyboard letters and numbers as well as other useful functions such as print and save. The user gazes at the letter they want and a small camera, built into the eye typer, records the eye movement and displays the selection on screen. At the time of selection the system will read out the letter or completed word. The eye typer can be programmed to learn words or phrases, which greatly increases the speed at which full sentences can be produced.

Systems software

Functions of the operating system

Systems software	This refers to programs that enable the computer to function effectively, to interact with the user, to communicate with peripheral devices and to manage the demands made upon its resources by applications software. The most important program in this category is the operating system but the category also includes utility programs such as virus checkers, and file management programs.

Operating systems (OS) provide a common platform for applications to run on. Without them each application would need to define its own way of communicating with the user, saving files to secondary storage, communicating with peripheral devices, etc. There are a number of competing OS on the market, the most commonly used being Microsoft Windows and Apple Mac. UNIX is an alternative OS popular with some business users and LINUX is a free system developed by an Internet-linked community of programmers.

Interrupt handling

Various hardware events such as mouse clicks, keystrokes, a message from an external source, etc. generate a particular type of signal called an interrupt. It is a signal that needs an immediate response, so the OS has to manage any ongoing processing jobs while dealing with it.

Memory allocation

The OS ensures that adequate memory resources are available for the task being performed by the user. This task has become more critical as multi-tasking (i.e. the ability to perform two or more different actions at the same time) has become the norm.

Backing storage

The OS organises the storage and retrieval of data from the hard disc drive and other secondary storage devices. In order to maintain efficiency it must be able to locate specific files quickly. It maintains a directory for this purpose.

Communicating with peripheral devices

A computer may be linked with any number of peripherals, including: a mouse, keyboard, printer, scanner, etc. The OS ensures that device drivers are in place and the computer can receive and send instructions to these devices effectively.

Application software

Operating system

Hardware

Examples of utility software

Virus checkers	A virus checker is a valuable piece of software that maintains an updateable directory of the 'signatures' – i.e. tell-tale sections of code – of known viruses. If noticed, a warning can then be sent to the user.
File management	Software of this type helps users to keep their files in logical order, ensuring optimal use of disc space and speed of retrieval. It might also offer facilities for compressing files and repartitioning the hard disc drive.
Security	Usually associated with network systems, software of this type allocates passwords, defines user access rights, maintains a log of computer usage, etc.

Application software

Different types of software

Generic/application software	This is software that is most commonly used by businesses and home users to perform day-to-day tasks such as writing a letter, running statistical analysis or keeping records. Word processor, spreadsheet, database, presentation, web author and graphics are all examples of application software. Each package is designed to perform a general task involving one or more types of data. They can be customised to look and perform tasks desired by the user.
Specific task software	This is software which is only designed to perform a certain task, such as payroll calculations or picture organisers. They are limited in what they can do and lack flexibility with regard to customising the package and linking it to alternative systems to automatically capture data or transfer it to another system. This kind of software will only do what it claims and very little else, which for some users may be perfectly adequate.
Bespoke software	Bespoke software is software designed to do a predefined and clearly stated task. It is often referred to as tailor-made software because it is only fit to perform the task it has been designed to do. An example of this may be the payroll system for a shipping firm. At first glance it appears that specific task software could be used. However, the shipping company may require more than the standard functions of the specific task software. They may specify that the system must convert staff payments into the employee's native currency and automatically transfer it to their bank accounts on the fifth day of each month. By tailoring the system to the exact requirements of the user, the software solution is likely to be to specialist and focussed for one business, and would not suit a similar business even though its requirements may be almost the same.

Integrated packages

One way of dealing with the problem of moving data between different applications is to use an integrated package. An integrated package provides the user with a 'suite' of applications which perform different tasks while sharing many of the same features. Most domestic users, when they buy a computer, find an integrated package already installed, the most popular being Microsoft Office and Lotus SmartSuite. These integrated packages provide access to a select range of generic software, including a word-processing package, a spreadsheet program, a database, a graphics program and presentation software. The advantages and disadvantages of such an approach are set out below.

ADVANTAGES OF AN INTEGRATED PACKAGE	DISADVANTAGES OF AN INTEGRATED PACKAGE
• The movement of data between applications is made easy. The separate modules are specifically designed to link with the other components in the package. • It is generally less expensive to purchase the integrated package than to purchase all the components separately. • There are often many common features (e.g. user interface design, keyboard shortcuts, etc.) which makes it easier for the user to learn how to use the different components.	• The user, almost inevitably, pays for functionality that they don't need and will never use. • If a user purchases an integrated package, they are obliged to use all the modules. While some modules may be effective, others may be less so. The user may have been better advised to purchase those applications separately. • Running an integrated package will require more memory resources than would be the case if the user only installed those applications they needed.

Desirable features of software packages

Help files

Good software will provide the user with a comprehensive set of help files. These files should cover all queries a user – even an inexperienced one – is likely to have. The opportunity to enter key words to drive the search for help is a desirable feature as well as being easy to search and setting out responses in a clear, accessible format.

Search facilities

The user should be able to search through files to find a particular item of information. The search process should not be over-complex and should allow for a range of different criteria to be used, e.g. using Boolean operators such as 'and', 'or', 'not', etc.

Editing facilities

The software should allow the user to make changes to existing files, to add new information, amend existing data and delete unwanted data. Standard cut/copy/paste operations are useful editing tools that can be used in a variety of contexts.

Upgrade paths

If the software is a newer version of an existing software package, it should allow the user to upgrade existing files without any loss of data. Upgrade releases should be managed so that they cause the user the minimum of disruption.

Desirable features of software

Macro capabilities

A macro is a short program that the user creates. It consists of a set of coded instructions that automate an action or procedure. The macro can then be activated when a keyboard shortcut is pressed or an icon is clicked on.

Data portability

There are often problems when data has to be transferred from one application to another. A good application will provide facilities to transfer data to other programs, without the user having to go through a complicated process.

Report generators

A report is a printed summary of information. There is a range of applications that need to be able to generate customised reports, e.g. databases, accounts packages, data analysis programs, etc.

Application generators

Some programs allow the user to create their own customised applications. Database programs, for example, let the user define the file structures and user interfaces to create an 'application within an application'.

Templates

Templates are predefined documents that can be used to create documents that conform to a basic format but differ in detail. Many companies have a range of form letters that they send out, e.g. a payment reminder.

Templates can also be used for data capture forms, generic report writing, memos, etc. They are often used in conjunction with a facility that allows the user to merge data held in a data source (e.g. a database) with a word-processed document. This facility may be used if a business wants to send the same form letters to all the clients in their database. Users can create their own templates or use the ones provided by the application.

Word-processing applications

Word-processing programs are among the most commonly used pieces of computer software. This is true both of the domestic market and the business environment. Fast, efficient text-processing programs have largely replaced all forms of typewriter and paper-and-pen technology in office environments. They allow the user to enter data, usually via a keyboard or a speech recognition system, and for that data to appear in text format on the screen, as if it were being typed on to paper. The text can then be formatted (i.e. its appearance changed), edited, saved as a document and printed. Most word-processing programs have WYSIWYG (what-you-see-is-what-you-get) functionality, i.e. the appearance of the page on the screen is the same as that which will be printed out. This helps the user determine precisely the desired configuration of the page.

Word-processing programs are valuable for a wide variety of users, including secretaries who have to produce letters and other documents, students who have assignments to write and authors creating manuscripts for books and articles, etc.

Some key functions of a word-processing application

Editing

This is possibly the greatest advantage of word-processing programs over other methods. The user can keep returning to a document, amending it, adding new text, deleting old text, etc. without having to worry about starting the whole document again or damaging the presentation of the finished copy. The program allows the user to move blocks of text around, either by clicking and dragging or by using the cut/copy/paste facility. If, for example, the user wished to copy one block of text into a number of different documents, they could copy it to the clipboard (a temporary store) and then paste it into the appropriate documents.

Other tools that help the user edit a document include the facility to find and replace a specific word or phrase in the document, a function for checking the spelling and a word-count function.

Templates

Templates are predefined documents that can be used to create documents that conform to a basic format but differ in detail. Many companies have a range of form letters that they send out, e.g. a payment reminder. The message and the layout of the document remains the same (i.e. it provides the template) but the details of the customer and how much he owes changes every time the letter is sent.

Templates can also be used for data capture forms, generic report writing, memos, etc. They are often used in conjunction with a facility that allows the user to merge data held in a data source (e.g. a database) with a word-processed document. This facility may be used if a business wants to send the same form letters to all the clients in their database. Users can create their own templates or use the ones provided by the application.

Formatting

Formatting means altering the appearance of the text on the page. This can entail changing the size of the text, its colour, its alignment on the page, whether or not it is emboldened/ italicised/underlined, etc. Most word- processing programs come with a set of fonts – i.e. styles of writing – installed. The user can choose the font that is most appropriate for the document that they are creating. Other aspects of formatting include setting the paragraph style, determining the line spacing, establishing the style that will be used for bullet points, inserting page numbers, headers/footers, etc. All of these formatting elements can be used in conjunction with each other to create a document that has an appearance consistent with its purpose and audience.

Importing objects

When word-processing programs were first produced all they could do was process text. As they have developed, so they have grown in sophistication and now rival desk top publishing programs in terms of the functionality they offer. For example, the user is now able to import a wide range of different objects into a document. A graph created in a spreadsheet program can be inserted into a document, as can images downloaded from a digital camera or retrieved from a clip-art library. Graphs and tables created in another application can be inserted as linked objects. This means that when they are updated in the source application they are also updated in the word-processed document. The inserted object can be formatted in a number of different ways, e.g. its properties can be set so that text 'wraps' around it.

Advantages of word-processing programs

Advantages	Disadvantages
• The main advantage of word-processing over type-written or hand-written documents is that the user can keep going back to the document and amending it. Previously this would have meant retyping/rewriting the whole document or spoiling its appearance with crossings-out and/or correction fluid. • Large documents can be saved economically and searched for quickly. • If correct security and back-up procedures are followed, the data held in a word-processed document will be securely stored. • The quality of the final presentation far outstrips any comparable method, especially if imported graphics are used to enhance the appearance of the document.	• The only real disadvantages are generic, i.e. concern about security and loss of data. • There are those who suggest that the ease with which form letters can be produced has led to a decline in the personalised letter and a concomitant growth in the 'pseudo-personalised letter'.

Mail merge

'Mail merge' is a commonly used facility that can be found in most word-processing applications. It allows the user to insert merge fields into a template. These merge fields then draw upon data held in a data file, thus creating a number of individualised documents from one template. Typically, this facility will be used for addressing letters to a group of individuals whose details are held by an organisation, e.g. a customer list. This is more efficient than having to address each letter individually and so is widely used by organisations that regularly send letters to clients or customers, e.g. banks, schools, hospitals. The system allows the user to draw on data held in different applications and so is a good example of a way in which data held in separate programs can be integrated. This integration is easier to achieve when working with an integrated 'office' suite.

How mail merge works

DATA SOURCE

Title	F.Name	Surname	P.Code
Mr	Alan	Wright	PV3 6YH
Miss	Sophie	Jones	PV16 9KT
Mr	Adam	Paul	PV5 8TY
Mrs	Helen	Lamb	PV16 8RD
Ms	Nisha	Omar	PV3 7PY
Miss	Kelly	Peake	PV16 6RE

The data may be held in a **database**, word processor or spreadsheet, either in a table or in a query that combines related tables and sets parameters for what data should be included.

Title	F.Name	Surname	P.Code
Mr	Alan	Wright	PV3 6YH
Miss	Sophie	Jones	PV16 9KT
Mr	Adam	Paul	PV5 8TY
Mrs	Helen	Lamb	PV16 8RD
Ms	Nisha	Omar	PV3 7PY
Miss	Kelly	Peake	PV16 6RE

The data may be held as a distinct **data file within the word-processing application**. It may be in tabulated format or a comma separated values (.csv) file.

Title	F.Name	Surname	P.Code
Mr	Alan	Wright	PV3 6YH
Miss	Sophie	Jones	PV16 9KT
Mr	Adam	Paul	PV5 8TY
Mrs	Helen	Lamb	PV16 8RD
Ms	Nisha	Omar	PV3 7PY
Miss	Kelly	Peake	PV16 6RE

The data may be held in a **spreadsheet**. Although not primarily designed to act as a text-based data store, spreadsheet applications can function in this way

A querying function may be used to determine which of the records held in the data file will be used as the source of the document, e.g. by selecting only those customers that live in certain postcode district.

A template is created that contains the information to be communicated, together with 'merge fields'. These will be populated with the names, addresses, etc. from the selected records when the document is merged. This template can be saved and re-used as required.

Shureshine Cleaning Co.
Unit 3b
Warwick Rd
London
SW26 5TG

17th March 2002

Dear <<Title>> <<Surname>>

Please find enclosed
details of ....

Shureshine Cleaning Co.
Unit 3b
Warwick Rd
London
SW26 5TG

17th March 2002

Dear Mr Wright

Please find enclosed
details of ....

The template is merged with the source data and either sent directly to the printer or used to create a new document file. The document file will consist of one individualised copy of the template for each of the records contained within the data source.

Spreadsheets

What is a spreadsheet?

The spreadsheet is generally credited with being the application that first persuaded business users that the PC could run programs that would be of use to them. In 1982 Lotus introduced Lotus 1-2-3, a spreadsheet program that allowed users to store and process numerical data. Its main appeal lay in the fact that it looked like an electronic version of the ledger books that accountants, and other business users who worked with figures, were used to. Its introduction led to a massive growth in the market for IBM PCs and began a decade of unprecedented growth for the computer industry.

A spreadsheet is an information processing tool that organises data into rows and columns. Modern spreadsheet programs are extremely versatile and may be used for creating graphical displays or as simple databases. Their predominant use, however, remains the storage and processing of statistical – and especially financial – data. Their facility for embedding automated mathematical and statistical functions makes them the ideal electronic replacement for the accounts book, inventory sheet and budget summary.

The uses of spreadsheets

ACCOUNTS

Columns and rows ideally replicate the layout required to perform accounts-type work. Household budgets, monthly cash flow sheets and complex company accounts are all made possible by deploying simple spreadsheet functionality which calculates to 100% accuracy. Simple addition and subtraction can be enough for basic financial work whilst pivot tables and lookups may be necessary for more detailed work. For any type of arithmetic a spreadsheet can be set up to accept variable data and perform calculations to give desired outputs such as profit figures, total budget available or the amount left to spend after household bills are settled.

DATABASE

Details relating to an individual product, item, person or any entity can be kept in list order and later used to merge with other software. A spreadsheet's design prompts natural list production similar to the table layout in a database. Such lists can quickly be sorted into specified orders such as largest to smallest, or alphabetical order. They can also be filtered to display only what the user wants to see. Such lists can utilise the formulas available to automatically calculate the data entry in further columns which can be filled down or across to save having to enter the same formula each time a new record is added. A spreadsheet database can be used as a source file for mail merging with a word processors.

GRAPHICAL DATA REPRESENTATION

Numerical data is often best displayed in graphical form to aid the ease with which it can be interpreted by humans. By looking at a graph or chart it is quicker to ascertain the busiest time of the year for the sale of certain products, or when the temperature was coldest in a particular region. Pie charts helpfully show how a resource has been shared and can visually show what element dominates the particular resource. For example, a budget of £100 can be divided between several departments. A pie chart will clearly show which department has the biggest share and which has the smallest. For control purposes this can be useful information. Some spreadsheets include map functions which can be used to display trends in various regions by colour coding or presenting a percentage figure at a certain point in the map. The production of graphs and charts needs some tutoring to start with, but after some familiarity the process is quite simple, as it incorporates the use of wizards that prompt for labels and offer various views the data can take before a final image is produced. Another key feature is that when the data used to construct the chart or graph is changed so the view of the chart or graph also changes.

STATISTICAL ANALYSIS

Spreadsheets are perfectly suited to performing statistical analysis. Data can be fed in automatically using data logging equipment, barcode readings, various types of scanners or the keyboard and various details can be extracted. For example, maximum and minimum values can be displayed; averages, mean, range and other mathematical work can be applied. Statistical data relating to exam results is produced each year to show the national average of A*–C pass grades, whilst at a reduced scale schools will be producing similar details relating to how certain classes performed under various teachers in various subjects. Such data can be used to aid planning and decision-making for the new academic year. Statistics are commonly used to argue cases for selection of sports teams by looking over the field of likely candidates and their previous scores with the bat or times on the track. Government agencies are also fond of using statistics to prove how well the economy is growing and the rate at which national spending on long-term projects is increasing. Finally, though, a 'health warning' should be applied to all statistically manipulated data because with careful massaging and clever tweaking statistics can be and are used to prove just about anything.

Spreadsheets (continued)

Spreadsheets – evaluation

Advantages	Disadvantages
• The use of spreadsheets has become ubiquitous in environments where financial and/or statistical data have to be managed. • They can perform a full range of mathematical calculations with a high degree of precision in a fraction of the time it would take a human. • Cells, spreadsheets and workbooks can be dynamically linked, so that updating of associated data is automatic. • Properly protected and regularly backed-up, they can be used to provide a secure and economical store for large volumes of statistical data. • They can provide a user-friendly means of creating graphical representations of statistical data. • They can be used for modelling scenarios based on 'what-if' projections. They can thus aid decision-making.	• There are no obvious intrinsic disadvantages to using spreadsheet software over traditional, manual methods. The problems that might be faced are generic to computing, i.e. vulnerability to loss of data, virus attacks, unauthorised access, etc. There might be some concern about keeping critical data in an environment that isn't 100% secure, but this was equally the case with the traditional methods. • Some users may find it difficult to adapt to working with electronic spreadsheets and this may lead to errors being made. • Spreadsheets can appear very powerful but it takes time to become a competent user and to learn which of the complex formulae are best suited to the task being carried out.

Modelling

The ability to set up a spreadsheet to insert various data into predefined cells means that those using them can produce a variety of outputs to test different scenarios. For example, a model of how fast checkout staff in a supermarket can serve each customer can help to work out average queue times per customer. By increasing the number of staff packing or working the till the queue time should show different outcomes and help management decide how many staff they ideally need if they want to keep queue times to an acceptable level. This is known as running 'What If' scenarios.

What IF I employed more staff
What IF I employed less staff

The system should adjust the output to potentially show what could happen if the decision is taken. Another example, used by scientists is to produce models which predict what will happen to the Earth if pollution keeps on rising or the ozone layer continues to be depleted. By increasing the temperature value in the model the scientist can be given predictive data relating to the speed at which the ice caps will melt. Each rise in temperature should show the amount of time reduced.

Issues associated with modelling

• Modelling brings with it many benefits: it is cheaper than building prototypes; it can represent complex phenomena in a simplified format; it can compute data in a fraction of the time it would take humans; it can suggest future trends in business, society, the natural world, etc.
• Some programs oversimplify complex phenomena by computing some but not all of the relevant data. Consequently, models are produced that don't take into account all the variables involved.
• Some phenomena are bound by rules and laws that are well understood, e.g. the relationship between mass and energy. Other phenomena are less well understood, e.g. the factors affecting population growth. None the less, some computer models are based on incompletely understood rules and laws. Moreover decisions are made on the basis of the predictions such models produce. A good example of this is the debate about global warming: different countries are making different commitments to the reduction of greenhouse gasses (partly) on the basis of which predictive model they adhere to, yet all of these models are based on an incomplete understanding of major climatic change.

Presentation software

Presentation software has been welcomed by anyone who wishes to display information intended for an audience. Used in conjunction with a projector and audio equipment, presentation software utilises tools which make presenting information more dynamic and interesting. Text and images can be timed to appear in a predetermined manner (animated) at a given time or at the click of a mouse. Sound effects, music and recorded verbal audio can be added along with video files. Teachers, university lecturers, those involved with corporate training and students all use presentation software to convey findings to more than one person. The ability to combine a range of different data into a logical and simple layout has attracted many types of users who are able to constantly add to or amend their presentations to enhance what they have done after each show, sales pitch or lesson.

Some key functions of presentation software

FORMATTING

The appearance of each individual slide can be changed in a number of different ways. Formatting allows the user to determine the properties of any text that is used: the slide background, borders, bullets, graphics, etc. Properties that can be changed include: size, position on the page, colour and order priority. Many programs also offer formatted templates. These provide a colour-coordinated outline that the user can customise as necessary. The whole slide show can be formatted so that it looks the same, to promote a consistent corporate identity.

IMPORTING OBJECTS

The program not only allows the user to insert any text that they wish, but also to import different objects. These objects may include graphs created in a spreadsheet document, images taken from a clip-art library, a table from a word-processed document, etc. The object may be embedded in the slide-show or linked so that it automatically updates. The more sophisticated presentation programs allow the user to import video clips and sound files. By using these facilities it is possible to create an exciting multimedia presentation.

CREATING A SHOW

The user can customise, to some degree, the way in which the slide-show runs. If it is necessary for the person giving the presentation to control the pace of the show, the transitions can be made to occur on a mouse click or a key stroke. Alternatively, if the slide show can run automatically, the transitions may be set to a timer. This approach might be used if the show is being set up to run on a TV monitor in a continuous loop. The way in which the show starts and ends can also be defined by the user.

ANIMATED TRANSITIONS

One set of functions to be found in a presentation package relate to the way that text and graphics appear on the screen. Instead of the text just appearing, it can be made to 'fly' in from one side, emerge gradually in a 'chequerboard' pattern, spin in from the centre, etc. Such effects liven up the slide-show and make it more interesting for the audience. Similar functions can be used to define the way in which one slide transmutes into another, e.g. as one slide finishes it 'dissolves' into the next. This is known as a transition.

Advantages and disadvantages of using presentation software

ADVANTAGES	DISADVANTAGES
• The quality of presentation is superior to that which can be produced by photographic slides and overhead transparencies. • It has the potential to utilise full multimedia facilities, thus expanding what material can be included in the presentation. • The finished document can be economically stored, easily edited and used again as often as necessary without any diminishing of quality. • The user has much more control over the final appearance of the slide show. • It can run automatically – in 'loop' mode – on a TV monitor, e.g. as used in exhibits, etc. • Presentations can be attached to websites and downloaded by interested parties.	• Some files, especially those that contain multimedia elements, can take up a lot of memory resources. • In order to show the presentation effectively, a good quality computer projector is required. These can be costly. • As with all computer-based technology, there is the danger of the document being lost or corrupted as the result of a system crash or security breach. • The quality of the presentation is dependent on user skill level. • Some people rely too much on presentation software and this can irritate the audience after a while.

Web-browsing software

How web browsers developed

The World Wide Web had its inception at the end of the 1980s at the Geneva base of the European Organisation for Nuclear Research. It was designed (by scientists Tim Berners-Lee and Robert Cailliau) to be a communication tool that would help physicists all over the world share their data and ideas. It took a while for this idea, generally considered to be one of the most revolutionary of the twentieth century, to take hold. By June 1993 there were just over 100 websites, mostly based in scientific centres and universities and accessed by only a few informed academics. What was needed for the idea to gain widespread acceptance was an application that would allow the general user to access and read websites.

In 1993 Marc Andreesen, a student at the University of Illinois, led a team that developed the first web browser application. The browser, which was called Mosaic, was an immediate success. In 1994 he developed it as commercial application and launched it as Netscape Navigator. Its widespread acceptance by general users led to the explosive growth of the World Wide Web. By January 1996 there were 100,000 registered websites. To date, there are approximately 108 million websites with roughly 27 pages each, which totals 29.7 billion web pages. By the time this book reaches the shelves this figure will be even higher.

The main function of a web browser

The primary function of a web browser is to use the Internet to request web pages. The web page arrives as an HTML file. The browser interprets this and displays the results.

```
<!DOCTYPE HTML PUBLIC "-//W3C//DTD
HTML 3.2 Final//EN">
<html>
<head>
<title>Oxford University Press - OUP - UK
Official Home Page of Oxford University Press
- Oxford Books</title>
<!--META TAGS TO AID SEARCH ENGINE
DESCRIPTION-->
<meta http-equiv="Content-Type"
content="text/html; charset=iso-8859-1">
<META http-equiv="PICS-Label"
content='(PICS-1.1
"http://www.rsac.org/ratingsv01.html" l gen true
comment "RSACi North America Server" for
"http://www.oup.co.uk" on "1999.10.12T10:30-
0800" r (n 0 s 0 v 0 l 0))'>
<meta name="author" value="OUP England -
enquiry@oup.co.uk">
<meta name="description" content="Oxford
University Press UK - dictionaries, educational,
academic and scholarly books.">
```

The user requests a web page by clicking on a hyperlink or typing in the website's URL into the address box. The browser sends the request to the user's Internet Service Provider or to a direct network link. The request is then made to the server hosting the desired website. The host sends back an HTML (Hyper Text Mark-up Language) file that contains all the information needed to create the web page.

The HTML file is read and interpreted by the browser. It uses the detailed instructions embedded in the code to construct the requested page. Some sections of the code relate to the overall appearance of the page, other sections contain addresses of files (e.g. graphics files) that need to be downloaded.

The page is gradually constructed on the screen. Some aspects of the page 'arrive' more quickly than others which is why web pages construct themselves in stages. The browser also needs to be able to launch helper applications (or plug-ins) in order to include certain types of files, e.g. audio files. If certain components of the page (e.g. a specified colour) are not available, the browser uses appropriate substitutes.

Other facilities offered by web browsers

Web browsers have grown in sophistication and now offer a number of additional functions to support the user. These include:

Favourites	A way of storing the addresses of those websites the user visits most often.
History	A function that allows the user to maintain a record of recently visited sites.
Navigation	There are a number of navigation options available, including the facility to return to a previous web page, to return to the home page, to cancel the downloading of a page, etc.
Search	Most users go to a search engine site (e.g. Google) to search for a particular item, but web browsers come with their own search facility.
Security	The user can determine their own security settings, ensuring, for example, that only websites that have been approved are downloaded.
Links	Browsers display links to popular websites, or to a page with links that come under a certain category heading (e.g. music, news, sport, etc).
Email	The user can access and compose emails via the browser.

Web-authoring software

One of the most revolutionary aspects of the Internet is the way it allows users with varying levels of experience and only minimum resources to create their own websites. This facility has led to an increase in small-scale enterprises challenging the market domination of established companies and, indeed, creating entirely new markets. It has also meant that special interest groups have been able to express their views and communicate with like-minded people around the globe, by-passing the commercially controlled mass media. In order that individuals with little or no programming experience can produce websites, software has been developed that facilitates this in a user-friendly way. This is referred to as web-authoring software.

Functionality of web authoring-software

CODE VIEW

Web pages are visual representations of programming code, usually HTML. However, most web-authoring packages don't require the user to write any code at all. Rather, they enable the construction of a page via a graphical user interface, where objects are 'dragged and dropped' on to a page template. However, some users will want to examine and amend the underlying code. An effective program will allow this to happen.

FORMAT

The final look of a web page is something that the user will want to determine. The program should offer formatting facilities such as:

- Colour options for backgrounds, text, simple graphical objects, e.g. lines, boxes, etc.
- Font and point size options for text objects
- Positioning of objects on the page and general layout items, e.g. columns, tables, etc.

OBJECT ACCESS

In addition to text, websites often contain graphical objects. A web-authoring program will allow the user to access these objects (e.g. by providing a clip-art library), import them into a document and manipulate them once they are there. More sophisticated packages will enable the importing of animated graphics, video clips, sound files, etc.

LINKS

Web pages usually contain links to other related pages. These are hypertext links, the activation of which sends a request for a different web page to be downloaded. The web-authoring program will allow the user to add new links to the site. These hyperlinks may simply indicate the URL that is being requested, e.g. www://http/oup.co.uk, or the URL may be activated by clicking on a graphical object.

TEMPLATES

Many web-authoring packages are aimed at the general user and so assume that they will need help in constructing their website. This help can take many forms including templates (i.e. outline website structures that just require details to be added) and wizards (i.e. series of dialogue boxes that take the user through a procedure one step at a time).

CGI

CGI stands for Common Gateway Interface and is a protocol that standardises the way that users can interact with a website. For example, the user may wish to include an interactive form as part of their site, i.e. where a visitor can register details or take part in a transaction. This requires the construction of CGI script. Many web-authoring programs enable this process without the user having to write any code.

Graphics software

Characteristic features of graphics software

Graphics software is designed to allow the user to store, manipulate and print graphical images. There are different varieties of graphics software, each designed for a different purpose, but they share some common characteristics:

Manipulation	The user can move images around the page, resize them, 'crop' them (i.e. extract sections) and, depending on the sophistication of the program, change their perspective, e.g. 'flip' the entire image from right to left.
Modification	The properties of the image (line width, colour, texture, brightness, etc.) can be adjusted, either in relation to individual components of the image or to the image as a whole. In this way the user can alter the overall look of the image.
Importing	The user should be able to import images from various sources and work with them in the document. Programs usually allow importing from scanners, digital cameras and clip-art libraries. Some programs are particular about what file formats can be used. In such case the image files will need to be converted before they can be used.
Stored files	In addition to allowing users to import their own images, many programs come with their own image banks. These may consist of general clip-art libraries or specialist graphic objects that could be needed for the specific program, e.g. software to help people design gardens will have available graphical representations of fences, lawns, plants, etc.
Graphical tools	Those programs that allow users to create their own images provide computerised versions of typical graphical tools, e.g. brushes, pencils, spray paints, etc. that create analogous effects.

Varieties of graphics software

COMPUTER-AIDED DESIGN (CAD) PROGRAMS

- CAD programs are designed to be used by professional designers, architects, engineers, etc. The level of sophistication in such programs makes them unsuitable for the general user.
- They use vector-based images rather than bit-maps as this allows for a greater level of precision, especially when the image needs to be manipulated.
- They allow the user to view objects from different perspectives and to model them at different stages of development, e.g. a car may be shown both as a skeletal design and as the finished product.
- Sophisticated CAD programs are able to calculate material costs based on the size of the product or building, and the amount of manpower required to construct over various timescales.

PHOTO-MANIPULATION PROGRAMS

- Increasingly, people are using digital format cameras to take their photographs and computers to store them on. This is true both for professionals and general users.
- Photo-manipulation software has grown in popularity. Consequently, there are a variety of programs on the market, some aimed at the professional, some at the home user. The functionality is broadly the same but the level of sophistication differs.
- The programs work with bit-mapped files, allowing the user to manipulate the size and shape of the image. A bank of effects facilitates modification of the image, e.g. a colour image can be made to appear in black and white.

PAINT/DRAW PROGRAMS

- Paint/draw programs facilitate the creation of images by the user. The program provides a 'blank canvas' and a set of graphical tools to work with. These tools are computerised equivalents of pencils, brushes, crayons, paint sprays, etc.
- The image is built up by the user, using different colours and textures. It can then be edited and modified, with elements changed and new effects added.
- Programs of this kind are used by both the general user and professional artists working in computer-generated formats. There are a number of programs aimed at young children.

Hardware needs

Memory store	Graphics programs generally use more memory resources than text-based programs. If this is not allowed for, computer performance will be affected as more and more images are stored on the system.
Input devices	Specialist input devices can be used to gain a great degree of precision (e.g. a digitiser tablet) or to mimic the effects of real graphical tools (e.g. a light pen).
Printers	Specialist printers (e.g. graphical plotters) may be needed by professional users and even home users will need a good-quality printer and specially formatted paper if they are going to achieve good-quality finished products.

Databases: introduction

What is a database?

A database is a systematically organised store of data. Increasingly, the term database refers to computerised systems, but databases can also be manual. Before computers, manual systems such as card index files, filing cabinets, libraries, etc. were used to organise data and so can be defined as databases. Computers have the ability to store large amounts of data in a compact space and to process it speedily. These two facilities make them ideally suited for database work and organisations of all sizes now use computers to sort, store, interrogate; and manage their data. Databases vary enormously, in terms both of scale and architecture, but there are certain elements that are common to almost all database systems:

* Data is organised in tabular structures where each row constitutes one record and each column defines a field.
* Users are able to add new records, amend existing records, and delete unwanted records.
* Users are able to interrogate (or 'query') the database, i.e. ask it to show which records fulfil certain criteria.
* Users can output the results of queries as reports. These can be viewed on-screen or printed out as hard copy.

How does a database work?

ID	Forename	Surname	Dept

A file structure is created that organises the data into fields (e.g. ID, forename, etc.) and records (each row is one record).

DATA ENTRY FORM

ID	1
FORENAME	John
SURNAME	Stevens
DEPT	Finance

A user-friendly data entry form is used to add new records and amend existing records.

ID	Forename	Surname	Dept
1	John	Stevens	Finance
2	Michael	Lee	Marketing
3	Sally	Atkinson	Finance
4	Harinda	Singh	Hum Res
5	Shima	Begum	Finance
6	Helen	Doods	Marketing
7	Duane	Courcy	Hum Res
8	Tony	Yip	Ops
9	Julia	Wallace	Ops

The table is populated with records which can then be interrogated.

DEPARTMENT REPORT QUERY

DEPARTMENT	Finance

A form is used to set the parameters of a query. In this case the user wants to extract the names of all those who work in the finance department.

ID	Forename	Surname	Dept
1	John	Stevens	Finance
3	Sally	Atkinson	Finance
5	Shima	Begum	Finance

The query is run and selects only those records that match the criteria. In this case those records where 'finance' is the entry in the 'dept' column.

Department personnel report

Dept: Finance

ID	Forename	Surname
1	John	Stevens
3	Sally	Atkinson
5	Shima	Begum

A report can now be created based on the information returned by the query. The report can be stored and recreated using different data as and when required.

Who uses databases?

A wide variety of individuals and organisations use databases; below are just a few examples:

Police forces use databases which store images of known criminals and fingerprints, and use them to match evidence and witness statements collected after a crime has been committed.

DATABASES

Schools use databases to keep records of pupils, their assessment data, the timetable they follow, etc.

Hospitals maintain databases of patients, doctors, treatments, etc. This is used to administer consultations, admissions, etc.

Businesses of all sizes maintain databases to keep track of sales, stock purchases, etc. and to analyse their performance. Databases also help companies identify trends in order to target specific markets.

Properties of data held in a database

A database is generally made up of data organised into tables.

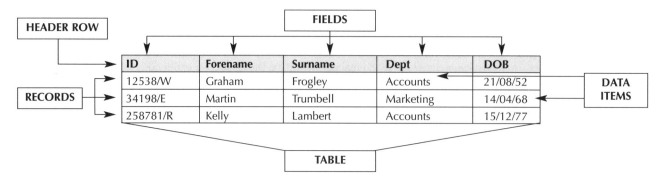

When a database is being created it is important to define what properties each data item will have, i.e. how it will be stored. This is undertaken at the design stage and involves setting field properties. The field properties will determine how each item in that field will be stored.

Field size
The maximum size of a data item can be set as a field property. This facility helps to ensure optimal efficiency in memory use. For example, if a data item will never exceed 10 characters, that would be set as the maximum field size.

Validation
A validation rule can be set at this stage. The validation rule will determine the conditions that a piece of data must meet if it is to be stored in a particular field. If it does not meet those conditions, it will be rejected.

Format
Some data items will be entered in a set pattern. The most obvious example is a date which will usually be entered as DD/MM/YY. This format can be set as a field property thus ensuring consistency in the way that the data is held.

Key field
A key field provides a unique identifier for each record. It usually consists of an identification code. This field is used in a relational database to link to other tables. A field, and hence the data items stored in that field, is either defined as a key field or it is not.

FIELD PROPERTIES

Index
When a field is indexed each record is given an order number. This index information is stored separately and can be used to speed up the sorting and searching of records. Key fields are often indexed as are any fields that are regularly used as a primary sort field.

Data types
In order to optimise database efficiency, data needs to be held in the most appropriate way, i.e. the correct data type. The following are the most commonly used:

Text/alphanumeric Used for data that will be wholly text, text and number combined, or numbers that will not be used in calculations (e.g. a telephone number).

Numeric Used for data that consists of numbers that may be calculated. This data type may be further specified as integer, double precision, single precision, floating point, etc.

Currency Used for data that represents an amount of money. The precise nature of the currency (dollar, euro, sterling, etc.) will need to be specified.

Boolean In a Boolean field only two data items are permitted: true and false. This is sometimes represented as yes/no, on/off, etc.

Memo A memo field allows longer text entries. It is useful where continuous prose (e.g. in a 'Notes' field) is required.

Date/time This data type is suitable for all data that represents a particular date or time.

Example – the properties of two data items

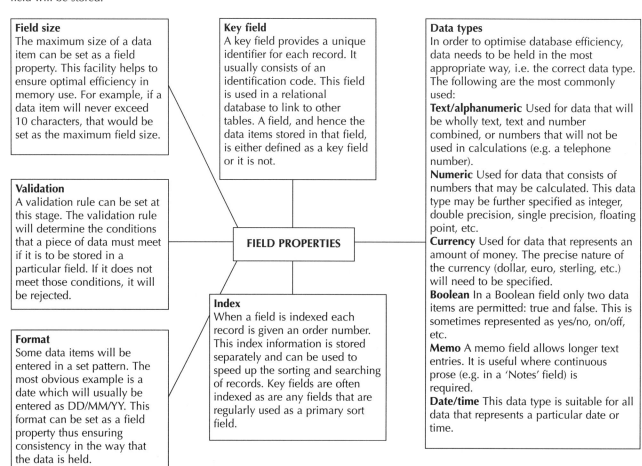

Data Item: 12/09/86	
Field name	Date_of_Birth
Field description	Employee's birth date
Index	No
Key field	No
Validation	Must be <([Now])
Data type	Date/time
Format	DD/MM/YY
Field size	8 characters

Data Item: North West	
Field name	Region
Field description	Define employee's base region
Index	No
Key field	No
Validation	Must be drawn from Region table
Data type	Text
Format	-
Field size	25

Flat-file systems

What is a flat-file system?

A flat-file system refers to a database where all the data is held in a single table or file. Below is an example of a flat-file database that might be used by an electrician to keep a record of work completed.

Job No.	Customer	Contact No.	Address	Estimate	Completion	Amount paid
A113	Mr K Jones	0309 224567	23 High St Sutton SM1 8YG	£330.75	12/01/02	£335.00
A114	Mrs R Tennet	0309 556213	14 Eastfield Rd Wallington WA4 5RT	£240.00	15/01/02	£230.00
A115	Mr P Suliman	0309 872136	4 Jones Avenue Sutton SM6 7TY	£195.00	25/01/02	£210.50
A116	Mr P Suliman	0309 872136	4 Jones Avenue Sutton SM6 7TY	£500.00	15/02/02	£560.50

Even though this is a relatively simple system with limited data, some of the problems inherent in flat-file systems are already evident:

Data redundancy   This is an important concept in database design. It refers to the unnecessary duplication of data. In the table above, data will be repeated each time the electrician does another job for the same customer. The unnecessary duplication of the customer's details constitutes data redundancy.

Data integrity   The integrity of data is its correctness, i.e. the extent to which it truthfully represents the original source information. One of the problems of maintaining integrity arises when updating occurs. In the example above, if Mr Suliman changes his phone number, it must be updated in every record where his name occurs. If it were left undone in one record, the data associated with Mr Suliman would no longer be wholly correct.

Flat-file systems in organisations

In the early days of computers, organisations would store data in separate files, each file related to a functional area of the organisation. The data held in such systems was manipulated and interrogated using software called 'file management systems'. This is shown in the diagram below.

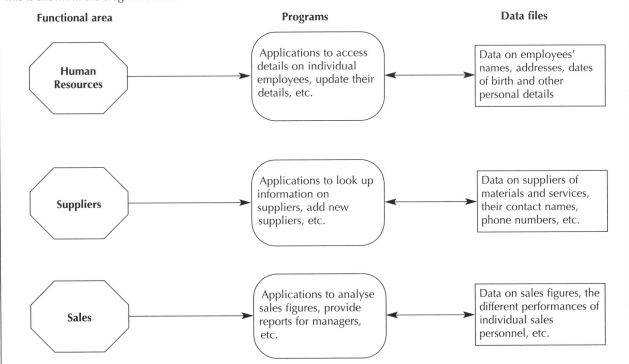

In such a system, problems related to data integrity and data redundancy are multiplied many times over. It is likely, for example, that data related to individual products would be stored both in the 'Sales' data files and the 'Suppliers' data files. Such data would be held more than once – leading to data redundancy. The integrity of such data would also be under threat. If the details of a product were changed in the 'Suppliers' file, procedures would be needed to ensure that it was updated in any other data files where it occurred. Such procedures would be difficult to maintain.

Another factor has to be taken into account when separate but overlapping data files are used – that of data consistency.

Data consistency   When data is held in more than one file it should be stored in a consistent form. In the example above, there would be data on sales personnel in both the 'Sales' file and the 'Human Resources' file. If in one file the date of birth was held as a text data type (e.g. 21 September 1960) and in the other as a time/date data type (e.g. 21/09/60) the data would be incompatible.

Relational databases

What is a relational database?

Relational databases were first developed in the 1970s by Edgar Codd as a way, initially, of providing a more flexible system for responding to spontaneous requests for management information. As they developed it was found that they also helped to solve many of the problems associated with data redundancy, data integrity and data consistency associated with flat-file systems. The key difference between relational databases and flat-file systems lies in the creation of separate tables that are related to each other. The diagram below uses the example of the electrician's data file.

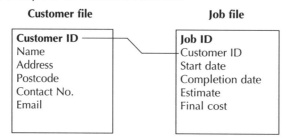

All the data associated with the customer is now held in one file and all the data associated with each job is held another file. In order to create a connection between the two sets of data, a relationship must be created by using two **key fields.**

Primary key   A key field is a unique identifier, usually some type of code number. The primary key is the start point of a relationship and will only occur once in that file. In this case each record in the customer file will describe the attributes of one customer and one customer only. That customer will be uniquely identified by the customer ID field.

Foreign key   The foreign key is the destination point of the relationship. It remains a unique identifier as regards the customer, but may occur more than once in the Job file, i.e. because the customer may have more than one job completed by the electrician.

The records might now look like this:

Customer ID	Customer	Contact No.	Address	Email
KJ2245	Mr K Jones	0309 224567	23 High St Sutton SM1 8YG	Kjones@serveme.co.uk
RT5562	Mrs R Tennet	0309 556213	14 Eastfield Rd Wallington WA4 5RT	–
PS8721	Mr P Suliman	0309 872136	4 Jones Avenue Sutton SM6 7TY	Psulxx@onserve.co.uk

Job No.	Customer ID	Start Date	Estimate	Completion date	Final cost
A113	KJ2245	05/01/02	£330.75	12/01/02	£335.00
A114	RT5562	13/01/02	£240.00	15/01/02	£230.00
A115	PS8721	20/01/02	£195.00	25/01/02	£210.50
A116	PS8721	10/02/02	£500.00	15/02/02	£560.50

As you can see, the Customer ID field acts as the **primary key** in the Customer file and the **foreign key** in the Job file, thus enabling a relationship between the two tables.

What are the advantages of a relational database over a flat-file system?

Data integrity	There is no need to change data in more than one table. If a customer's details require updating this only needs to happen once, i.e. in the Customer file. All references to that customer in any other file (i.e. via the primary key) will automatically reflect the update.
Data redundancy	In a well-designed relational database there should be no 'repeating attributes', i.e. no piece of data should be unnecessarily repeated.
Data consistency	Because the attributes of any one entity (e.g. a job, a customer) are contained within one file, there is no risk of the same attribute being stored in a different format in a different file.
Flexibility	A relational database can be queried with greater flexibility than a flat-file system. Data drawn from different files can be combined in a variety of ways, producing better-quality information.
Greater efficiency	Data only has to be inputted once and this saves on time and human resources. The memory space required is also less and this saves on computing resources.

Querying databases: 1

The prime function of a database is to store data in an organised way so that users can interrogate and manipulate that data. There may be many reasons why users may wish to undertake this process, e.g. identifying a group of records that share specified qualities; calculating totals based on the information held in records; updating the details of a specified record or group of records; viewing data in different combinations and formats, etc. Databases usually allow users to define and store their own queries. The nature of the query will depend on the task it has to perform. Below are some examples of different querying techniques.

A select query – single criteria

A select query extracts a sub-set of data from a table or more than one linked tables. Criteria are used to establish which records will be extracted.

TABLE

Product_ID	Prod_Name	Cost_price	In_Stock
CA/34/99	20m Cable	£12.65	21
CA/56/98	Cable Ties	£4.50	6
CO/73/99	Connectors	£2.35	5
SW/86/98	Switches	£4.67	17
FC/54/99	Fine Cable	£16.78	9

QUERY

	Product_ID	Prod_Name	Cost_price	In_Stock
Criteria				<8
Sort		Ascending		

RESULT

Product_ID	Prod_Type	Cost_price	In_Stock
CA/56/98	Cable Ties	£4.50	6
CO/73/99	Connectors	£2.35	5

A select query – multiple criteria

Sometimes it is necessary to set more than one criteria. Boolean operators (e.g. 'AND', 'OR', etc.) can be used to make the selection criteria more specific.

TABLE

Product_ID	Prod_Name	Cost_price	In_Stock
CA/34/99	20m Cable	£12.65	21
CA/56/98	Cable Ties	£4.50	6
CO/73/99	Connectors	£2.35	5
SW/86/98	Switches	£4.67	17
FC/54/99	Fine Cable	£16.78	9

QUERY

	Product_ID	Prod_Name	Cost_price	In_Stock
Criteria			>£4.00	<20
Sort			Ascending	

RESULT

Product_ID	Prod_Type	Cost_price	In_Stock
CA/56/98	Cable Ties	£4.50	6
SW/86/98	Switches	£4.67	17
FC/54/99	Fine Cable	£16.78	9

An update query

An update query can be used to change data in a table. This function is especially useful when block updates, e.g. a price change, need to be made.

TABLE

Product_ID	Prod_Name	Cost_price	In_Stock
CA/34/99	20m Cable	£12.65	21
CA/56/98	Cable Ties	£4.50	6
CO/73/99	Connectors	£2.35	5
SW/86/98	Switches	£4.67	17
FC/54/99	Fine Cable	£16.78	9

QUERY

	Product_ID	Prod_Name	Cost_price	In_Stock
Update to			£13.15	
Criteria		= "20m Cable"		

RESULT

Product_ID	Prod_Type	Cost_price	In_Stock
CA/34/99	20m Cable	£13.15	21
CA/56/98	Cable Ties	£4.50	6
CO/73/99	Connectors	£2.35	5
SW/86/98	Switches	£4.67	17
FC/54/99	Fine Cable	£16.78	9

A query with calculated totals

Queries can be used to make calculations based on the data held in tables. In addition to the formula used here, queries can show averages, sums, counts, etc.

TABLE

Product_ID	Prod_Name	Cost_price	In_Stock
CA/34/99	20m Cable	£12.65	21
CA/56/98	Cable Ties	£4.50	6
CO/73/99	Connectors	£2.35	5
SW/86/98	Switches	£4.67	17
FC/54/99	Fine Cable	£16.78	9

QUERY

Product_ID	
	= Cost_price*In_Stock

RESULT

Product_ID	Value of stock
CA/34/99	£265.65
CA/56/98	£27.00
CO/73/99	£11.75
SW/86/98	£79.39
FC/54/99	£151.02

Querying databases: 2

What is SQL?

Database applications usually provide users with a user-friendly means of constructing queries, whereby the user can specify the parameters of the query, the data they wish to interrogate, and the form they would like the results presented in. This approach works well at a basic level but can be restrictive when the needs are more complex. For example, a developer may be trying to create an application that draws on data held in different databases, running on different platforms. She will need to write her code in such a way as to communicate with a range of database formats. In order to meet this need a set of 'query languages' has emerged. These languages give users a common platform from which to interrogate and manipulate data held in different databases. The most widely used of these languages is Structured Query Language (SQL).

SQL is not as easy to use as database programs that provide user-friendly interfaces for the construction of queries. It is a complex computer language with its own vocabulary, grammar and syntax, all of which need to be learnt if it is to be used effectively. It can also be time-consuming to write out extensive SQL code. There are, however, programs that help the user write SQL code and its flexibility and robustness make it a boon for developers. It can deal with complex, multi-faceted relational database queries and is now widely accepted as a standard for interrogating and manipulating data.

SQL example 1

TABLE (PRODUCTS)

Product_ID	Prod_Name	Cost_price	In_Stock
CA/34/99	20m Cable	£12.65	21
CA/56/98	Cable Ties	£4.50	6
CO/73/99	Connectors	£2.35	5
SW/86/98	Switches	£4.67	17
FC/54/99	Fine Cable	£16.78	9

SQL STATEMENT

SELECT Product_ID, Prod_Name, Cost_Price, In_Stock
FROM Products
WHERE Products.In_Stock < 8
ORDER BY Prod_Type

RESULT

Product_ID	Prod_Type	Cost_price	In_Stock
CA/56/98	Cable Ties	£4.50	6
CO/73/99	Connectors	£2.35	5

In this example the 'SELECT' clause of the code indicates which fields should be displayed in the result, the 'FROM' clause indicates the table where the data resides, the 'WHERE' clause defines the criteria that will be used to define the extracted data and the 'ORDER BY' clause determines how the result will be sorted.

SQL example 2

TABLE (PRODUCTS)

Product_ID	Prod_Name	Cost_price	In_Stock
CA/34/99	20m Cable	£12.65	21
CA/56/98	Cable Ties	£4.50	6
CO/73/99	Connectors	£2.35	5
SW/86/98	Switches	£4.67	17
FC/54/99	Fine Cable	£16.78	9

SQL STATEMENT

UPDATE Products
SET Products.Cost_price = "£13.15"
WHERE Products.Product_Name = "20m Cable"

RESULT

Product_ID	Prod_Name	Cost_price	In_Stock
CA/34/99	20m Cable	£13.15	21
CA/56/98	Cable Ties	£4.50	6
CO/73/99	Connectors	£2.35	5
SW/86/98	Switches	£4.67	17
FC/54/99	Fine Cable	£16.78	9

In this example the 'UPDATE' clause indicates the name of the table in which the data items to be updated reside, the 'SET' clause indicates the field to be updated, and the 'WHERE' clause defines the criteria that must be met if the records are to be updated.

Using queries to create reports

One of the prime functions of a database is to provide reports for the user. These reports, which can be presented on-screen but are more often printed as hard copy, provide information in an appropriate format for the user. The precise nature of the report's format will depend on the use to which the user is going to put the information. For example, a distribution manager may want a simple printout of drivers' phone numbers, whereas as a senior manager might want a monthly summary of sales figures in graphical form. The format will be determined by the user.

How a query can be used to create a report

A DVD store keeps its data in a relational database. It has tables for data on Customers, DVD, Loans, Suppliers and Miscellaneous Sales. The tables are related to each other using key fields. Below are extracts from the customer file and the loan file.

CUSTOMER FILE

Customer_ID	Name	Surname	Address	Town	Code
12/578/AF	Miss K Stevens	Stevens	12 The Grove,	Newton	NW3 7YT
12/987/PH	Mr T Koways	Kowaya	34 West Street	Newton	NW3 8YH
12/960/LK	Mr F Greene	Greene	14 High Road	Forsham	FS4 9RE
13/97/LH	Mrs D Patel	Patel	3 Grand Drive	Newton	NW3 8TT
13/652/PF	Mr L Wai Lun	Wai Lun	12 Wick Ave	Forsham	FS4 3ES
13/041/UG	Miss F Rogers	Rogers	15 Smiley Street	Newton	NW4 6RS
12/749/SA	Mr J Nunn	Nunn	11 Lode Cres	Yale	NW6 5GT

LOAN FILE

Loan_ID	DVD_Id	Customer_ID	Date_out	Date_Back	Paid
1	128/AC	12/578/AF	12/01/02	13/01/02	£3.50
2	134/RO	12/960/LK	12/01/02	13/01/02	£3.50
3	453/AC	12/578/AF	12/01/02	13/01/02	£3.50
4	774/HO	13/652/PF	12/01/02	13/01/02	£2.00
5	325/CO	12/749/SA	12/01/02	13/01/02	£3.50
6	467/CO	13/652/PF	12/01/02	13/01/02	£3.50
7	552/AC	12/578/AF	12/01/02	13/01/02	£2.00

The DVD store owner want to offer his best customers 'Gold Card' status and so he needs to produce a report that will tell him who his best customers are. He uses a user-friendly interface to create the query.

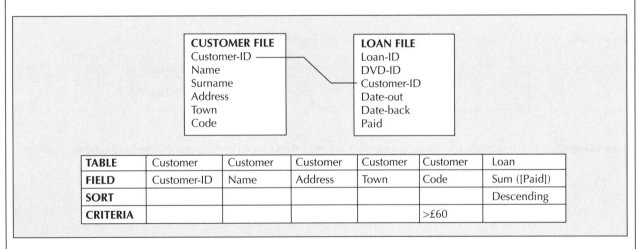

CUSTOMER FILE
Customer-ID
Name
Surname
Address
Town
Code

LOAN FILE
Loan-ID
DVD-ID
Customer-ID
Date-out
Date-back
Paid

TABLE	Customer	Customer	Customer	Customer	Customer	Loan
FIELD	Customer-ID	Name	Address	Town	Code	Sum ([Paid])
SORT						Descending
CRITERIA					>£60	

This query has selected the fields that will need to be shown in the report, determined the order in which it will be sorted (i.e. with the customer who has spent the most money shown first) and set the criteria that will be used to extract the data from the tables (i.e. only those customers whose total loans exceed £60 will be included). The two tables that will be needed are linked together (i.e. related) by the Customer_ID key field. A report can now be generated which uses the above query as its data source.

GOLD CARD CUSTOMER REPORT

Quarter: January 1st – March 31st

Name	Address	Town	Code	Total value of loans during last quarter
Miss K Stevens	12 The Grove,	Newton	NW3 7YT	£90
Mr T Koways	34 West Street	Newton	NW3 8YH	£86
Mr F Greene	14 High Road	Forsham	FS4 9RE	£78.50
Mrs D Patel	3 Grand Drive	Newton	NW3 8TT	£65.00

Entity relationship modelling

Before a database can be designed and implemented, it is necessary to model the underlying data elements. There are various methods for doing this, one of which is entity relationship modelling. Three key concepts involved in this process are:

Entity   An entity is a person/object/event/concept on which data can be held. In a hospital database the following would all be entities: patient, nurse, treatment, ward, bed, appointment, test, etc.

Attribute   Each entity has a series of attributes. These describe different properties of the entity. Using the above example, the attributes of a patient would include age, weight, home address, dietary needs, etc.

Relationship   In a relational database, entities will relate to each other in some way. For a example a doctor will treat a number of patients, a nurse may be attached to a particular ward, etc.

Entity relationship modelling involves the creation of diagrams that show which entities will need to exist in the database and how they will need to relate to each other.

In the example below the database is for a veterinary surgery. The following entities might be identified: patient, vet, owner, room, appointment, treatment, nurse and test. The diagram should indicate how these entities relate to each other.

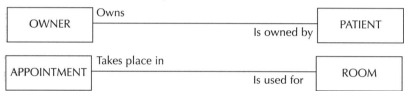

Another aspect of the diagram will be the *types* of relationship that exist between the entities. There are three types of entities:

One-to-one   In this example each vet is allocated one room. It is only possible to have one vet attached to one room at any time.

One-to-many   In this example a vet makes a number of appointments – i.e. one vet, many appointments.

Many-to-many   In this example one animal/patient may see more than one vet and one vet may see any number of animals.

In databases, many-to-many relationships cause difficulties so they are usually joined together via another entity, using two one-to-many relationships. In this example one vet will make a number of appointments and one patient may make many appointments.

In this way a diagrammatic model is built up. It identifies all the entities that will be contained in the database and an indication of the way in which they relate to each other. This then provides a sound basis for designing the resulting database.

Normalisation: 1

What is normalisation?

Normalisation is a formal procedure undertaken during the design stage of database development. It entails creating a robust and valid database structure through a process of 'atomisation', i.e. breaking down the tables into the smallest possible units. Normalisation then involves the creation of a logical structure of related tables in which data will be stored. If completed effectively, it will help in the creation of an efficient, flexible, easy-to-query database. The ideal structure will ensure data consistency and data integrity, and eradicate the unnecessary repetition of data, i.e. data redundancy.

Normalisation is a staged process, usually consisting of a first, second and third normal form. At each stage the structural design is improved. The following illustrates how this process would be undertaken. It is not meant to represent a full data model and there are many other attributes one would expect to see in a database of this kind.

First normal form

Rule *A table is in first normal form when it contains no repeating attributes or groups of attributes.*

Student_ID	Forename	Surname	Course_ID	Course_title	Lecturer_ID	Lecturer_name
24500/V1	James	Sawyer	PY/12AS IT/12AS MA/12AS	Psychology Information Technology Mathematics	AG PHG BD	Mr Gardner Miss Graham Dr Duckham
34567/V1	Lisa	Terry	CH/12AS IT/12AS PH/12AS	Chemistry Information Technology Physics	DD PHG VC	Mr Davenport Miss Graham Mrs Cadwell
54783/V1	David	Brown	MS/12AS EN/12AS HI/12AS	Media Studies English History	LP KN JF	Mr Peterson Miss Nichols Mr Forrest
671200/V1	Steven	Moody	PY/12AS BI/12AS GE/12AS	Psychology Biology Geography	AG AM LS	Mr Gardner Miss Munir Mr Stone
439456/V1	David	Powell	IT/12AS FR/12AS GR/12AS	Information Technology French German	PHG ABL GJ	Miss Graham Mme Bailey Mr Jemson

In this table there are repeating attributes of the 'Course' entity, i.e. the course details are repeated for each student. In its present state, this data table would not satisfy the rule for the first normal form. It is therefore categorised as un-normalised. In its current form this set of data would not be able to function effectively as a database. In particular, problems would be caused when the user wished to update records, add new records or delete records no longer needed.

In order to move this data into the first normal form, it is necessary to split the table into two entities: student and course.

Student_ID	Forename	Surname	Course_ID
24500/V1	James	Sawyer	PY/12AS
24500/V1	James	Sawyer	IT/12AS
24500/V1	James	Sawyer	MA/12AS
34567/V1	Lisa	Terry	CH/12AS
34567/V1	Lisa	Terry	IT/12AS
34567/V1	Lisa	Terry	PH/12AS
54783/V1	David	Brown	EN/12AS
54783/V1	David	Brown	HI/12AS
54783/V1	David	Brown	MS/12AS
671200/V1	Steven	Moody	BI/12AS
671200/V1	Steven	Moody	GE/12AS
671200/V1	Steven	Moody	PY/12AS
439456/V1	David	Powell	IT/12AS
439456/V1	David	Powell	FR/12AS
439456/V1	David	Powell	GR/12AS

Course_ID	Course_title	Lecturer_ID	Lecturer_name
PY/12AS	Psychology	AG	Mr Gardner
CH/12AS	Chemistry	DD	Mr Davenport
MS/12AS	Media Studies	LP	Mr Peterson
IT/12AS	Information Tech	PHG	Miss Graham
MA/12AS	Mathematics	BD	Dr Duckham
PH/12AS	Physics	VC	Mrs Cadwell
EN/12AS	English	KN	Miss Nichols
HI/12AS	History	JF	Mr Forrest
BI/12AS	Biology	AM	Miss Munir
GE/12AS	Geography	LS	Mr Stone
GR/12AS	German	DJ	Mr Jemson
FR/12AS	French	ABL	Mme Bailey

This data is now in the first normal form because there are no repeating attributes or groups of attributes. There is, however, data redundancy: the students' names are being repeated unnecessarily. This will be dealt with in the move to the second normal form.

Normalisation: 2

Second normal form

> **Rule** *In the second normal form there will be no partial key dependencies.*

In this case the columns 'Forename' and 'Surname' are dependent on the Student_ID field, i.e. each entry in the Student_ID column is unique and there is a student name uniquely dependent on it. However, Forename and Surname are not uniquely dependent on the 'Course_ID' field, i.e. any number of student 'Forenames' and 'Surnames' may be linked to an entry in this column. There is, therefore, partial dependency.

The solution to this is one often used in relational databases: separating two entities in a many-to-many relationship by inserting a third entity. In this case many students can take many courses but to leave the tables in this form would not work well in a relational database, so they are linked by a third table called 'Enrolment'.

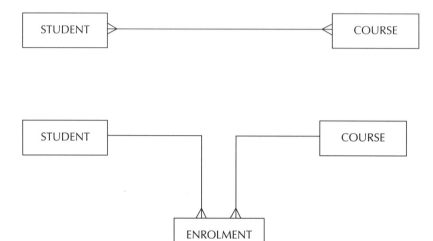

This would result in the following table structures:

STUDENT

Student_ID	Forename	Surname
24500/V1	James	Sawyer
34567/V1	Lisa	Terry
54783/V1	David	Brown
671200/V1	Steven	Moody
439456/V1	David	Powell

COURSE

Course_ID	Course_title	Lecturer_ID	Lecturer_name
PY/12AS	Psychology	AG	Mr Gardner
CH/12AS	Chemistry	DD	Mr Davenport
MS/12AS	Media Studies	LP	Mr Peterson
IT/12AS	Information Tech	PHG	Miss Graham
MA/12AS	Mathematics	BD	Dr Duckham
PH/12AS	Physics	VC	Mrs Cadwell
EN/12AS	English	KN	Miss Nichols
HI/12AS	History	JF	Mr Forrest
BI/12AS	Biology	AM	Miss Munir
GE/12AS	Geography	LS	Mr Stone
GR/12AS	German	DJ	Mr Jemson
FR/12AS	French	ABL	Mme Bailey

ENROLMENT

Student_ID	Course_ID
24500/V1	PY/12AS
24500/V1	IT/12AS
24500/V1	MA/12AS
34567/V1	CH/12AS
34567/V1	IT/12AS
34567/V1	PH/12AS
54783/V1	EN/12AS
54783/V1	HI/12AS
54783/V1	MS/12AS
671200/V1	BI/12AS
671200/V1	GE/12AS
671200/V1	PY/12AS
439456/V1	IT/12AS
439456/V1	GR/12AS
439456/V1	FR/12AS

The database structure is now in the second normal form because there are no partial key dependencies.

Normalisation: 3

Third normal form

Rule   *In the third normal form there are no non-key dependencies.*

After a disposal of any partial key dependencies in the second normal form, the last task in the normalisation process is to eradicate any non-key dependencies. In this case the 'Lecturer_name' field is dependent on the 'Lecturer_ID' field and not the 'Course_ID', as is the case with the second normal form. It is therefore necessary to create a new table called LECTURER. This will contain the unique 'Lecturer_ID' field and the 'Lecturer_Name' which is dependent on it.

STUDENT

Student_ID	Forename	Surname
24500/V1	James	Sawyer
34567/V1	Lisa	Terry
54783/V1	David	Brown
671200/V1	Steven	Moody
439456/V1	David	Powell

COURSE

Course_ID	Course_title	Lecturer_ID
PY/12AS	Psychology	AG
CH/12AS	Chemistry	DD
MS/12AS	Media Studies	LP
IT/12AS	Information Tech	PHG
MA/12AS	Mathematics	BD
PH/12AS	Physics	VC
EN/12AS	English	KN
HI/12AS	History	JF
BI/12AS	Biology	AM
GE/12AS	Geography	LS
GR/12AS	German	DJ
FR/12AS	French	ABL

LECTURER

Lecturer_ID	Lecturer_name
AG	Mr Gardner
DD	Mr Davenport
LP	Mr Peterson
PHG	Miss Graham
BD	Dr Duckham
VC	Mrs Cadwell
KN	Miss Nichols
JF	Mr Forrest
AM	Miss Munir
LS	Mr Stone
DJ	Mr Jemson
ABL	Mme Bailey

ENROLMENT

Student_ID	Course_ID
24500/V1	PY/12AS
24500/V1	IT/12AS
24500/V1	MA/12AS
34567/V1	CH/12AS
34567/V1	IT/12AS
34567/V1	PH/12AS
54783/V1	EN/12AS
54783/V1	HI/12AS
54783/V1	MS/12AS
671200/V1	BI/12AS
671200/V1	GE/12AS
671200/V1	PY/12AS
439456/V1	IT/12AS
439456/V1	GR/12AS
439456/V1	FR/12AS

The tables are now in the third normal form. This now provides the logical basis for a database structure.

Database notation

When the normalisation process is being documented a conventional form of notation is used. In this form, the above example – in the third normal form – would be written out like this:

STUDENT (<u>Student_ID</u>, Forename, Surname)
COURSE (<u>Course_ID</u>, Course_Title, Lecturer_ID)
ENROLMENT (<u>Student_ID</u>, <u>Course_ID</u>)
LECTURER (<u>Lecturer_ID</u>, Lecturer_Name)

It should be noted that the entity is written in capital letters, the attributes are placed inside the brackets and separated by commas, and the key fields are underlined.

Organisational database strategy

Database reources that an organisation might use

Data warehouse	Data warehousing involves storing data that is produced by Transaction Processing Systems. Data held in data warehouses can be 'mined' to discover patterns of association, sequences, groupings, etc. This can be of value to the organisation.
Company database	Company databases will contain a wide range of information that relates to the core activities of the organisation. The nature of the organisation will determine the precise nature of the data, but typically it will consist of a combination of operational data (e.g. sales, purchases, stock levels, etc.) and other data that the organisation needs to run its business (e.g. client details, suppliers, employees, etc).
Proprietary databases	Proprietary databases are collections of data related to a particular business area, e.g. detailed reports on global purchasing trends. Organisations develop them so that they can market them commercially. Other organisations with an interest in that business area then pay to have access to them.

Using databases

Data held in various databases can be combined and interrogated in different ways. The resulting information can be used by the organisation for different purposes, including:

Strategic planning	The senior management of an organisation must make plans for its future. Data mining can indicate trends that will help it determine the optimal areas of development.
Self monitoring	Operational data held in company databases can be used by the organisation to monitor its own performance and to relate it to the performance of competitors.
Communication	Databases will contain details of customers, clients, suppliers, employees, etc. These can be used to facilitate efficient communication, e.g. using a mail merge facility.
Decision-making	Decision support systems draw upon data held in company and proprietary databases in order to aid the decision-making process.
Environment monitoring	It is essential that a business remains informed about changes in the environment in which it operates. Failure to do so might mean that competitors gain market advantage.
Legislative compliance	Organisations must ensure that they comply with legislation, especially – in this context – data protection legislation. Secure and well-organised databases make this easier to manage.

Factors determining a database strategy

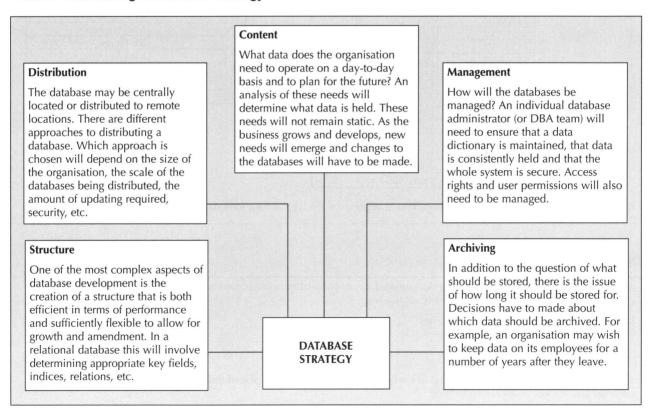

Database management systems: 1

What is a database management system?

A database management system (DBMS) is a method for managing the interface between the data that an organisation stores and the programs that it uses to access that data. Typically, an organisation will store its data in a series of connected data files, e.g. a relational database. Various users will then need to access this database in order to perform a variety of functions on it, e.g. updating, querying, appending, etc. These different users will not all need to access the same data files. For example, a user in human resources may need to access only the 'Employee' and 'Wages' files whereas someone working in the warehouse department may need access to the data held in the 'Stock' and 'Orders' files. A DBMS manages these different needs in an organised and efficient manner.

How does a DBMS work?

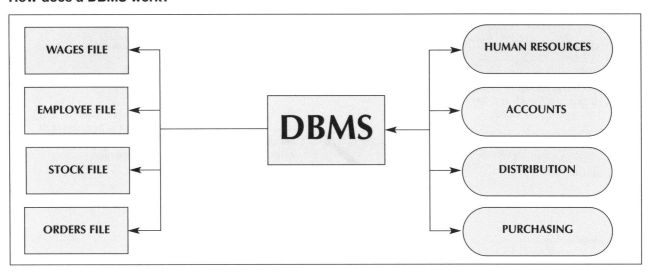

Functions of a DBMS

The DBMS should:

- Allow a variety of users to perform standard database procedures: creating new files, updating existing records, deleting unnecessary records, extracting sub-sets of data, producing reports, etc.
- Ensure that data is securely held and its integrity is protected. Part of the security strategy should include organised back-up and recovery procedures.
- Create and maintain an up-to-date data dictionary. A data dictionary is a stored record of all the different elements of a database – i.e. names of tables and fields, data types used, relationships between different tables, validation rules, etc.
- Organise appropriate user access procedures. It may be necessary to restrict which data files users have access to and what actions they can perform on the data – i.e. some users may have read/write access, other may have read-only access.

Advantages and Disadvantages of a DBMS

Advantages	Disadvantages
<ul><li>There is a greater degree of data standardisation within the organisation. Users are obliged to use the same data definitions and work within the confines of the data dictionary.</li><li>Security is improved because the database is centrally located and access to it can be controlled.</li><li>Data is independent from the programs that interact with it. This means that new programs can be created without developers having to worry about creating or amending underlying data structures.</li><li>It is an economical use of organisational resources. The data only has to be stored once. It can then be accessed by the different functional areas of the organisation. This creates savings in terms of hardware and memory requirements.</li></ul>	<ul><li>The creation and maintenance of a large scale DBMS will be costly. It is likely to require expensive hardware, considerable memory resources and high-specification processing devices. Cost may also be incurred acquiring the necessary staff expertise.</li><li>Security procedures have to be detailed and extensive if an organisation's data resources are all centrally located. The organisation is more vulnerable to a disastrous data loss and so will need a well-maintained disaster recovery policy.</li><li>Database management systems are complex products. In developing associated programs, developers will need to understand all of their workings. The training and additional time that this might involve will add to development costs.</li></ul>

Database management systems: 2

The client–server approach

Many organisations take advantage of client–server technology to optimise the efficiency of their database management system. The users have client software on their machines and the network server runs DBMS server software. When a user wishes to query the database, the request is sent to the server. The server selects, sorts and returns the requisite records to the client. The user can then use the returned information as they wish. An example of this process is shown below:

An administrator in a hospital wishes to produce a report on patient waiting times during the past month.

She has client software installed on her machine and a user interface that allows her to set the parameters of her query. The query is sent to the network server which has DBMS server software installed.

The server searches the appropriate data files, selecting those records required by the user. In this case it will need to search the 'Patient' and 'Outpatient Treatment' data files. The selected records are then returned to the client workstation.

The user has a stored report on her machine. This report has been created by the user so that it can be regularly produced. It can now be populated by the returned records and printed.

The advantages and disadvantages of a client–server approach

✓ A large number of users can gain access to a centrally located database. This is more cost-effective than installing the same database on all users' machines.

✓ When a query is run only the required data is returned, this cuts down on network traffic and so improves performance.

✓ Centralised database management enhances security and helps to optimise data integrity and data consistency.

✓ Clients can be authorised not just to view data but also to update, amend and delete records. This increases flexibility.

✗ Initial purchasing and maintenance costs are higher.

✗ It is more complicated – and therefore more costly – to produce applications that are client–server-enabled.

✗ There is reliance on one main server with all the attendant dangers this implies.

✗ A large volume of data requests may overwhelm the network and slow down communications. For this reason, many organisations have developed distributed databases (see page 00).

The role of a database administrator

A database administrator (DBA) is an individual within an organisation who has overall responsibility for overseeing the organisation's data resources. Depending on the size of the organisation, that person may lead a team, delegating various responsibilities as necessary. The responsibilities characteristically associated with the role are set out below.

Training

The DBA is responsible for ensuring that all relevant personnel understand the way the database works. This training will need to be appropriately targeted for users at different levels. Senior managers, for example, will need to know what information requests can reasonably be made. Users at an operational level may need to learn how to run simple queries or update existing data files.

Security

The DBA must ensure that the database is secure from all the usual internal and external threats. Data integrity must be maintained, e.g. through the use of validation programs. This work may involve liaising with other individuals/teams who have an overall organisational responsibility for security. It will also involve the development of an effective back-up and recovery strategy. There will also need to be a database focus to the organisation's disaster recovery procedure.

Maintenance

Maintenance work can take various forms, including:

- ensuring that any changes to data structures – e.g. the creation of a new table – are compatible with the overall database architecture;
- dealing with problems encountered by users, and making necessary corrections to the database;
- managing the implications for the database of any general changes to the ICT infrastructure.

Access and authorisation

A DBMS will involve a number of different users accessing different parts of the database. It is the responsibility of the DBA to ensure that users only access those aspects of the system that they need to. It may also be necessary to give different users different rights in regard to the actions they can perform, e.g. setting read-only, read/write access. A DBA may also take responsibility for maintaining a password system.

Liaison with other departments

The DBA will need to liaise with various individuals whose work might impact upon the database. One critical aspect of this liaison is the communication with program developers. In a database management system, where programs and data are independent of each other, it is critical that developers understand the structure of the database. Liaison will occur at various stages of the development life cycle, ensuring that programs read from and write to the database effectively.

Performance monitoring

How well the database operates will have a significant effect on the overall functioning of an organisation's ICT systems. The DBA should monitor the effectiveness of the database, perhaps using benchmark tests to investigate how efficiently it is performing critical tasks, e.g. how long it takes to run a particular query. Following such monitoring, it may be necessary to amend the structure of the database in order to improve its efficiency.

Database security

In addition to all the established ICT security issues, there are specific issues associated with data integrity that those responsible for database management need to be aware of. A relational database contains a number of different tables linked by key fields. One property that a link between tables might have is 'referential integrity'. This means that when a user modifies the data in one table, linked data in other tables may also be affected.

In the example below, the user has deleted a customer from the Customer file. In the related Orders table, all of the orders made by the customer are also deleted. This may be exactly what is required but, equally, the organisation may want to use all the data in the Orders table for its own analysis, regardless of whether or not a customer is on its lists.

Customer_ID	Name	Surname	Address	Town	Code
12/578/AF	Miss K Stevens	Stevens	12 The Grove,	Newton	NW3 7YT
12/987/PH	Mr T Koways	Kowaya	34 West Street	Newton	NW3 8YH
12/960/LK	Mr F Greene	Greene	14 High Road	Forsham	FS4 9RE
13/97/LH	Mrs D Patel	Patel	3 Grand Drive	Newton	NW3 8TT
13/652/PF	Mr L Wai Lun	Wai Lun	12 Wick Ave	Forsham	FS4 3ES
13/041/UG	Miss F Rogers	Rogers	15 Smiley Street	Newton	NW4 6RS
12/749/SA	Mr J Nunn	Nunn	11 Lode Cres	Yale	NW6 5GT

RUN DELETE

Deleting this record will result in associated records in linked tables being deleted.

Proceed   Cancel

Order_No.	Customer_ID	Value	Date	Staff_code
3345	12/578/AF	120.65	14/02/02	TL
3346	13/97/LH	335.75	14/02/02	TL
3347	13/652/PF	1234.50	15/02/02	SA
3348	12/578/AF	367.00	16/02/02	DF
3349	13/652/PF	639.00	16/02/02	FD

Establishing user/group permissions

It is the responsibility of the database administrator (DBA) to ensure that different users have only the access they need to perform their tasks. Accidental data loss, such as was illustrated in the example above, should not occur if user access is properly controlled. Each user should have an account that establishes which tables she can have access to and what processes she is permitted to perform. In a large organisation it may be more efficient to divide users into groups, allocate individuals to the groups and set permissions in relation to the groups. Additional security can be provided by obliging users to use a password system and by coding in warning messages before certain actions (e.g. deleting a record) are performed.

Below is an example of the way in which permissions may be set for an individual user.

USER

ALLOCATE USER GROUPS
USER NAME: P. TATE

Groups:		Sec. Level	
Accounts	✖		
Hum Res	✔	1	✖
Production	✖	2	✔
Sales	✖	3	✖

The user belongs to a group that has been defined as Human Resources Level 2. This group comprises those employees who belong to the Human Resources department and have been given level 2 security clearance.

GROUP PERMISSIONS
GROUP: HUM RES   SEC LEVEL 2
TABLES:

Customers	✖	Emp. hours	✔
Orders	✖	Pay detail	✔
Order details	✖	Suppliers	✖
Employees	✔	Deliveries	✖

Users will need access to several related tables, including Employees, Wages, Hours Worked, Health Record, etc. They will also require access to certain reports, forms, queries, etc.

USER ACCESS LEVEL
USER: P. TATE   SEC LEVEL 2

TABLE: EMPLOYEES

Add new record	✔	Modify table	✖
Delete record	✔	Block update	✖
Edit record	✔		

Users will be need to perform different actions on each of the database objects that they have access to. 'Read Access' means that they can only look at the data in a table whereas Read/Write Access means that they can both look at the data and modify it. In some cases they may be able to modify the design of the object.

Distributed databases

What is a distributed database?

Organisations often have systems that rely on databases that must be accessible by users working in functionally diverse and geographically remote areas. One method of providing this service is to have one large database, stored on a mainframe computer and accessed via a wide area network. There are, however, drawbacks to such an approach:
- there is over-reliance on a single storage location which could crash and put the whole system out of commission;
- query processing may not be efficient, especially when many demands are being made at the same time;
- it may not be the most efficient use of the organisation's computing resources.

Declining processing costs and improved network communications have enabled the development of an alternative approach based on the distribution of databases across a number of different locations. This approach is referred to as a distributed database system.

Four approaches to distributing a database

Partitioned database

The remote databases download the portion of the database that they require for their local needs. Changes are made at a local level. The central database is then updated, usually via an overnight batch process.

Duplicate database

The whole database is replicated and downloaded to each remote location. In a similar way to the partitioned system, changes made at a local level are justified with the central database later.

Central index

The central index holds key indexing data, e.g. customer's name and ID number. The full data file is held and kept updated at a local level. Users can query the central database. The index is then used to direct the user to the location of the complete data file.

Network query

The central processor operates as a kind of search engine, querying all the remote databases, before returning the data from whichever location it is held in. All databases are stored and updated at a local level.

Advantages and disadvantages of distributed databases

Advantages	Disadvantages
- There is a reduction in risk of a central failure putting the whole organisation out of action. - It is a more efficient use of an organisation's processing and storage resources. - There is increased speed of response to local queries and less chance of excess data traffic jamming the system.	- Depending on the system used, there is an increased possibility of data integrity being compromised, i.e. as a result of running two versions of the database in parallel. - As a consequence of the decentralised nature of the system, there is a greater security risk. - There is a greater dependence on high-quality communications systems.

The process of evaluating software

When an organisation decides that it wishes to acquire new software, it will be the task of an individual or team to evaluate available software solutions. The aim of this process is to ensure that the software chosen will meet all of the users' needs in a cost-effective manner. In a centralised system, this task will fall to the ICT department. They will need to establish the users' needs, evaluate possible solutions and advise management on the best purchase.

Software evaluation report

Prior to a major software purchase well organised companies will insist that a software evaluation report be submitted to senior management. The report will consist of the following headings:

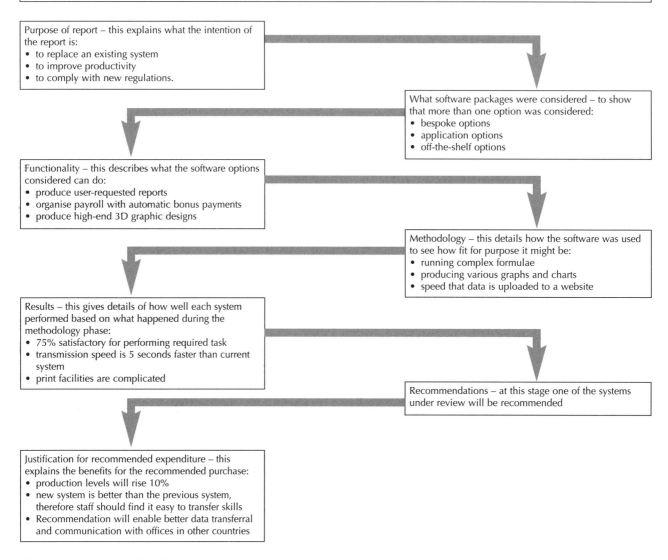

Purpose of report – this explains what the intention of the report is:
• to replace an existing system
• to improve productivity
• to comply with new regulations.

What software packages were considered – to show that more than one option was considered:
• bespoke options
• application options
• off-the-shelf options

Functionality – this describes what the software options considered can do:
• produce user-requested reports
• organise payroll with automatic bonus payments
• produce high-end 3D graphic designs

Methodology – this details how the software was used to see how fit for purpose it might be:
• running complex formulae
• producing various graphs and charts
• speed that data is uploaded to a website

Results – this gives details of how well each system performed based on what happened during the methodology phase:
• 75% satisfactory for performing required task
• transmission speed is 5 seconds faster than current system
• print facilities are complicated

Recommendations – at this stage one of the systems under review will be recommended

Justification for recommended expenditure – this explains the benefits for the recommended purchase:
• production levels will rise 10%
• new system is better than the previous system, therefore staff should find it easy to transfer skills
• Recommendation will enable better data transferral and communication with offices in other countries

The process of evaluating software

1. Determine criteria	In order to evaluate anything systematically, the first step is to determine what will be the relevant criteria for making the decision. In the case of software this will include: cost, reliability, compatibility, etc: These criteria may then be placed in a rank order to determine their priority or weighted according to how critical they will be in reaching the decision.
2. Gather information	Information about what products are available will need to be collected. The software vendors will send out their own promotional material and in some cases will contact directly those in charge of software acquisition. Further information may be found on the Internet, in magazines and newspapers and by speaking to users in other organisations.
3. Evaluate possible choices	Once the possible choices have been established, each choice needs to be evaluated using the established criteria. This may be achieved by taking a demonstration copy through a series of benchmarks tests designed to assess its performance. It would also be valuable to gather comments from potential users and to assess the likely impact on the organisation's ICT infrastructure.
4. Make decision	Having been through the above processes, the individual/team is in a position to make a decision. The decision may take the form of a 'recommendation to buy' report which would be sent to a senior manager. In this instance, the report should also justify the choice, indicating how the choice was arrived at and what criteria were used.

Criteria for evaluating software

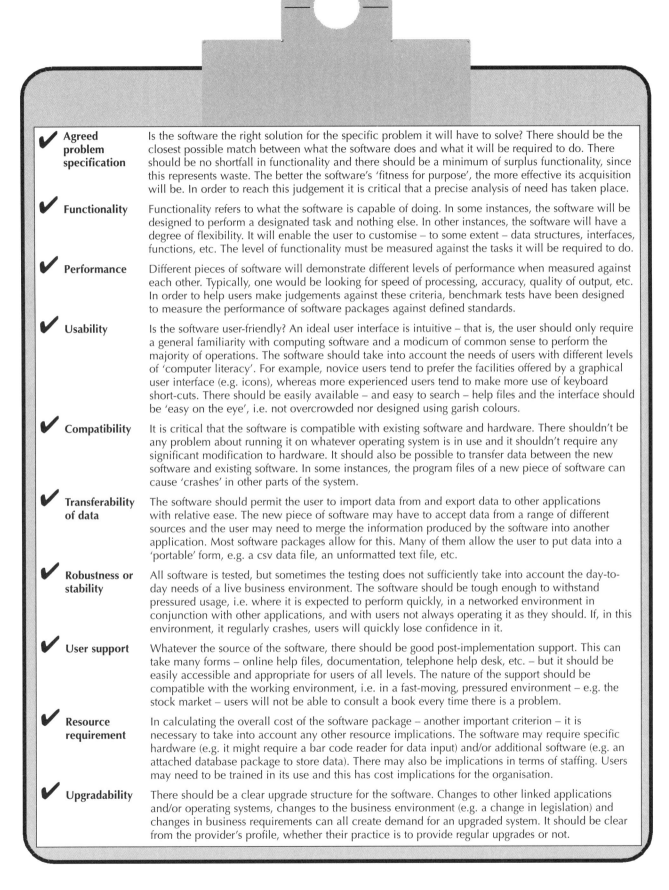

✔ **Agreed problem specification**

Is the software the right solution for the specific problem it will have to solve? There should be the closest possible match between what the software does and what it will be required to do. There should be no shortfall in functionality and there should be a minimum of surplus functionality, since this represents waste. The better the software's 'fitness for purpose', the more effective its acquisition will be. In order to reach this judgement it is critical that a precise analysis of need has taken place.

✔ **Functionality**

Functionality refers to what the software is capable of doing. In some instances, the software will be designed to perform a designated task and nothing else. In other instances, the software will have a degree of flexibility. It will enable the user to customise – to some extent – data structures, interfaces, functions, etc. The level of functionality must be measured against the tasks it will be required to do.

✔ **Performance**

Different pieces of software will demonstrate different levels of performance when measured against each other. Typically, one would be looking for speed of processing, accuracy, quality of output, etc. In order to help users make judgements against these criteria, benchmark tests have been designed to measure the performance of software packages against defined standards.

✔ **Usability**

Is the software user-friendly? An ideal user interface is intuitive – that is, the user should only require a general familiarity with computing software and a modicum of common sense to perform the majority of operations. The software should take into account the needs of users with different levels of 'computer literacy'. For example, novice users tend to prefer the facilities offered by a graphical user interface (e.g. icons), whereas more experienced users tend to make more use of keyboard short-cuts. There should be easily available – and easy to search – help files and the interface should be 'easy on the eye', i.e. not overcrowded nor designed using garish colours.

✔ **Compatibility**

It is critical that the software is compatible with existing software and hardware. There shouldn't be any problem about running it on whatever operating system is in use and it shouldn't require any significant modification to hardware. It should also be possible to transfer data between the new software and existing software. In some instances, the program files of a new piece of software can cause 'crashes' in other parts of the system.

✔ **Transferability of data**

The software should permit the user to import data from and export data to other applications with relative ease. The new piece of software may have to accept data from a range of different sources and the user may need to merge the information produced by the software into another application. Most software packages allow for this. Many of them allow the user to put data into a 'portable' form, e.g. a csv data file, an unformatted text file, etc.

✔ **Robustness or stability**

All software is tested, but sometimes the testing does not sufficiently take into account the day-to-day needs of a live business environment. The software should be tough enough to withstand pressured usage, i.e. where it is expected to perform quickly, in a networked environment in conjunction with other applications, and with users not always operating it as they should. If, in this environment, it regularly crashes, users will quickly lose confidence in it.

✔ **User support**

Whatever the source of the software, there should be good post-implementation support. This can take many forms – online help files, documentation, telephone help desk, etc. – but it should be easily accessible and appropriate for users of all levels. The nature of the support should be compatible with the working environment, i.e. in a fast-moving, pressured environment – e.g. the stock market – users will not be able to consult a book every time there is a problem.

✔ **Resource requirement**

In calculating the overall cost of the software package – another important criterion – it is necessary to take into account any other resource implications. The software may require specific hardware (e.g. it might require a bar code reader for data input) and/or additional software (e.g. an attached database package to store data). There may also be implications in terms of staffing. Users may need to be trained in its use and this has cost implications for the organisation.

✔ **Upgradability**

There should be a clear upgrade structure for the software. Changes to other linked applications and/or operating systems, changes to the business environment (e.g. a change in legislation) and changes in business requirements can all create demand for an upgraded system. It should be clear from the provider's profile, whether their practice is to provide regular upgrades or not.

Approaches to acquiring software

When an organisation needs a software application to perform a specified task, it has to choose how it will acquire that application. There are four basic choices and they are outlined below. In making the choice, the organisation will apply the criteria set out on page 59.

Approach	Customising existing off-the-shelf software	Purchasing a specifically designed, off-the-shelf application	Paying for a customised solution by an external software provider	Developing the application using an in-house team
What is involved	Applications such as spreadsheets and databases include functionality which allows them to be tailored to the specific needs of an organisation. The ability to construct intuitive user interfaces and logical data structures can be achieved by users with a limited level of skill.	Specialist applications are developed and marketed with specific end users in mind. These applications have the functionality to complete business-specific tasks, e.g. a package designed to manage the end-of-year accounts of a small business.	Software providers are companies whose business is to sell customised solutions to different organisations. The provider would work alongside the organisation to determine its needs, design the solution and implement the finished application.	Some organisations have 'in-house' development teams. These teams develop applications to meet the needs of the organisation. Some of their work will involve the customisation of generic applications, some of it will involve developing applications from scratch.
Strengths of this approach	**Cost** Because commercially available generic packages have such a large market, the purchase cost is relatively low. **Reliability** The application will have been through an extensive testing procedure, including testing in a variety of business environments. **Upgrading** If improved releases of the package become available, it will be easy to install them. **Time** The application has already been tested, so it can be implemented quickly. This will, however, depend on how many customisations are required.	**Cost** The relative cost of such packages is low, though there is less functionality for the money than with a generic package. **Fitness for purpose** An application can be chosen which will fit closely with user requirements. As more specialist applications become available, the easier this becomes. **Time** The application can be implemented straight away. However, it will take time to configure it for the specific data structures of the organisation.	**Fitness for purpose** The user is paying for the application and so can determine exactly what is produced. It is therefore likely to fit closely with the user requirements. **Minimal change** Sometimes, with an off-the-shelf application, organisational procedures and policies have to change in order to fit in with the limitations of the applications. With a customised system this can be avoided. **Support** The extent and type of support can be geared to the needs of the organisation.	*The strengths of 'Customised solution by external provider' apply. Additionally:* **Close liaison** The developers and users work alongside each other. A constant dialogue can be created where the user requirements – including changes to these requirements – can be quickly communicated to the developers. **Strengthening of organisational resources** Some organisations feel that having an in-house development team can give them a competitive edge, i.e. because they are able to respond more quickly to changes in the market.
Weaknesses of this approach	**Fitness for purpose** Even with customisations, the application is unlikely to fulfil precisely the organisation's requirements. There is also likely to be 'waste functionality', i.e. tasks that the application can perform but which will never be needed. **Inherent weaknesses** Despite extensive testing, some commercially successful packages have inherent problems or bugs. Without access to the source code there is little the user can do about this.	**Lack of flexibility** Applications of this kind tend not to allow the user to customise extensively. This can mean that the application determines how information is processed. This can be restrictive. **Support** The quality of post-implementation support can vary considerably and will depend on the calibre of the vendor. In some cases it can be minimal. **Documentation** This is likely to be restricted to what the vendor provides.	**Cost** Costs tend to be high. The more complex the requirements, the higher the cost. **Time** The process can be slow and made longer by failing to ensure the original analysis identified the exact requirements of the system. Having to back-track or make inclusions can cause significant delays. **Reliability** Because testing is necessarily limited, problems can occur after implementation, i.e. when the application is being used in a live business environment.	*The weaknesses of 'Customised solution by external provider' apply. Additionally:* **Continuity** Development teams keep changing, especially in today's climate where ICT professionals change jobs regularly. This can lead to problems, e.g. the originator of a piece of coding is no longer available to explain how an aspect of the application works.

Human–computer interface (HCI)

Introduction

HCI is concerned with how humans communicate with information systems. The obvious method of entering data by keyboard is the traditional starting point but there are many more considerations to think about. Data entry, screen layouts, psychological factors, actually operating the system as well as obtaining outputs are just some of the elements which need to be discussed. If a user has difficulties using a system, the chances of its popularity and effective deployment to a wider audience will be hindered. Every type of user will have different requirements from a system and it is up to software designers and developers to ensure that these needs are satisfied.

There are a number of defining characteristics of a sophisticated HCI, including:

Online help	Almost all software packages contain online help files. This means that users can access help without having to resort to books and manuals. The quality of these help files varies considerably and a sophisticated HCI will provide a comprehensive and appropriately targeted help facility. This may consist of a searchable index of topics, step-by-step 'how-to' guides, wizards for working through complex procedures, pop-up screens with tips for the user, etc. Highly sophisticated systems can 'learn' what sort of help the user needs most often and ensure that the availability of such help is prioritised.
Differentiated interactions	A sophisticated interface will allow different users to perform the same action in different ways, thus accounting for different levels of expertise and individual user preference. For example, a commonly performed action is 'cutting and pasting'. The interface may allow the user to perform the action via a menu item, a keyboard short-cut, clicking on icons or using a pop-up menu activated by clicking the right-hand mouse button.
Multi-tasking	Modern operating systems allow the user to multi-task, i.e. run several applications at the same time, switching easily between them. Interfaces will need to take this into account at the design stage, e.g. by providing minimise and maximise functions.
Customisation	Sophisticated systems often allow the user to customise the interface. This may involve changing the screen configuration (e.g. using different colours or font sizes), creating customised toolbars, developing personalised templates, etc.

The creation of a sophisticated HCI has implications for the resources required. These implications include:

Processing resources	The more sophisticated the interface, the more demands it will place on the central processing unit.
Main memory	Sophisticated HCIs require a large memory capacity to run, not least because they contain a considerable number of graphical objects.
Backing storage	An application with a sophisticated HCI will require more storage memory, whether this is on an applications server or a local hard drive.
Development resources	A sophisticated HCI will take more time to develop, may need more people to work on it, and will require more testing. This will have a knock-on effect on development costs.

Factors to take into account when designing a user interface

Task	The first question to ask in relation to interface design is: what is the program designed to do? The interface design should be consistent with the overall aims of the program. So, for example, if the program is a sophisticated business decision support system, designed for use by strategic management, the design elements should reflect this, e.g. muted colours, business-like graphics, minimum clutter, etc. Equally, if it is a program designed to help home users design their garden, the interface may be colourful and 'fun'.
User expertise	While it is not always possible to know in advance what level of expertise a program's users will have, designers can make a reasonable estimate of their likely skill level. If, for example, a business-specific accounts package is being designed, it is reasonable to assume that the users of such a package will be familiar with programs designed to manipulate numerical data. The most challenging interfaces in this regard are those for programs that might be used by everybody from complete novices to computer professionals, e.g. a generic spreadsheet package.
User preference	Some interfaces take into account the desire of users to create screen configurations that suit their particular needs. Such interfaces allow the user to configure some elements of the screen design in accordance with their own preferences. For example, the arrangement and selection of icons on a tool bar might be changed so that they are consistent with the functions that the user employs most frequently.
Resources	Graphical design elements need more memory resources than text-based ones. This can, in some cases, lead to a strain being put on resources and a concomitant diminishment of performance. This is particularly evident when a memory-heavy interface is loading up. With the increased memory and processing power of computers this is less of a problem than it used to be, but still something that some system designers may need to account for.

Psychological factors in HCI design

Psychological factors involved in designing effective user interfaces

If a computer interface is to be effective, it must be designed with the needs of the user in mind. Users come in all shapes and sizes: they have differing levels of expertise, different attitudes towards computers in general, and they use their computers for different reasons. Those responsible for designing interfaces must consider the various ways in which users will interact with their hardware/software, and design systems that will make those interactions positive experiences. Some of the specific psychological factors that should be taken into account are set out below.

Allowing personalisation/customising

While it is desirable that a user interface should share common elements with other interfaces, users also like to be able to customise their screens. Through the process of customisation the user is exerting a degree of control over the computer and expressing their personal preferences in regard to the look and feel of the interface. This can make users feel less 'at the mercy' of their computers. Customisation may be at a relatively simple level, e.g. adjusting the configuration of screen colours, or at a more sophisticated level, e.g. creating personalised toolbars with custom-built commands.

Avoiding information overload

Humans can only cope with so much information at one time. Experiments into the capacity of short-term memory have shown that it can hold only 7 ($\pm$2) pieces of information. Furthermore, that information is only held there for approximately 20 seconds. After that, it must be transferred to the long-term memory or it will disappear. The designers of user interfaces should therefore avoid bombarding users with more information than they can cope with. Nor should the interface expect them to remember more items of information than can be stored in the short-term memory. This can be achieved through designing uncluttered screens, concise message boxes and menus that aren't too extensive.

Using existing cognitive structures

Cognitive structures are the (conceptual) mechanisms we use to make sense of the world and process new information. New information will be processed most easily if it fits smoothly into our current understanding of the world around us. Computer users are most likely to learn how to interact with a new program if its interface (a) is similar to what they have already experienced in other programs (b) is consistent with their general experience (e.g. 'escape' means the same in computer terminology as it does in real life) and (c) responds in a logical manner, e.g. moving the mouse in one direction elicits a similar, proportional movement by the screen pointer.

Reducing fear

For some users, computers are a source of fear. This fear, sometimes referred to as 'technophobia', may be summarised thus: ease with computers is increasingly expected by society in general and employers in particular; if a person is apprehensive about using computers, she will be disadvantaged at work and may even lose her job. To such users the computer represents a threat to their well-being, a threat that they don't feel equipped to cope with. The effective interface will take account of this fear, especially in the case of applications aimed at the general user, e.g. by offering an easy way of rectifying an erroneous action.

Minimising frustration

Frustration occurs when one wishes to achieve a certain objective and is prevented from doing so. A build-up of frustration leads to increased stress and, in the view of some psychologists, aggression. Many users experience frustration in relation to computers. The most common complaint is that the computer 'won't do what I want it to'. In other words, the interface is not providing a sufficiently transparent mechanism for the user to issue commands to the computer and receive information in return. The more that is at stake for the user, e.g. the shorter the time available in which to prepare for a critical meeting, the more pronounced the frustration.

Physical factors in HCI design

When creating HCI systems, designers need to take into account the way in which the user will physically interact with the computer. The keyboard plus mouse input/screen output is the most typical model but there are others. When using computer game programs, for example, one might use a specialised input device such as a joystick, 'steering wheel' or generic game-playing device in order to make the most of the game's facilities. The challenge for designers is to create an HCI that is intuitive — i.e. the nature of the interactions closely resembles the interactions humans experience in the real world. The design process includes a consideration of the following factors:

Purpose	The nature of the interface will be partially determined by the program it is designed for. If the program is a graphics package designed to allow the user to draw images directly on to the screen, an appropriate input device will need to be used – a stylus or light pen, for example. The way in which this device interacts with the program will need to built into the overall program design.
User	Some programs are designed for an individual user, some for a small group of users and some for the general user. The physical nature of the HCI may be able to take into account the needs of likely users. For example, an educational program designed to be used by young children could be designed with their needs in mind, e.g. use of bright colours, interactions with pointing devices that aren't too finely calibrated, simple commands in a large font, etc.
Environment	The general environment where a program will be used may also affect the way the interface is designed. For example, a CAM system designed for use in an industrial environment would need to be robust enough to deal with the rough handling it may receive and not be oversensitive to dirt or noise.
Health and safety	It is important that normal use of the system should not result in short-term discomfort or long-term injury for the user. Awareness of this issue has led designers to develop more ergonomic keyboards that lessen the chance of regular users developing repetitive strain injury.
Users with disabilities	Some programs are specifically designed for users with disabilities, e.g. a voice-activated system for those with visual impairments. Those responsible for designing HCI systems intended for use by the general public, an interactive museum information system for example, should take into account the needs of users with disabilities.

Different ways of interacting with computers

Voice input

There are a number of systems that work on the basis of voice recognition. They can range in sophistication from simple command systems to voice activated text processing. Being able to 'talk' to computers directly is clearly a desirable facility, but there are a number of inherent difficulties involved, e.g. the changes in pronunciation created by regional accents.

Graphics devices

Graphic designers, architects and others working in a similar field need to be able to interact with computers in a very specific way. For example, they may wish to 'draw' an image on the screen in the same way as they would if they were doing it on paper. Standard pointing devices are not always adequate for this. Light pens and digitising tablets are used in this context.

Game-playing devices

The computer games market is highly competitive. One way in which manufacturers have sought to gain an advantage over their rivals is through the development of sophisticated interaction devices. The joystick and 'steering wheel' were examples of this but this market has seen a major transformation with the advent of the Wii console which uses wireless controls that can be used as virtual sports equipment, weapons or in conjunction with fitness sessions. The motion through the air of the controller is revolutionising modern game playing.

Pointing devices

The mouse was first developed in 1963 but didn't come into general use until the introduction of the Apple Macintosh PC in 1984. It is now established as a standard means of communicating with a graphical user interface. The mouse is becoming more sophisticated with the introduction of wireless devices, programmable functions and motion-sensitive devices that can move a pointer in three dimensions.

Touch screens

Touch screens allow the user to press parts of the screen to activate different functions. Simple systems may use pressure pads, more sophisticated ones have an infra-red matrix over the screen that identifies the point being touched. Such systems are often used in public places, such as bars and clubs which allow customers to order food and drinks from their tables without having to wait for a waiter to come and collect the order. Travel agents also use this technology to allow potential holiday makers to navigate around resorts and find information about various excursions.

Biometric systems

Biometric systems are those that can 'read' individuals' biological attributes, e.g. iris-recognition devices that can decode the unique configurations of the subject's eye. The most widespread use of such devices is in security systems, where they can be used to check the legitimacy of an individual seeking entrance to a room, building, and within the past few years in laptop and desktop computer systems.

Types of user interface: 1

There are various types of user interface available. The preferred choice largely depends on the skill level of the user, the task the system is designed to perform and how familiar the individual is with certain stages of computer evolution. Those who are involved with developing system and other types of software will interact with systems in a different way from the more general user. For different tasks and various skill levels there are alternative options which allow the operator to make the system do what they want it to do in the most suitable way.

Command line interfaces

Command line interfaces were the first visual user interfaces to be employed and, despite their intrinsic limitations, are still regularly used. The most common example of usage is the MS-DOS interface which can be used to perform a number of system operations such as creating directories and deleting files. As can be seen from the screen shot below, the interface requires the user to type in coded commands which the computer then performs. This means that the user must learn the coded commands. For this reason, command line interfaces tend to be used mainly by technically oriented computer professionals (network managers, for example) rather than by ordinary users. For those users that have learned the commands, this approach can be an efficient method of communicating with the computer.

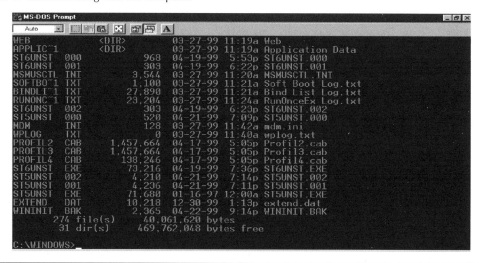

Graphical user interfaces

The graphical user interface (GUI, pronounced 'gooey') is now the standard mode of computer–user interface for the keyboard/mouse/monitor set-up. GUIs have the following defining characteristics (usually referred to as the 'WIMP interface'):

W The screen is organised into **windows**, i.e. overlapping frames that can be viewed singularly or in combination with other windows.

I Graphical features are used as short-cuts for the user, i.e. instead of having to type in a command they can click on an image – or **icon** – that symbolises the action.

M Menus are presented to the user so they can select a command from a predefined list. These menus may be presented as 'pop-up' screens or as 'pull-down' lists on a **menu** bar.

P A **pointing device** is used to move around the screen, to locate where on the screen the user is working and to identify which command is to be issued.

There are clear advantages to this approach to computer–user interfacing:
- The user does not have to learn a specific computer language to communicate with the computer.
- The use of graphical images provides effective short-cuts that are particularly useful as a 'way in' for novice users.
- The mouse provides an 'intuitive' method of communicating instructions, i.e. our hand movements correspond precisely to the movements of the pointer on the screen.
- There is a reduction in ambiguous instructions – i.e. because menus offer a limited range of options the user has to choose a command that the computer will understand.

One significant disadvantage should be noted: GUIs require more memory and processing resources to run effectively. The more sophisticated the GUI, the more this is the case.

Types of user interface: 2

Natural language interface

This type of interface suits those users who like to communicate with their system by using actual words, phrases or sentences in order to get results or create outputs. By using natural language there is no need to learn complex programming languages or set procedures. Systems driven this way have a data entry space where a request is typed. Search engines and software help facilities are driven by using natural language. A user types in their request and a range of options are returned, provided the entry has been spelled correctly. The limitation of such a system is that many words can have more than one meaning, which means that sometimes the output is not what the user wants. In order to maximise the chance of getting the interface to output what is wanted the words entered need to be precise and in context with other carefully chosen words. Entering too many words can return millions of responses. Attempting to use a natural language interface for other applications may not be appropriate. For example, a mouse click may be more efficient than typing in a lengthy command and also gets over the problems created when words are spelled incorrectly on entry.

Menu-driven interface

A menu-driven interface restricts the operator to the options provided by the system, usually shown on a screen. They can be found, in their simplest form, on automatic teller machines (cash points). The user inserts a card, enters a pin number as security and uses the keypad to navigate the system and make selections. It can be surprising how many options are available with just a few buttons. The Apple IPod MP3 player is also menu driven and with few buttons on the device itself opens up a whole host of different functions and options. Mobile phones incorporating touch screen technology also make use of the menu-driven interface. Such interfaces are intuitive to use, displaying pictorial icons, which makes them ideal for novice users and few entry mistakes are made due to the limit number of options available. Boosting simplicity in use means that this interface is very popular because it takes very little time to learn and compliments the touch screen technology that is currently becoming ever-more prevalent on mobile devices and in the commercial and education sector in the form of electronic whiteboards.

Customising an interface

As has been stated, many applications allow the user to customise the interface to fit in with their particular needs. Some of the ways in which this might be achieved are set out below:

Toolbars

Toolbars generally sit at the top and sides of a screen and contain icons that can be clicked to perform actions. Which toolbars one has and which icons they contain can be determined by the user. In some cases the user can create their own functions, i.e. by using macros, and develop a customised toolbar to execute these functions.

Menus

Both drop-down and pop-up menus can be customised so that they only contain items the user knows that they will need. This helps to speed up menu use by reducing clutter.

Font

The font refers to the appearance of written text on the screen. The size of the font can be changed as can its colour and style. This may be just a matter of personal preference for the user, or it may reflect a more important need, e.g. a user suffering from a visual impairment may need text of a certain size and colour to be able to see it properly.

Templates

A template is an outline document that provides a generic framework for writing individual documents. If, for example, a standard letter is regularly sent by an organisation, this can be set up as a template. When a letter needs to be produced, the template can be used to create the document. The user will just need to add in or amend individual details, e.g. the name of the addressee.

Screen view

The screen view can be changed to allow the user to see more or less of the document that they are working on. The screen shown, for example, allows the user to see the full width of the page, including margins.

Screen colours

The configuration of the screen colours may also be changed. The de facto standard for screen appearance uses grey, blue, black and white for different elements of the screen design. Research into visual perception has shown this to be an effective combination, but individual users may be happier with a different arrangement of colours.

63

Speech recognition systems

Speech recognition systems

The majority of communication between human beings entails people talking to each other. What we wish to communicate is contained in the meaning of the words we utter and qualified by our tone of voice and the secondary signalling of body language and facial expression. Creating a human–computer interface that mimics this intuitive mode of communication has proved to be an enormous challenge for the computer industry. The systems that have been developed to facilitate such interaction are still lacking in sophistication and are not yet in widespread use. The problem lies in the fundamental limitation of all computer systems: the need to reduce everything to digital data – i.e. a series of 0s and 1s – in order to process it. The human voice, with all its ambiguities and subtle nuances, has proved particularly resistant to this reduction. None the less there are software applications that allow users to speak directly to computing systems. These systems may be simple, e.g. voice-activated commands, or sophisticated, e.g. word-processing systems that translate the user's speech into text-based data, but they work in essentially the same way.

The user speaks into a microphone, ideally one able to filter out background noise. The quality of the microphone will be a key factor in determining the accuracy of the system. The first stage of the process is for the user to 'train' the software to recognise the particular properties of their voice. This usually involves reading a 'script' of commonly used sounds into the microphone. The computer then creates a database of vocal references to take account of regional pronunciations, individual vocal inflections, speech defects, etc.

The speech generates an analogue signal which the computer needs to translate into a digital format in order to be able to process it. An analogue-to-digital converter samples the analogue signal every 10–20 milliseconds and assigns a digital value, thus creating a sequence of 0s and 1s that represent the pitch, volume, phoneme length of the vocal input. This data is then compressed to speed up transfer and processing and adjusted to take account of background noise, the properties of the microphone, etc.

The software contains a database of known phonemes (sound units such as 'ee', 'aw' 'oh', etc.). The incoming data is compared with the binary values of the stored sounds and, using an acoustic probability method, the best match is found. Phoneme values are then combined and compared to a database, or lexicon, of known words, and a set of probable matches is found. The software then uses a 'natural language component' to reach a judgement about what the most likely choice is. This can then be displayed on the screen.

The screen displays the chosen word. The user may decide it is incorrect and effect a correction. In some cases the computer may be 'unsure' which choice to make. It will then query the user using a dialogue box to present the possible choices. The user may also choose to make corrections once the words have appeared on the screen. Some software has the capacity to 'learn' as it goes, i.e. it 'remembers' when mistakes have been made and factors them in to future decisions.

Advantages and limitations

Advantages	Limitations
• When working effectively, it is quicker and less monotonous than keyboard entry. • It is hands-free which can be of value in some environments, e.g. an operating theatre. • It can be used by users with disabilities, allowing them to communicate without having to use a keyboard.	• It is, at the moment, a developing technology and so many of its 'bugs' have yet to be ironed out. • It finds it difficult to deal with homonyms (words that sound the same but have different meanings, e.g. 'there', 'their' and 'they're') of which there are many in the English language. • Punctuation can be a problem: the user has to say 'comma', 'paragraph', etc.

Careers in ICT

Introduction

Increasingly, there are more and more ICT-related jobs being created, as the use of computer systems expands. Graphic designers, Bank clerks, teachers, administrators and estate agents all need to be competent users of ICT if they are to take advantage of the benefits ICT can offer. Within organisations who rely heavily on ICT there are several roles which need to be accounted for.

Project manager

Project managers oversee the development of new ICT systems. They are responsible for a process that begins with identification of a problem and ends with the evaluation of an implemented solution. They will then oversee the development of the system, the testing process and the implementation. Finally they will undertake a post-implementation evaluation of the system to determine which aspects of it have been successful and which have not.

Key skills

- Interpersonal skills
- Meticulous attention to detail
- Analytical mind
- Logical approach to problem solving
- Strong written and verbal communication skills
- An understanding of the interaction between business operations and technology

Computer programmer

Computer programmers write the code that tells the computer how and when to perform the functions specified in the system design. They need an understanding of general programming structures and principles (e.g. iteration, conditional clauses) and a specialist knowledge of programming languages e.g. C++, Visual Basic. Their work involves:

Coding: writing step by step instructions in the appropriate language.
Compiling: putting the whole program together and converting it into binary code.
Debugging: testing the program, finding errors and correcting them.
Maintenance: amending the original code if errors occur after implementation.

Key skills

- A logical approach to problem solving
- Ability to concentrate on one task
- Ability to learn effectively
- Attention to detail
- Jargon-free communicator

Website administrator

Website administrators supervise and maintain an organisation's website. They are responsible for all aspects of the website, including: creating content or incorporating content provided by others, creating and amending the logical structure of the site, running the web server software, creating and updating graphic elements, evaluating the effectiveness of the site, etc.

Key skills

- Adaptability – ability to respond to changing circumstances
- Good design skills
- Technical knowledge of the Internet
- Strong verbal and written communication skills

System analyst
System analysts organise and analyse all the elements of the system (user needs, available resources, impact on existing system, etc.) and design an appropriate solution.

System designer
System designers specify the particular files and records to be used, the nature of the user interface and sequence of processing, etc. The designer also dictates the order in which the system will be constructed, the timescale for each section and the format for the on-screen and hard-copy outputs.

Testers
Testers ensure that the system works as specified by the end user. This involves constructing a test plan to ensure that all the elements the system is supposed to cover function as requested. A range of test data will be run through the system and the results will be logged and reviewed.

Network administrator

Network administrators take responsibility for the security and administration of networks. Their work may involve: overseeing the installation of new hardware and ensuring its network compatibility, maintaining network hardware and ensuring that problems are fixed, setting up user accounts and passwords, ensuring that the network is secure and that users are using it legitimately, ensuring that there is an effective back-up system.

Key skills

- Strong technical knowledge
- Practical problem-solving skills
- Understanding of the overall technology needs of the organisation
- Good interpersonal skills

The ICT professional: qualities required

In addition to the specific technical skills required by ICT professionals, there are personal qualities that it will be advantageous for them to possess. These qualities, which are described in more detail below, relate to the type of work ICT professionals are called upon to do.

Problem-solving skills ICT work often involves devising solutions to problems. A logical approach to problem-solving will therefore be a great asset. Effective problem-solving involves identifying the nature of the problem, translating the user's requirements, designing and evaluating a range of possible solutions, and testing a chosen solution. This type of work is an essential component of systems development, computer programming and post-implementation user support.

Communication skills Effective communication is clear, accurate and appropriate for the intended audience. ICT professionals will need to be able to communicate effectively, both verbally and in writing. They will need to explain systems to users, provide documentation, give presentations, write/speak to clients, etc. The language and terminology they use must be pitched at an appropriate level for the person they are communicating with.

Interpersonal skills A good deal of ICT work involves team work and the effective ICT professional will be able to work well with others. Interpersonal skills include: the ability to listen to and empathise with the views of others, the capacity to resolve conflicts in a peaceable manner, a willingness to support others when they need it, etc. Without these skills, the behaviour of the individual may damage the productivity of the team.

Initiative Initiative is the ability to instigate new ideas and set projects and ideas in motion. The effective ICT professional will not wait to be instructed, but will see new solutions to problems and the fresh potential of new technologies. This is an especially important quality in ICT managers, who are constantly looking for new ways of using ICT to improve efficiency and enhance the success of the organisation.

Learning skills Everybody has the capacity to learn, but some people are more effective than others. Effective learners can pick up new skills and assimilate new knowledge quickly and efficiently. This is an especially valuable skill in ICT. Technologies are changing rapidly and new products come on to the market with increasing regularity. It is therefore advantageous to be able quickly to acquire the requisite skills and knowledge in order to put these new technologies to use.

Design skills There are some areas of ICT where the ability to create well-designed, easy-to-access screens or reports is essential. Programmers who are developing user interfaces need such skills, as do web-designers and those responsible for the production of documentation. Stylish and ergonomic hardware devices will be attractive to buyers, and therefore people capable of producing such designs will always be in demand.

Methodical approach A methodical approach is characterised by planned, structured working and meticulous attention to detail. This is an especially important skill in computer programming. A single error in a line of code can create huge problems at the testing stage, problems that can set the project back weeks and result in additional costs. A methodical approach will help to minimise these errors.

Organisational skills ICT work involves planning, scheduling and resourcing projects. If an ICT project is to be successful, it has to be well-organised so that the resources required are available, the work is completed on time and everybody working on the project knows what they have to do. This skill is particularly important for those involved in project management.

The system development life cycle (SDLC)

What is the development life cycle?

- New information systems are developed as responses to problems in an organisation, i.e. when existing systems cannot provide an appropriate solution to a specified problem. This process is cyclical because as one system is completed, new requirements become apparent and the process begins again.
- In large organisations the development of new systems can be an enormous undertaking, involving significant human and non-human resources, a time frame measurable in years, and a considerable amount of capital investment.
- For this reason it is a process that must be approached in a systematic and methodical way. Formal methodologies have been developed which break down the process into a series of distinct activities, with measurable outcomes at the end of every stage.
- **Formal methods** are necessary because managers need to be able to identify what stage of development a particular project has reached. Also, people involved in the project need to be accountable for completing specified tasks. This is easier to monitor and control if a set procedure – one that is known to all parties involved – is rigorously followed.
- The breakdown of distinct activities helps to create **clear time scales** for task completion. Without this, the project can easily over-run. If a project significantly over-runs, the finished system may no longer be of use to the organisation.
- At the end of every stage of the life cycle there will be a '**deliverable**', i.e. a specified element of the development (a feasibility study, a finished program, etc.) will be completed. This allows managers to judge whether or not the system is developing along expected lines. If it is, an '**approval to proceed**' can be given; if not, the process can 'loop back' a stage in order to correct the problem.
- The traditional approach, which is summarised in the diagram below, allows for considerable management control but is not without drawbacks. The end users are consulted in the early stages of the process but may not be consulted in the latter stages. This absence of a feedback loop through all the stages of development can lead to user dissatisfaction with the final product.

A summary of the system development life cycle

Each stage of the process outlined below is described in more detail on pages 70–74.

SYSTEMS INVESTIGATION The stage at which the problem is initially identified. The question is asked: how will a new system provide a solution to this particular problem? Consideration is given to the resources that will be required and a feasibility study is undertaken to determine the potential costs and benefits of the proposed development.

SYSTEMS ANALYSIS The stage at which the existing system is described and evaluated; the user requirements for the new system are determined; an analysis of the data which will be used in the system is undertaken; and the way in which the new system will solve the problem is outlined.

If the system fails to get approval to proceed, it loops back to an earlier stage.

SYSTEMS DESIGN At this stage all of the different elements of the solution are designed in line with the requirements set out in the systems analysis. This will involve creating design specifications for hardware, software, databases, telecommunication/network links, personnel and procedures.

SYSTEMS IMPLEMENTATION This involves several, clearly defined substages: acquiring hardware, acquiring software, preparing users, training personnel, preparing data, installing the system, testing the system, running the start-up, and overseeing user acceptance.

SYSTEM MAINTENANCE/EVALUATION An installed system needs to be checked periodically to ensure that it is working as it should. Any errors in the program will need to be fixed and users will need access to support. The whole system will need to be evaluated in order to determine to what extent it has fulfilled its original aims.

The SDLC: investigation phase

System request

The investigation phase comprises the first stage of the System Development Life Cycle (SDLC). It entails the identification of a possible project, an initial consideration of its feasibility and a preliminary investigation into the implications of undertaking the project.

The SDLC begins with a Systems Request. Systems Requests may be instigated by teams and/or individuals within the organisation and engendered by a combination of internal and external factors, as shown in the diagram below.

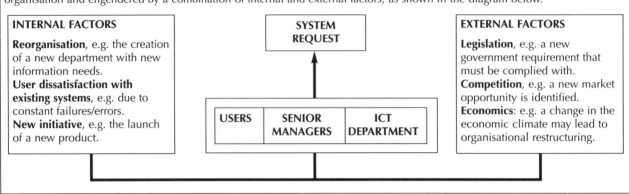

INTERNAL FACTORS

Reorganisation, e.g. the creation of a new department with new information needs.
User dissatisfaction with existing systems, e.g. due to constant failures/errors.
New initiative, e.g. the launch of a new product.

SYSTEM REQUEST

USERS | SENIOR MANAGERS | ICT DEPARTMENT

EXTERNAL FACTORS

Legislation, e.g. a new government requirement that must be complied with.
Competition, e.g. a new market opportunity is identified.
Economics: e.g. a change in the economic climate may lead to organisational restructuring.

Feasibility study

The next stage of the investigation phase is the production of a Feasibility Report. A feasibility study considers the system request from different perspectives (usually defined as Economic, Operational and Technological) to determine whether it is advisable for the organisation to undertake the project.

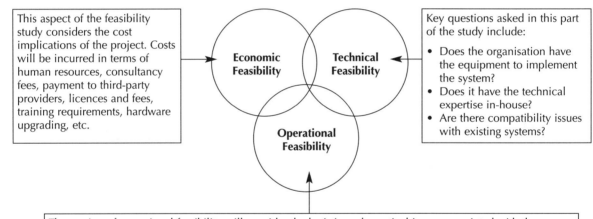

This aspect of the feasibility study considers the cost implications of the project. Costs will be incurred in terms of human resources, consultancy fees, payment to third-party providers, licences and fees, training requirements, hardware upgrading, etc.

Economic Feasibility

Technical Feasibility

Operational Feasibility

Key questions asked in this part of the study include:

- Does the organisation have the equipment to implement the system?
- Does it have the technical expertise in-house?
- Are there compatibility issues with existing systems?

The section of operational feasibility will consider the logistic and practical issues associated with the implementation of the system. What impact – positive and negative – will it have on the day-to-day work of users? What training will be required? Will organisational restructuring be necessary as a consequence of its impact?

Preliminary investigation

If the Feasibility Report advises that the project is worth pursuing, the next stage is to undertake a preliminary investigation. This results in a report to management, the components of which are shown in the diagram below.

AN UNDERSTANDING OF THE PROBLEM The report needs to undertake preliminary analysis into the true nature of the problem and the way in which the proposed solution would solve that problem. What are the key issues that the project will encounter?

BENEFITS What advantages will the organisation gain from undertaking the project? What material/non-material benefits will stem from the new system and will they outweigh the costs incurred?

PRELIMINARY INVESTIGATION REPORT

COSTS What costs will be incurred if the project is undertaken? Costs should be defined not only in monetary terms but also in relation to human resources, time and opportunity costs.

SCOPE AND CONSTRAINTS What will be the scope of the project? Will it be implemented in just one functional area or will it be enterprise-wide? What effect will the implementation of the system have on other systems and procedures? The constraints are the restrictive conditions that the project will have to work within, e.g. a fixed budget and time frame.

The SDLC: analysis phase

The analysis phase, which is designed to investigate the requirements of a new system in detail, can be divided into three distinct sections: determining requirements; analysing requirements; report production.

Determining requirements

During this stage the individual(s) responsible for systems analysis must gather information about the status of the existing system and the requirements of the new one. This entails defining a set of questions, deciding on which sources of information to use and determining the most appropriate information-gathering technique to use.

What questions need to be asked?

- What function does the current system perform?
- What are the shortcomings in the current system that the new system will eradicate?
- What data will be required for the new system?
- What are the sources of the data?
- How will the data be collected and inputted?
- What outputs will be required by the new system?
- How will the new system interact with existing systems?

What sources of information can be used?

External sources, including:
- customers/clients
- suppliers
- government agencies
- consultants
- competitors.

Internal sources, including:
- direct users
- indirect users
- senior managers
- technical support staff
- existing policies, reports, organisational documents
- existing systems and procedures.

What information gathering techniques can be used?

- Structured interviews with individuals, i.e. questions determined in advance.
- Unstructured interviews with individuals, i.e. open-ended discussion.
- Observation of existing practice.
- Reading of documentation, policies, journals, manuals, etc.
- Questionnaires to users.
- Examination of documentation/outputs related to current system.
- Visits to other similar organisations.

Techniques and tools

The collected data will be used to gain a clear understanding of the status of the present system and the requirements of the new system. In order for this process to be effective the raw data needs to be presented in an appropriate format. There are several analytical techniques that can be applied to achieve this.

Data Flow Diagram (DFD)

DFDs represent diagrammatically the relationship between different systems in the organisation and how data moves around those systems. They contain four main components: Entities (e.g. customers); Processes (e.g. computing total sales); Data Flow (i.e. the origin, destination and direction of any transference of data); Data Store (any location where data is held, e.g. a customer data file).

Structured English

Structured English is a method for describing the logical processes that will be undertaken in the new system. It is similar in style to coding language, and focuses on the key building blocks of sequence, selection and iteration:

For each RECORD in ORDERS if TOTAL VALUE => £500.00 Then print RECORD.

Decision table

A decision table is a graphical representation of the way in which a process may be determined by different conditions.

CONFIRM ORDER				
CONDITION	1	2	3	4
Credit available	Y	Y	N	N
Item in stock	Y	N	Y	N
Confirm	X			
Don't confirm		X	X	X

The systems analysis report

When the analysis has been undertaken a report is presented to the manager(s) responsible for approving the next stage of development. The report will cover the following areas:

- An evaluation of the current system, i.e. its strengths and weaknesses from the users' point of view.
- A detailed description of the user requirements that will be met by the new system.
- A description of the organisation's needs that the new system will meet.
- A description of how the new system will work, i.e. how it will meet the above requirements.

Collecting data and information

Methodologies

The way in which data is collected should be a carefully planned operation. There are several tried and tested methods which can be used. It is important that the most suitable methodology is chosen to ensure that the data collected conforms to the criteria relating to what constitutes good quality data. In some cases interviews will be more appropriate than observations and questionnaires likely to yield better results than reading documentation.

Several key elements need to be considered prior to selecting a methodology. The first is budget. The company funding the research may have limited financial resources and which would limit what they are able to do. Likewise those who are well endowed with cash could opt to spend small fortunes each time they are analysing or collecting data and information. The cost should be relative to the size of the organisation. Another factor to consider is time. How quickly does information need to be gathered? If it is collected in a rush careless errors could creep in. If it is collected slowly and methodically the system requirements may have changed by the time the results of the analysis are ready.

The most common methods used for collecting data and information are listed below:

Interviews

These can take place on a one-to-one basis or with a group of people. It is important that the questions asked are direct and relevant and that a skilled, well trained interviewer is used. Skilled interviewers are able to ask questions based on answers given that may be more helpful than sticking rigidly to a script.

Interviews with staff who currently use the system can be revealing and highlight needs that had been overlooked or were unexpected. Interviews should be conducted when those involved are not going to be disturbed and can concentrate fully on what they are being asked. Distractions like phone calls and staff dropping in and out will not help produce good information on which to base the analysis. Often several interviews will help focus the production of the results although valued judgments can mean that common agreements are not reached, or may be slightly clouded.

Observations and visits

In some cases it is more appropriate to watch how staff use software or perform operations than it is to talk to them. Staff may not have time to fill out lengthy questionnaires or sit for an interview. It is important that the observer is well trained and knows what they are looking for. Time delays, crashes, interruptions are a few of the things that can be noted and may contribute towards the production of a better system. Observations can be quite long processes spanning over several weeks as various staff and managers are watched as they go about their everyday tasks.

Reading documentation

Companies will produce a lot of historical documentation in the form of reports or minutes taken from meetings. By reading through the content of such publications clues can be gathered which could be useful indicators as to what would be useful within a new system. This can also be a lengthy process, but by using contents pages and looking for key sub-headings some time can be saved. Also actually having to locate documents or files can hinder progress.

Questionnaires

Questionnaires are a popular first choice used by people who are asked to gather information. They can also be economical to reproduce and distribute. However, there can be significant costs involved in hiring people to ask others to fill out questionnaires and collect responses. Another issue is the response rate from questionnaires which are posted. Often the returns can be quite small which means that summarizing the results is quick, but the actual combined results are taken from a sample too small to be deemed useful. Questionnaire designing is a very complex process and can tie up personnel over a long period of time to ensure that what they produce collects all the information in the form that is useful. Occasionally the process is rushed and ambiguous questions are included and a lack of thought is given to layout or areas where the respondent might like to provide further information. Questionnaires require someone to filter through them and analysis the results.

Specification

At this stage of the system development life cycle the exact requirements (specified objectives) of the system need to be given in detail. All features must be clearly identified and recorded in order to pass onto the designers who are charged with making the blueprints for the final system. The specification will need to be presented to the intended end users to ensure that all of the initial requests and needs are included. The specification is also used to aid with the draft of the test plan where the requested functionality is put through its paces to ensure the system does what it is supposed to do and all the requested features have been included.

Each point in the specification should carry some form of justification too. This means that any features built in have been thought through and are included for a specific reason. Failing to clearly document and approve what the system must do could lead to problems later when it is discovered that key points have been omitted.

A system may be required to keep track of houses sold by estate agents over a period of time. To arrive at a specification with any purpose this request must be broken down into small components to arrive at precise user requirements.

Some of the details which could be included are:

System must:
- Store and display the price of each house for sale.

Why?
To aid with calculating total sales for each estate agent.
- Store and display a picture of each house for sale.

Why?
This can be used for future valuation purposes and may link to a 'For sale' database within the organisation.
- Store and display the number of rooms in each house for sale.

Why?
To highlight if a particular estate agent is better or worse at selling certain sized properties.
- Allow the end user to easily extract details of sales for each employee in a chosen month in less than three mouse clicks.

Why?
The head office is keen to extract this information quickly and does not have the skills to build queries to achieve this request.
- Provide a data entry box to capture the name of each estate agent limited to 30 characters.

Why?
The name of each estate agent is required to identify who has sold what, and a limit on data entry saves storage space and reduces processing time.
- Provide a data entry box to record the contact details for each estate agent including mobile and email details.

Why?
So that details of bonus payments or commission can be passed on to each estate agent.

This list is just the tip of the ice berg, but with such details, almost a checklist, the system design can take place with more certainty.

The SDLC: design phase

There are two aspects to the design phase: logical design and physical design. The logical design specifies how the new system will fulfil the requirements identified in the analysis phase. The physical design specifies the hardware, software, data files, etc. that will be required to put the logical design into action.

Elements of the logical design

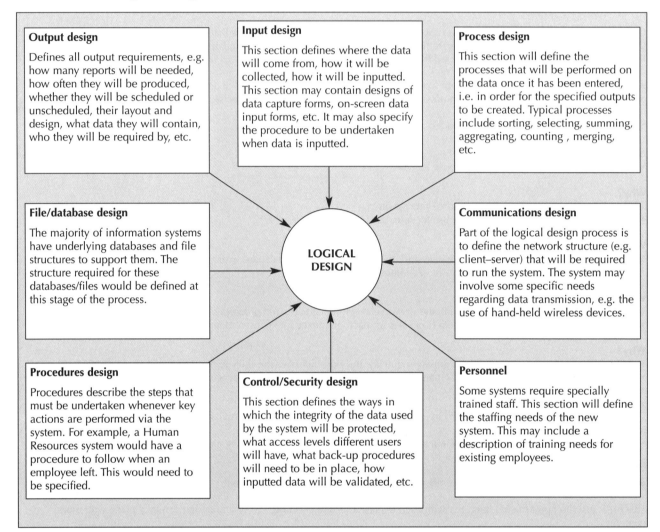

Output design

Defines all output requirements, e.g. how many reports will be needed, how often they will be produced, whether they will be scheduled or unscheduled, their layout and design, what data they will contain, who they will be required by, etc.

Input design

This section defines where the data will come from, how it will be collected, how it will be inputted. This section may contain designs of data capture forms, on-screen data input forms, etc. It may also specify the procedure to be undertaken when data is inputted.

Process design

This section will define the processes that will be performed on the data once it has been entered, i.e. in order for the specified outputs to be created. Typical processes include sorting, selecting, summing, aggregating, counting , merging, etc.

File/database design

The majority of information systems have underlying databases and file structures to support them. The structure required for these databases/files would be defined at this stage of the process.

LOGICAL DESIGN

Communications design

Part of the logical design process is to define the network structure (e.g. client–server) that will be required to run the system. The system may involve some specific needs regarding data transmission, e.g. the use of hand-held wireless devices.

Procedures design

Procedures describe the steps that must be undertaken whenever key actions are performed via the system. For example, a Human Resources system would have a procedure to follow when an employee left. This would need to be specified.

Control/Security design

This section defines the ways in which the integrity of the data used by the system will be protected, what access levels different users will have, what back-up procedures will need to be in place, how inputted data will be validated, etc.

Personnel

Some systems require specially trained staff. This section will define the staffing needs of the new system. This may include a description of training needs for existing employees.

Elements of the physical design

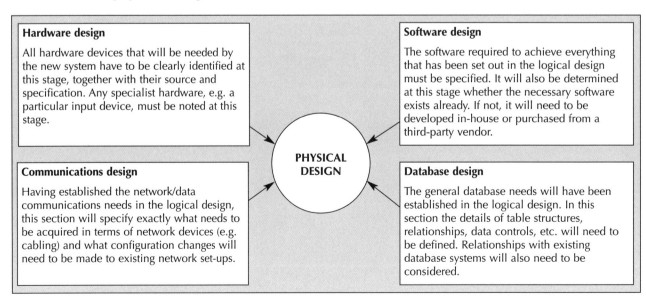

Hardware design

All hardware devices that will be needed by the new system have to be clearly identified at this stage, together with their source and specification. Any specialist hardware, e.g. a particular input device, must be noted at this stage.

Software design

The software required to achieve everything that has been set out in the logical design must be specified. It will also be determined at this stage whether the necessary software exists already. If not, it will need to be developed in-house or purchased from a third-party vendor.

PHYSICAL DESIGN

Communications design

Having established the network/data communications needs in the logical design, this section will specify exactly what needs to be acquired in terms of network devices (e.g. cabling) and what configuration changes will need to be made to existing network set-ups.

Database design

The general database needs will have been established in the logical design. In this section the details of table structures, relationships, data controls, etc. will need to be defined. Relationships with existing database systems will also need to be considered.

The SDLC: implementation phase

The implementation phase is when the system specified by the design stage is constructed, tested and put in place. There are three distinct stages:

Building The designs created during the previous stage of the SDLC are used to create the system. This may be undertaken by in-house teams or it may be devolved to third-party providers. The main focus during this stage will be the creation of programs using standard programming languages, although some database design and document production will also be involved.

Testing The completed system must be tested thoroughly. A rigorous testing programme will be undertaken, with the system being tested both in the programming environment (alpha testing) and in an environment more akin to the live environment it will actually operate in (beta testing). There will be a final testing phase after the system has been installed (user acceptance).

Installation The completed, tested program will need to be installed in the environment where it will operate. This involves more than just installing it on a server. The installation process entails preparing users (i.e. ensuring they will be in a position to work with it efficiently), preparing the site (e.g. ensuring the hardware that will be running it is of a sufficiently high specification) and preparing the data (i.e. ensuring that the data that will be needed for the program to run is accessible).

Installation strategies

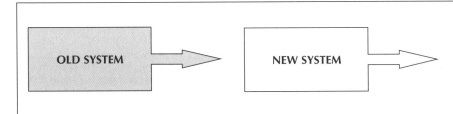

DIRECT CONVERSION entails disengaging the old system and starting up the new system on a specified date. It is the least time-consuming strategy but the highest risk. If there is a problem with the new system, it is difficult to re-engage the old system.

PHASED CONVERSION is less high risk than direct conversion since it allows for a 'grace period' when the old system can still be used if the new system has problems. It can be time-consuming and involve more staff if the system needs to be installed at several locations. It is considered to be a moderate risk strategy.

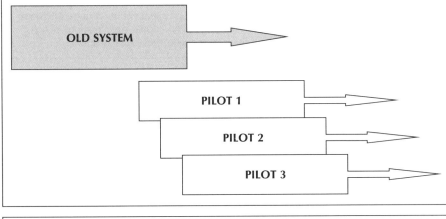

PILOT CONVERSION is again considered to be a moderate risk strategy. It entails installing the new system in one area of the organisation and looking for problems before installing it in another area. Depending on the number of pilots involved, this process can be time-consuming but it does aid the 'bug-fixing' process.

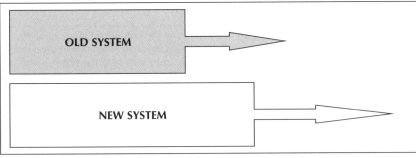

PARALLEL CONVERSION is considered to be the lowest risk strategy. The new system is run alongside the old system. The outputs of both the old and new systems are compared and reconciled. When the new system seems to be running well the old system is disengaged. This approach can be expensive in terms of system resources.

Testing

Testing is a critical phase in software development. Most programs are written by teams of people, with each team member working on a different aspect of the application. These different aspects all have to be brought together in order to create a system ready for implementation. Before the system can be fully implemented it must be subject to a rigorous test procedure. If an application is not tested properly and, as a consequence, there are problems when the user operates it, the software provider's reputation will be damaged and they may lose business.

What is involved in testing?

- Testing will involve the construction of a comprehensive plan based on the content of the specification and that covers every aspect of the system, specifies the types of tests that will be performed on it, defines what the outcome of these tests should be, and notes what remedial action might be required.
- Testing should be conducted using three types of data: typical/normal (the type of data that might normally be entered); erroneous (data that might feasibly be entered but is none the less incorrect); extreme (data that is highly unlikely to be entered). The aim of this process is to take into account all the possible mistakes that a user might make.
- Testing is an iterative process – i.e. if a problem is found at any stage in the process, the process reverts to an earlier stage, corrects the problem and picks up the testing procedure from that point.

The different stages of testing

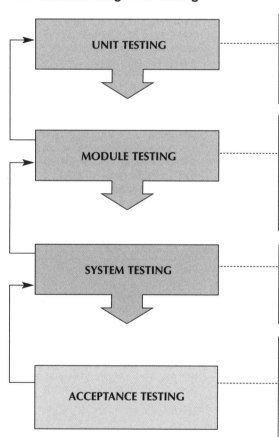

A unit is a self-contained section of programming designed to perform a specific action. For example, a unit might consist of a subprocedure that makes visible a previously invisible command button, or a function that calculates the average of a set of inputted values. Each of these units must be tested to ensure they perform the action correctly, using both typical and erroneous user actions.

A module is a linked collection of units that make up a clearly delineated aspect of the overall system. For example, an accounting system may contain a module that manages the procedure for the end of a tax year. Such a module would consist of subprocedures and functions that would update calculations, create a new week structure, etc. Each unit will have been tested during the previous stage. What must now be investigated is whether these units all work together, i.e. whether actions performed in one unit can affect the performance of another.

A system is the sum total of all the elements required by an application. System testing ensures that all the modules work together and they connect effectively with any data sources that will be required. System testing should also recall the original functional specifications of the system and ensure that the system meets these specifications.

Acceptance testing is where the system is tested in something approximating the 'live' operational environment in which it will have to function. This is often performed in a specially designed 'test environment'. A test environment creates a copy of all the programs, data files, stored procedures, etc. that the organisation currently uses. The data in this test environment will be exactly the same as that in the 'live' environment but won't be affected by any changes made to it during the testing procedure. The system can now be tested to see if it will function under normal operational conditions.

Alpha and beta testing

Alpha testing takes place in the development environment. It is usually undertaken by those responsible for creating the program, though final users may also have an input. The process is essentially that outlined above, i.e. proceeding through a series of stages, using typical, erroneous and extreme data to see where the program falls down. This first stage is necessary because fundamental problems may come to light and this will mean reverting to an earlier stage of development.

Beta testing involves releasing the fully tested application to real users who will then use it in a live environment for a test period. During this time the users may notice problems with the system which they can then report to the software producer. This approach allows software vendors to put their application though a 'dry run' in a variety of live environments over a period of time. They can thus identify and correct shortcomings before fully releasing the product on the market

The SDLC: maintenance and evaluation phase

It is also important that the new system should be evaluated. The outcome of the evaluation will help those responsible for its implementation to judge whether the expenditure on the new system has been justified. The evaluation must also reflect the original specification in order to ascertain that what has been produced matches what was initially requested. A thorough evaluation also helps to improve the quality of future developments by highlighting what worked well and what caused problems.

Areas to be covered in a post-implementation evaluation

ACCURACY

A critical test for any system is the accuracy of its output. Erroneous information, produced as a result of processing errors, can have disastrous consequences. Of course, this will have been covered during the test procedure but it is important to ensure that accuracy is maintained during day-to-day operations.

QUALITY OF OUTPUT

One of the main functions of any information system is to produce high-quality information. The outputs must be judged against the criteria that are used to determine quality of information, i.e. is the information complete, accurate, reliable and available to the right person at the right time in a suitable format?

USER SATISFACTION

If users don't like using a system they will try to avoid doing so. If they have no choice, they will become disgruntled and therefore less effective. The users should feel comfortable using the system and confident that any problems they do encounter will be resolved quickly.

CONTROLS AND SECURITY

The system should be fully protected from unauthorised access and the integrity of the data it uses should be comprehensively protected. It should comply fully with legislation (such as the Data Protection Act) that stipulates the level of security required to protect personal data.

Evaluation report

ORIGINAL OBJECTIVES

During the early stages of system development, a set of objectives should have been established. The system should fulfil these original objectives. For example, if one of the objectives was to improve customer service, a judgement must be made as to whether or not this has been achieved.

RELIABILITY

The reliability of a system can be judged on the basis of how often it breaks down. A reliable system should be robust enough to survive in a busy, working environment, where users may subject it to 'rough treatment'.

COMPATIBILITY

The system should fit seamlessly into the general working environment. It should be able to 'communicate' when necessary with existing systems. There should be no deleterious effects on existing systems as a consequence of its implementation.

PERFORMANCE

The system should run at an appropriate speed. Advances in technology have resulted in users having high expectations of computer performance – i.e. they become impatient if the response is not instantaneous. Speed of performance in the operational environment therefore needs to be evaluated.

Approaches to gathering information for the evaluation report

Quantitative tests	Performance monitoring software can be used to determine speed of processing and accuracy of output.
Interviews	Users can be interviewed individually about the system. How do they feel about using it? What problems have they encountered? What has been the quality of support?
Error logging	One way of evaluating the reliability of a system is to analyse the errors that occur. This can be done through a help desk log or network-based error-logging software.
Questionnaire	A questionnaire can be given to all those who use the system, including managers who receive reports. The questionnaire can contain structured questions that will allow the development team to 'score' different aspects of the system.

Maintenance issues

Why do maintenance issues occur?

Even if a piece of software has been tested extensively, it may still be necessary to provide post-implementation maintenance. There may be a number of reasons for this, including:

- 'Bugs', which may not have been identified during the testing process, become apparent when the system is operating in a live environment.
- Users may, after a period of time, find a particular aspect of the software unsatisfactory.
- Changes in the business environment, e.g. a change in legislation, may mean that the software is required to perform tasks it wasn't originally designed for.
- A security issue, e.g. a virus threat, may emerge which means that the system requires an extra level of protection.
- The software provider may discover a way to make the application run more efficiently.
- New software or hardware may be purchased, the integration of which requires changes to existing systems.

When a maintenance issue emerges, the ICT manager will contact the software provider (or in-house team) and outline the nature of the problem. If the problem is a critical one, an immediate solution may be provided. If the change is non-critical, the software manufacturer may add it to a number of other changes and prepare a second release version of the original software. These new versions are numbered according to the sequence of release. For example, a change from version 1.3 to version 1.4 indicates that minor changes have been made, whereas a change to the whole number, from 2.3 to 3.0 indicates a significant upgrade.

Three types of maintenance

Corrective

This involves the identification of 'bugs' and errors that haven't been picked up during the testing process. For example, an application may crash every time it tries to connect to another application. This may not have been tested for and so may only emerge after a period of time in a live environment. The problem will be analysed and an appropriate solution will be designed, tested and implemented.

Adaptive

This occurs when the user or the vendor perceives a new need that could – or must – be catered for. These are referred to as enhancements, i.e. improvements to the system. For example, an accounting package may need to adapt in order to accommodate changes to tax legislation. As with corrective maintenance, the functionality required by the new need is defined and a solution is created.

Perfective

If a software provider has created an application that is generally popular and successful, it will want organisations to keep using it. It is therefore in its best interests to keep working on the software, seeking ways to make it perform more efficiently. In this respect software manufacturers are no different from soap powder manufacturers, i.e. in seeking to maintain their market share by regularly introducing 'new' or 'improved' versions of their product.

The pattern of maintenance types

This diagram shows the degree to which each type of maintenance is likely to take place in relation to the age of a system.

	Straight after implementation	Early operational period	Middle operational period	Late operational period
Corrective maintenance	HIGH	LOW	LOW	HIGH
Adaptive maintenance (minor amendments)	NONE	MEDIUM	MEDIUM	MEDIUM
Adaptive maintenance (major amendments)	NONE	NONE	MEDIUM TO HIGH	MEDIUM TO HIGH
Perfective maintenance	LOW	LOW TO MEDIUM	MEDIUM	LOW

Management information needs

Managers in organisations have a variety of functions depending on their position in the hierarchy and the nature of the organisation. There are, however, some generic functions that all managers have as part of their work. The ability of managers to perform these functions effectively may be enhanced by their use of information systems. Managers therefore have 'information needs'. The nature of these needs can be directly related to the management function being performed.

Function	Information needs
Planning Managers need to plan for the future, analysing current situations and forecasting future scenarios: • Establish goals • Define courses of action. • Plan resources – human and non-human.	• Schedules and costings. • Information about the local area. • Information about local bylaws.
Decision-making • Structured, i.e. predictable and planned for. • Semi-structured: there is an element of predictability about them but they are not susceptible to the rigid application of formulaic rules. • Unstructured decisions cannot be predicted or planned for. They arise as the result of unforeseen events and require managers to rely on their understanding of the situation and their judgement.	• The overheads. • Customer base. • The proximity of competitors. • Transport and delivery implications. • The success/failure rate of other similar businesses. • Availability of labour.
Control and monitoring • Maximum productivity. • Minimum waste. • Monitoring processes. • Success and failure. • Remedial action.	• Weekly sales figures. • Market research. • Wage sheets.
Coordination/liaison • Liaise with other managers and with subordinates. • Ensure that information flow is effective and in an appropriate format.	• Summaries of sales figures. • Communications from senior management of e.g. guidelines. • Personal information on employees.

What are Management Information Systems?

• Management Information Systems (MIS) are organised collections of people, procedures and resources designed to support the decisions made by managers. In order to make good decisions managers need access to timely, relevant and accurate information. An MIS is designed to produce this.
• The information usually comes in the form of reports. Some of these reports will be produced regularly (e.g. weekly sales figures), others will be produced on demand (e.g. sales figures for a specific branch). For the information in these reports to have value it must have been processed into an appropriate format. These reports are usually in 'hard copy' format but may also be available online.
• The information contained in these reports will be generated from various sources, both internal and external. External data may include stock market reports, market research, supply costing, etc. Internal data may include processed transaction data and data drawn from centrally held databases, e.g. personnel files.
• An MIS typically supports the functions of planning, controlling, monitoring and decision-making at all management levels, i.e. strategic, tactical and operational.
• Older MIS were relatively simple systems, designed to summarise and report on day-to-day operations at scheduled intervals. They did not have analytical/modelling capabilities and were designed to operate in an environment where information needs were known. Newer MIS are more flexible and include software that allows managers to create their own customised reports. More complex MIS are perhaps better defined as Database management systems.

Some qualities of an effective MIS

• It should be accessible to a wide range of users, including those with a relatively poor level of computer literacy.
• It should provide useful information by summarising data in an effective way to avoid information overload and by presenting it in the most appropriate format, e.g. by using graphs or tabulated formats.
• It should connect multiple levels of detail so that a user can start out looking at a high-level issue, then easily drill down to more detail where necessary to aid planning and decision-making.
• It should be flexible, allowing the user to extract specific sub-sets of data which have been ordered in the most useful way.
• It must be accurate. There should be no question about the credibility of the information being produced by the system.
• It should support a wide range of user skill levels.

The success or failure of an information system

Characteristics of a successful system

A successful information system:

- will be implemented on schedule and within the original cost constraints;
- will, through regular use, 'add value' to the organisation, thus justifying the time/money invested in its development;
- will be viewed favourably by users – they should consider the system to be supportive of their work;
- will have fulfilled the original objectives as specified at the start of the project;
- will be 'low maintenance', requiring only minimal post-implementation support and 'bug-fixing';
- will be fully integrated into the organisation's overall information strategy.

Factors contributing to the failure of an information system

Lack of formal methods

It is important that the approach taken to the development of systems is a formalised and systematic one. Systems development involves significant capital investment. There is, therefore, too much at stake for an *ad hoc* approach to be adopted. Formal methodologies allow managers to monitor the various stages of development and only authorise further progress if they are satisfied that the system is developing along expected lines. A haphazard approach to systems development is almost bound to lead to systems that fail to fulfil the above criteria for success.

Inadequate analysis

The aim of the analysis stage is to collect and organise *all* information that pertains to the new system. This involves a precise mapping of the existing information systems in the organisation. Existing hardware, software and procedures will also need to be fully described. If this information is not fully or correctly compiled, the developers will gain an inaccurate view of the system requirements. They will therefore design and produce a system based on this inaccurate view. The final system will inevitably be inadequate in regard to the original requirements.

Lack of management involvement in design

In large organisations the development of information systems is undertaken by ICT specialists. These specialists may not have a comprehensive understanding of the business area that they are designing the system for. In developing a new system, the developers should maintain a constant dialogue with managers of the area that the system is being developed for. Only in this way can the developers fully take into account the needs of the users and the specific information issues of the relevant business area.

SYSTEM FAILURE

Over-emphasis on computer systems

Information systems consist of a wide variety of elements, of which computer technology forms only one part. There is a danger that developers will focus all their attention on the development of software and the acquisition of hardware. If this occurs, the personnel involved in the system and the procedures that they follow will receive insufficient attention. Since any system relies on the successful interaction of all elements, this limited focus can lead to problems at the implementation stage.

Lack of management knowledge of ICT

Managers of specialist business areas are not always aware of all of the latest developments in ICT. This can mean that they can miscalculate what ICT systems are capable of. This in turn can lead to them making excessive or inappropriate demands. They can, for example, set out requirements that cannot possibly be met by developers working within the constraints of existing technology. Additionally, managers who do not understand the procedures of systems development can have false expectations about what can be achieved within a specified time/budget.

Lack of teamwork/inadequate standards of work

Systems are generally developed by teams of people, with each member of the team taking responsibility for different aspects of the development. In order for a system to be successful, all those professionals involved need to be adequately skilled in their areas, and professional and conscientious in their approach. It is also important that the team as a whole demonstrates a high level of co-operation, mutual support and effective communication. Failure to do so will almost certainly lead to system inadequacies.

ICT in manufacture

Manufacture represents the extraction or acquisition of raw materials and converting them into tangible products prior to being sold to a general market. The same principles still apply, but the processes involved have changed dramatically with the advent and explosion in use of ICT. Formerly, workers were classified by their trades and tended to stay within that trade for most, if not all, of their working lives. The demand for skilled craftsmen gradually reduced as the ability to undertake the same tasks became possible by pre-programmed machines. Instead of hiring someone to apply sharp tools to carve wood into impressive tables and chairs, employers take on computer-literate workers. They not only have the manual skills but are able to load programs which cut shapes and carve with 100% accuracy in a fraction of the time taken by a human. Of course, there is still some demand for personalised hand-made goods but these come at a premium price. For the mass market, mass production is required. Those who are able to respond quickly to a trend, and supply products to satisfy demands, are companies that tend to be flexible and deploy a successful IT strategy that monitors the markets, reports on consumer spending patterns and recommends additions to the business plan.

Practical uses of ICT in manufacture

Research and development
The ability to analyse market data is greatly enhanced by using computer technology. By identifying patterns in consumer spending and purchase habits, manufacturers are able to better predict and produce products likely to appeal and sell on the mass market. The option to locate regional trends or clarify the wants of a certain age group can be used to ensure that what the manufacturers finally produce is what the consumer wants. Colours, shapes, sizes, weights and price are a few of the important elements taken into account when gathering market data. Technology also helps to build simulations of products which aid with costing calculations as dimensions are matched to materials and suppliers. From an on-screen image the market can be tested again to ascertain if the virtual product matches expectations. The cost of building expensive prototypes is reduced because they are replaced by models which can be altered or enhanced and re-tested depending on what the data recommends.

Design

Blueprints detailing exact design specifications can be produced in specialist software. Alternative colours and sizes can be added and altered to view different designs. The use of ICT allows designers to be located in any part of the world, which means that when a specialist has finished on their particular area they can send the design onto the next designer who adds their section. The ability to quickly change the way a product looks without having to do a total re-draw is an obvious attraction.

Stock control

During the process of production it is important that the components used do not run out. If this happens products cannot be fully assembled and orders will be delayed. A delay such as this can damage business confidence and could mean a loss of business. Stock control systems know exactly how many components are in stock, how many are required to fully construct a product and how many finished products can be produced in one day. To reduce the risk of running out the stock control system will store a re-order level. As each component is used the system reduces the number in stock until that figure is at the re-order level. A fresh order will be placed automatically and will be designed to arrive 'just-in-time' (the actual name of the system adopted from production methods in the Far East) to ensure smooth production. The advantage of this is that storage space is not wasted holding stock that may not be used for a long time and customer orders are satisfied because all the required components will be present when required. The type of data that will be entered will include the quantity of the order to be produced and how long each product takes to make. The amount of wastage per product is also claimed to be reduced although it is not inconceivable that whole batches with similar faults still fall off the production line.

Marketing

When a product has been manufactured it needs to be sold and it is the job of the marketers to attracted customers. Graphical software is used to design advertisements for magazines, TV and billboards. Sophisticated monitoring software is often used to ensure that fast moving consumer goods (FMCG) are located in the place best suited to achieve optimum sales. ICT is used to plan sales displays which might vary from store to store. Marketing is also involved with collecting and analysing sales data and consumer trends. Simple software with basic arithmetic embedded can be used or bespoke packages can be designed to perform specified analysis. Such data is passed onto the research and development department who act on the information given.

Automated production

The need for humans to put products together has slowly diminished as they are replaced by robots or other automated technology which is able to work continuously and with a higher degree of accuracy. The initial financial outlay can be prohibitive and maintenance costs tend to be an issue but the advantages are appealing enough for companies to make the initial investment and look to upgrade every few years to the next piece of technology. Robots are able to perform tasks in inhospitable conditions and do not need to rest or be fed. The car industry was amongst the most publicised user of robotic technology and prompted the use within other areas when the benefits were made clear.

E-commerce

E-commerce is concerned with buying and selling, using IT. Soon after the Internet became the world's information share point, retailers saw the potential to reach millions of customers and uploaded their shop-fronts online. Traders were quick to appreciate the advantage of allowing customers to browse all their products from the comfort of their own home at any time, night or day.

There is now a range of entertainment, products and services online. Legal advisors, estate agents, supermarkets all use web space to generate income.

Some of the key features of online trading for businesses include:
- 24-hour trading, 365 days a year.
- Can reach a much larger potential customer base.
- No need for expensive premises and storage of products because orders can be satisfied as and when they are made.
- The site is dynamic so it is a lot easier to update with images and latest information than it is to reorganise a whole store.
- Customer information can be taken directly from customers through online order forms and later interrogated.
- Payments can be made directly using secure online payment methods.
- Fewer staff are required to sell products.
- Links from other sites can generate income.
- Search engines may produce more potential customers.
- Businesses can use the web to trade with other businesses.
- The head office can be based anywhere there is the technology to support it.

Some of the key features of online trading for customers include:
- Ease of communicating with the supplier is enhanced.
- Browsing for the best deals and making purchases from home.
- Comparing prices for similar products.
- Signing up for updates to new products.
- Making secure online payments.
- Shopping 24 hours a day, 365 days a year.
- Avoiding the expense of travelling to shops.
- Avoiding queues.
- Gathering information about products and reading reviews.
- Storing websites in a Favorites folder.
- Possible to benefit from cheaper prices because of the lower trading cost for the supplier.
- Checking availability of products.

Online auctions

With the advent of online auctions it is not only established businesses that are able to generate sales using the Internet. The biggest success in this category is eBay, which makes millions of pounds through the commission of sales through its website. Buyers are able to browse thousands of products and use search facilities to locate what they are looking for, bid and have their winnings posted. Sellers are able to reach a broader audience and sell just about anything they no longer want or need.

Banking

Online banking is another area which has taken off in recent years. The services provided in a high street bank are available online. It is possible to apply for loans, overdraft facilities, credit cards, and view investment opportunities. The transfer of funds from one account to another and pay bills is also common practice. Banks have gone to great lengths to ensure that their sites are secure by insisting on several levels of security before an account can be accessed. The hours that banks open is often the same as those that people work so they are unable to go to the bank. The online version provides all the facilities required except the ability to withdraw cash.

Making payments

By using technology consumers are able to pay for their purchases rather than using cash. 'Chip and pin' is the most recent development. A debit or credit card is inserted into a special reader which allows payments to be made only after the personal identification number (pin) has been entered. After it has been entered the customer's account is debited by the cost of the purchase and the seller's account is credited. The transfer of funds can take several days to complete in the UK, despite the fact that digital transfer should be able to reduce this to a matter of hours if not minutes. Banks are suspected of holding on to the transferred money and using it for their own gains before allowing it to leave their accounts.

Teleworking

Teleworking occurs when a member of an organisation arranges to work at home rather than in the workplace. In some instances telecommuting – or teleworking – is a full-time arrangement; in other instances an employee may choose to work from home only at specific times. This arrangement has become increasingly achievable through the use of computers, the availability of Internet/intranet links and advances in communications technology – e.g. fax machines, email, videoconferencing, remote desktop etc.

Conditions required for teleworking to take place

- The organisation needs to be engaged in the kind of work that can be done at home. There are many examples of this, the most common being: data entry, secretarial work (e.g. copy-typing), design work, etc.
- The organisation needs to be able to trust the employee to work from home effectively, or have a means of monitoring them.
- There needs to be appropriate hardware/software provision. In addition to a computer, this usually involves an email/Internet connection or a link to a company-wide intranet.
- An appropriate home-working environment needs to be available, i.e. a space where the employee can work without interruption.

Advantages for the employee

- **More flexible use of time** This can be particularly useful if the employee has other responsibilities, e.g. child-care, care for an elderly relative, etc.
- **Working in a known environment** Some people may prefer to work in a quiet, home environment rather than in a busy office.
- **No travelling involved** Some people live a considerable distance form their place of work. In such cases, teleworking will cut down on time and money wasted on commuting.

Disadvantages for the employee

- **Work is a social environment** Many people form social groups via their workplace and one in three people meet their future life partner at work. Telecommuting can lead to social isolation.
- **Some work requires interpersonal contact** Personal conversations form a vital part of the work process in any organisation. Direct, face-to-face interaction is sometimes the only way that information can be fully communicated.
- **Working at home is not always easy** There may be many interruptions and distractions, and this can make work difficult. Also the person may feel that their home now offers no escape from work.

Advantages for the employer

- **Reduction of the need for office space** If employees don't need desk space, the need for large offices decreases. This can cut down on rental/purchase costs. There may be other associated costs which can also be cut: electricity bills, maintenance staff, etc.
- **Hiring staff on the basis of productivity** Some employers need to hire staff on a short-term basis to complete specific tasks, e.g. batch processing.
- **Greater productivity** Some employees, working in the right environment and away from the distractions of colleagues, can be more productive.
- **Recruit the best** Some staff may be located in another country but their level of expertise may be worth the fee.

Disadvantages for the employer

- **Difficulty in monitoring the productivity of employees** The employer may be concerned that insufficient work is being done and there may not be any easy way of monitoring this.
- **There are security issues** An Internet link is always a vulnerable point in a networked system. When it is linked to a domestic PC, this is even more the case.
- **There may be initial costs** Communications links may need to be set up and the employee may need a work-dedicated terminal.

Videoconferencing

How videoconferencing works

1 Videoconferencing room

In some organisations specially prepared rooms can be booked. The room will be set up like a standard meeting room, organised so that people can talk to each other and give presentations. Additionally there will be some specific pieces of technology that will permit videoconferencing to take place. There will be at least one large monitor/screen so that the people in the room can see participants who are in another location. There will be at least one microphone to pick up the voice signals of the people in the meeting and at least one camera to capture the visual images of the participants. If there is more than one camera/microphone there will also need to be some sort of mixing/controlling device.

2 Signal conversion

People speak and interact as they would do at a normal meeting. The camera(s)/microphone(s) pick up the signals in analogue form. These analogue signals will need to be converted to binary code before they can be transmitted. This is achieved through the use of a device – called a 'codec' – which can convert analogue to digital signals and vice versa. An additional step at this stage might be to combine the audio and video signals into one combined file format. An example of this is the .AVI (*audio video inter-leave*) format which combines the two types of signals and has the effect of compressing the data, making it easier to transmit.

3 Compression

Transmission will be more effective if the data can be compressed, i.e. made smaller without any significant loss of quality. There are various techniques that can be used for file compression. The method that is used will depend on the resources available (some are more costly than others) and how critical the quality of the image/sound is. A typical compression technique used by videoconferencing is 'lossy' compression. The lossy technique involves focusing on areas of high contrast and removing some pixels (units of visual data) from the image. Minor background variations are therefore sacrificed but, in most cases, this does not result in a significant loss of image quality.

4 Transmission

Data is usually transmitted using an ISDN (integrated service digital network) line. ISDN transmits data in a digital rather than analogue form and supports simultaneous transmission of audio, video and computer data. This ensures that the video and audio data 'arrive' together. This makes it particularly useful for videoconferencing.

5 Destination

At the reception end the process is reversed. The data is decompressed where necessary, reconverted to an analogue signal and transmitted on the screen. The whole process is two-way so the capture/conversion/transmission procedure is repeated at the second location. In this way a live, two-way transmission environment is created.

Advantages	Disadvantages
Many organisations have employees based in several countries. Bringing these people together for meetings on a regular basis is almost impossible. When meetings have to take place, it may involve expensive international travel with all the difficulties and costs that this involves. Videoconferencing allows for regular meetings between differently located individuals. It has the advantage over telephone conferencing that one can see the face of the person one is addressing. It can also be used in conjunction with the Internet to facilitate presentations. An individual in one location can create and run a presentation (using presentation software). People in the second location can then view this on a monitor that is logged on to a dedicated website.	The main disincentive to the use of videoconferencing is cost. It is expensive to set up, maintain and run. In order to justify this cost it must be cost-effective for an organisation. This is most likely to be the case when an organisation has key people in remote locations who need to speak to each other on a regular basis. Another potential weakness of the system is that subtle communications between people (i.e. through facial expressions, body language, whispered asides, etc.) can be lost because they are not picked up by the camera/microphone or are lost in the compression/transmission process.

ICT in education

Schools are charged with preparing young people for life after school, and this includes access to and use of the tools they are most likely to encounter. The world of ICT has had a significant impact on the way people study and the way education is administered. A lot of the technology favours different learning speeds and does not, like some teachers, assume that everybody learns at the same pace and in the same way.

Distance learning

Those who struggle to attend traditional lessons because of commitments at home can take advantage of distance learning courses. Specialised sites are set up from which students can access and download theory (text files or podcasts) and assignments, and later upload completed work for assessment. The Open University is a prime example of an organisation that provides this service, offering a progressive route of study right up to doctorate level. The option to study by using a link to the Internet has provided many people with the opportunity to improve their academic profile.

Interactive learning

Learning by doing is a popularised educational theory and much technology has been developed in support of this notion.
* Teachers use interactive white boards to perform demonstrations or presentations to audiences.
* Online resources encourage learners to play games whilst learning new concepts and theories.
* Software has been written to work with touch screen technology which prompts pupils to use their fingers to make selections and control work areas.
* Digital photography and film making has become easier with the development of more intuitive software which means pupils can make their own revision DVDs to revise from, rather than reams of hand-written notes.
* Digital resources (CD-Roms and Websites) are often designed to track progress and report feedback relating to the students' performance. Less difficult or understood sections can be skipped and harder sections revisited through simple navigation. Detailed reports on class or an individual's performance can be obtained which helps the teacher plan activities and resources for future lessons

Administration

Some schools use swipe card systems to log pupil attendance. Such systems are linked to the main office which is able to produce reports showing who is missing from school. Automatic emails or text can be sent to parents or phone calls made to find out why the pupil is missing. Databases are also used to hold details of each pupil. Grades at various stages of the school career, contact details, medical information, and dietary requirements are just some of the details schools need to hold on behalf of the pupil.

Virtual learning environments

Moodle is an example of a VLE which, amongst many things, allows teachers to set up their own online areas where they can store resources and provide access to their classes. Pupils are able to log in, collect details of homework, download tasks, complete them and return them back to the site. The teacher can collect the homework from the site, mark it and provide feedback. VLEs provide tools which help to track student performance and even log the time work was uploaded or provide alerts when work hasn't been submitted. Multiple choice online tests can also be constructed which are automatically assessed and scores logged, as well as linked to alternative resources and chat facilities. These can be a novel way for a class to interact beyond the classroom.

Assessment

In some cases, after exams have been taken, the papers are taken and scanned into computer systems. Examiners are then able to access the papers online and carry out their assessment work. This method removes the need for examiners to receive packages through the post, find room to store and mark them, and then have to return them to the exam board for further sampling. It is common for an examiner to assess the same part of an exam over and over again. By only marking certain questions many times, examiners become more consistent with the marks they are awarding and the whole process is speeded up. The same response can be marked several times to ensure standards are being meet and the software used can produce multiple reports relating to the performance of each examiner.

ICT and health

The National Health Service in the UK has been able to use technology to prolong life and prevent disease. It has spent millions of pounds developing a variety of machines to assist with patient treatment, and to improve the quality of care given to those who need it. The ability to diagnose accurately and prescribe correct medicines are other areas that have gained benefits from ICT.

Making an appointment

This can be done online through a website facility. The patient can specify a time and select a GP and see if they are both free before the system makes the booking. On arrival touch screen technology is used to greet patients in some surgeries. By checking in through this type of system administration staff are free to carry out other duties.

Patient records

Patient records are kept in databases. Prior to seeing a patient the doctor will search for the patient's records and see what conditions or complaints and medicines they have had in the past. They will also check to see if they are allergic to any medication so that it can be avoided. The details in the database help build a profile of each person and aid with selecting the course of treatment most suited to the individual.

Expert systems

A doctor can use an expert system to help with diagnosis and prescribing the best remedy. A similar system is also available online. Symptoms are input into the system through a menu-driven system or natural language interface and one by one the system attempts to identify the complaint and recommend a treatment or ask further questions. The original data entered into the system is provided by experts who are trained to make real decisions. As the knowledge base and understanding of treatments and symptoms grows, so to does the capacity and usefulness of the expert system. Doctors cannot possibly know every complaint and every treatment so such a system can reduce the burden of having to try and remember everything there is to know.

Getting to patients

In the event of an emergency it is crucial that the ambulance arrives as quickly as possible. Satellite navigation systems enable drivers to find the address they are looking for and such systems can even recommend the best route to avoid known trouble spots and delays such as road works or recently reported traffic jams. By arriving with minimal delays lives can be saved. Some ambulances make use of on-board heart monitors which transmit data back to the hospital they are going to so that the waiting doctors have some data to help them prepare for the arrival.

NHS Online

The NHS has a helpful and easy to navigate system which allows people to find out all sorts of information to help keep themselves healthy. Dietary advice, self-medication treatments, help lines and contact information are all available. The ability to search and submit symptoms is also available as well as the latest news on emerging treatments. The facility to click on various parts of the body and select possible areas where advice is needed is a recent addition and easy for a non-experienced computer user to operate.

Plastic surgery - models

Plastic surgeons can use imaging technology to show a patient how they will look after surgery (provided all goes well). Being able to view the finished work before it has even happened helps plastic surgeons put patients at ease and allows patients the opportunity to comment on or suggest alternatives prior to treatment. During the procedure a wide range of monitoring devices are used to monitor the patient's heart rate and blood pressure to make sure that they are not in any trouble.

ICT in the home

In the 1970s it would have been quite rare to have noticed much in the way of ICT equipment or use in the home. In recent times, in the developed world, it would be rare to go into someone's home and not find any evidence of ICT. The owners of the equipment may or may not appreciate that they own ICT systems but they certainly appreciate the benefits that can be had.

Home computers/laptops

The cost of owning a home computer or laptop has fallen since they first hit the market. Sophisticated machines with fast processors, huge amounts of storage space and flat screen monitors can be found in homes up and down the country. By paying for an Internet connection from an Internet Service Provider home users can connect to the biggest network in the world. As soon as this connection is made they can potentially access any other machine on the planet and vice-versa. Affordable home computers open up millions of shop doorways on the screen, provide access to many services and information, and give instant exposure to the latest film, music and television news, including actual footage. The benefits of email communication allow families in different parts of the world to communicate with ease, use chat facilities, share photographs and use videoconferencing facilities. There are so many benefits to users of PCs that it would take several more books to cover them all.

Portable devices

Mobile phones can be used anywhere that there is a signal strong enough to receive and send calls. Such devices bring peace of mind to stranded motorists and allow people to communicate in an ad-hoc fashion to arrange meetings or share information and ideas. Mobile phones also allow the owner to send text messages to other mobile phones, which is useful when the person you are trying to contact does not answer the call. Mobile phones are able to store records of calls, can help organise lists of contact details and can even be used as tracking devices.

In recent years digital photographic technology has been combined with the mobile phone, which means people can take photographs as and when they please. By using blue tooth technology (no wires) the photographs taken can be transferred to a home computer system where they can be edited, stored in digital photo albums, uploaded to the Internet or sent as an email attachment.

Not only can mobile phones be used to make calls and take pictures, but the ability to listen to MP3 files has also been built into them. Therefore a mobile phone can be used for multiple purposes. Such devices have replaced the need to carry a camera, phone and walkman. The sound quality is often very good and the storage reasonable and likely to increase.

All this technology wrapped up in a neat plastic case doesn't stop there. Some mobiles have the functionality to surf the Internet, which means that all the advantages of using it can be achieved on the move. The interface for this technology has changed to touch screen with the arrival of the iPhone. Over the coming years the competitors will catch up and it will be common to see touch screen mobiles everywhere with huge amounts of storage space for thousands of songs and images, playing full length feature films and the ability to search the Internet from anywhere as the pursuit for greater signal strength continues.

Domestic appliances

Machines are now produced which can read digital signals on RFID tags placed in products which have been on the high street. Appliances such as fridges will know what has been placed inside them by reading the FRID tags. By networking the fridge it is possible for it to know when it is low on certain products, use its network capabilities to contact a supplier and place an automatic order for more. Online shopping favourites lists are already a possibility, making this 'far out' idea appear slightly more plausible. Washing machines, again reading RFID tags, can identify the garments in their drum, measure the weight and apply the appropriate wash setting.

Social networks

Many home users, and some who should be busy working in offices, use social network sites to locate and communicate with old friends. The most popular at the moment allows account holders to post pictures, send messages, build profiles, and even chat and play games with other users online at the same time. The built-in search facility has given many the opportunity to locate old school friends whilst some have even found love through networking through friends of friends.

Computer crime

What is computer crime?

Computers have given workers in most fields new tools to work with, tools that have made their jobs easier and allowed them to do things that were not possible before. Unfortunately, this is as true for criminals as it is for doctors, teachers and designers. It is sometimes thought that 'computer crime' is a new phenomenon but, as the categories below demonstrate, it is more the case that computers have provided new ways to commit old crimes. The facilities provided by computers – their speed of processing, their capacity to connect to international communication networks, the way in which many of their processes are hidden – make them valuable to criminals whilst creating new challenges – and new opportunities – for law enforcement agencies.

Categories of computer crime

Unauthorised access

This is usually referred to as 'hacking' or 'cracking'. Hacking involves infiltrating a system to which the individual does not have authorised access. The purpose behind this infiltration varies according to the individual. Some hackers see their activities as a form of game-playing, i.e. where they are matching their computer skills against those of an adversary. The gaining of access is sufficient for them. Others are more destructive in their intentions. They target organisations that they are antagonistic towards and, having gained access, commit acts of 'electronic vandalism', e.g. amending critical data.

Fraud–phishing

Developments in computerised systems have contributed to a growth in electronic transaction processing. This has led to a concomitant rise in computer-based fraud. Criminals have used computerised systems to steal people's credit identities. They then use those identities to make purchases or facilitate cash transfers. Another example of computer-based fraud is where individuals have gained unauthorised access to financial accounts and amended the details of those accounts to their advantage. There have also been examples of people setting up websites for companies that don't exist, and accepting people's credit card payments.

Publication of illicit material

Material such as hard-core pornography cannot legally be published and sold in many countries. However, the Internet is transnational in its scope and so illicit material can be created in a country where it is legal and viewed in a country where it is not. It is not possible at the moment to police an international 'ownerless' system such as the Internet and, consequently, individuals can publish illicit material with impunity. Another example is the publication of material likely to incite racial hatred. Were material of this kind to be made available through a shop, the owner and publisher could be prosecuted. Such material is freely available on the web.

Theft

Information stored on computerised systems has value. The code behind a piece of software, a database of consumer information, or the master copies of a new film, can be sold for profit and criminals are therefore motivated to steal such items. In some cases this theft can be achieved through a conventional break-in – i.e. the tapes or hard drives containing the data are physically removed. More often, however, the theft is achieved electronically. The system where the data/software/content is located is hacked into and the material electronically transferred to another site.

Industrial espionage

Some organisations try to gain an advantage over their competitors by illicitly gaining access to information about the competitor's marketing strategy, latest research, expansion plans, etc. In the past this would have been achieved through breaking-in, illegal photographing of documents, insiders passing out information, etc. Now it can be achieved through hacking into organisational databases and viewing the information they contain. This process can be achieved more easily if the perpetrators have accomplices working within the organisation.

Sabotage

For a variety of reasons an individual or individuals may wish to damage the effective functioning of an organisation. If they are able to gain access to that organisation's information systems, they can do a great deal of damage, both directly to the systems and indirectly by amending the way the systems operate. The motivation for such sabotage may be:

- personal – a grudge against an ex-employer;
- political – an attack on an organisation whose actions are disapproved of;
- economic – damaging the performance and reputation of a competitor.

Chat room dangers

Chat rooms are used by youngsters to type messages to friends who use the same system. Regrettably such systems are infiltrated by perverts and paedophiles who pretend to be of a similar age, sympathise with the issues being discussed, and attempt to arrange meetings with unsuspecting youngsters with the intention of abusing them. Good chat rooms publish safety advice which includes not giving out personal details, never meeting anyone without taking a friend with you and telling parents where you are going, and reporting someone who asks inappropriate questions. The police have used chat rooms to trap paedophiles and make arrests. The digital record of conversations and information found on the suspect's computer often makes the task of acquiring evidence much easier and a conviction more certain. The process of trying to trick youngsters into a meeting is known as 'grooming' and offenders will take their time over many months in an attempt to gain trust and confidence.

Protecting systems

Firewalls

ICT systems need to be in communication with the outside world. This often involves connection to publicly accessible communication systems. This creates an 'electronic gateway' that is difficult to police effectively. Firewalls have been developed to make this vulnerable area more secure. A firewall is a combination of hardware and software resources, designed to check the legitimacy of incoming messages and requests for service. Messages/requests whose source is questionable can be safely re-routed until the legitimacy of the communication can be verified.

Access procedures

Access to networks should be protected by password systems. These vary in the degree of security they offer. Simple, user-defined passwords are not very secure: people tend to use predictable formulae for setting passwords, e.g. their birthdays. Some organisations use specially designed passwords that change daily according to a designated pattern. Security can be further enhanced by setting different access levels – e.g. a junior employee may have read-only access to a piece of data, whereas someone more senior may have read/write access to the same data. Employees should be able to access only those areas of the system that they have been cleared to work on.

Encryption

Encryption may be used to make stored data more secure. Encryption involves taking a piece of data (cleartext) and translating it into a coded version of itself (ciphertext). Nobody can make sense of the data in its encrypted form: it will just appear as a collection of nonsense characters. In order to be able to make sense of it, the user must decrypt the ciphertext. This involves using a copy of the encryption key, i.e. a piece of software that translates cleartext into cipher text and back again. If an unauthorised individual managed to gain access to the data, it would be useless without access to the key.

Physical security

It is necessary to protect the hardware from theft and unauthorised access. A number of measures can be employed:
- Security guards: responsible for permitting access to the building, logging visits, patrolling the site, challenging intruders, etc.
- Secure areas: some equipment (e.g. main servers) may be held in a secure area with limited access. Such an area may be locked, alarmed and monitored by security cameras.
- Biometric access devices: newer security systems are based on biometric readings of individual's fingerprints, voice, iris pattern, etc.

Clerical procedures

The integrity of an organisation's data can be compromised by errors made at the point of data entry. In order to optimise data accuracy, there should be set procedures for data entry and a means to check the validity and – as far as possible – the accuracy of the data. This might involve batch-processing procedures, validation checks (e.g. range checks, presence checks, hash totals, etc.) and verification procedures, including double entry of data and confirmation of the accuracy of stored data with the original data source (e.g. confirming with a client that their address has been correctly entered). Security should be factored into the design of all procedures followed by users.

Training and education

The most effective way of preventing employees unintentionally compromising the security of systems and data is to ensure they are well trained. All employees whose work involves access to ICT systems should be aware of security issues. They should understand the importance of being security conscious and know how to avoid the types of errors that lead to problems. For example, it is not possible to prevent a virus being sent to an organisation via an email but, if staff are aware of the dangers of opening emails from unknown sources, the virus can be deactivated before it causes any damage. Security awareness can be reinforced through the use of posters, screen messages, etc.

Backing-up

Security measures, however effectively employed, are never sufficient to prevent loss or corruption of data. It is impossible, for example, to account for the damage done by an unforeseen terrorist attack. The most effective security measure is, therefore, the existence of a well-organised, carefully executed back-up procedure. This allows for recovery from even a disastrous loss of data or system failure.

Tape drive

T H R E A T S

Viruses

What is a virus?

A virus is a computer program that has been specifically designed to infiltrate a 'host' computer, to hide itself in that computer, and then, following a designated trigger event, perform actions that are, at best, an annoyance (e.g. an abusive screen message) and, at worst, catastrophically destructive (e.g. erasing all data on the hard drive). A virus is so called because, like its biological counterpart, it has the ability to replicate itself and spread to other 'hosts', infecting them as it does so. The first significant virus, known as 'Brain' appeared in 1986. It had the capacity to infect IBM PCs and was initially spread by students at the University of Delaware using floppy disks. Since then the number of viruses has grown exponentially and there are now many thousands of known examples. The media has tended to amplify the threat of viruses through its publicising of the effects of the most exotic examples ('Michaelangelo', 'Melissa', 'The Love Bug', etc.) The extent of the threat can, however, be overestimated. A combination of regularly updated anti-virus software and sensible computer usage will account for the threat posed by the overwhelming majority of viruses.

Types of virus

File viruses

A file virus attaches itself to an executable file (i.e. files with a .exe or .com file extension). It locates itself at the file's header. When the file is run, the virus replicates itself and spreads to other files. The virus can then begin its destructive work. The ExploreZip virus is a file virus that looks for Microsoft files and assigns a zero byte count to the file, thus ensuring its contents are wiped and unrecoverable.

Macro viruses

Increasingly the commonest form of virus, a macro virus, utilises the macro facility offered by Microsoft Office products. A macro is a simple program, which a user can write, to perform a specified set of actions. Generally speaking, any action that can be performed by the computer can be written in a macro. The virus is hidden in a simple file. Each time the file is opened it runs its hidden program. The macro might be programmed to wipe the contents of some or all of the user's files.

Avoiding viruses

Simple measures can be taken to ensure that computers are not infected by viruses. These include:

- install and continually update anti-virus software;
- virus-check all external storage media before using them;
- scan and check any software downloaded from the Internet;
- do not open email attachments unless their origin is known;
- avoid any software (especially games) that might have been illegally copied (i.e. pirated versions);
- do not boot up from a floppy disc.

Computers and law enforcement

Just as criminals have taken advantage of the new opportunities offered by developments in ICT, so too have law enforcement agencies sought to improve their performance through the application of new technologies. There are numerous examples of where technological developments have aided law enforcement. These include:

- The use of centralised databases to store details of crimes and criminals. These databases can then be queried to aid investigation into ongoing cases.
- Improved communication between law enforcement agencies at both a national and international level. Information about crimes committed in one country can be accessed in other countries. This has become more and more necessary as criminals take advantage of the same technology to 'globalise' their operations.
- Use of computing systems for analysing DNA, fingerprints, voice samples, etc. The speed of processing has led to the increased use of forensic evidence as a means of detection and to assist in the securing of convictions.
- Use of specific computer-based technologies – surveillance cameras, speed cameras, alarm systems – to help prevent crime and catch those who break the law.

Legislation: 1

How does legislation impact on the organisation?

All organisations have to operate within a legal framework. There is a wide range of laws – local, national and international – that apply to organisations and failure to comply with them can make a company liable to legal action. Because an organisation is responsible for the actions of its employees while they are at work, it must ensure that those employees are fully aware of their rights and responsibilities under the law. In order to achieve this, organisations develop policies that establish a rule-based framework to ensure that employees do not contravene existing legislation. From an ICT perspective, there are some key pieces of legislation that affect organisations based in the UK. Their implications for organisational policy are discussed below.

IMPLICATIONS FOR ORGANISATION	ENFORCING AND CONTROLLING THE LEGISLATION
The Data Protection Act The main aim of this legislation is to protect the rights of individuals who have data held on them by organisations. Under its terms the organisation is held responsible for the security, accuracy and conditions of use of the data it holds. Organisations that do not comply with the terms of the DPA can be prosecuted. It is therefore critical that all data-using organisations have procedures in place to ensure that data is held securely, that its accuracy is maintained and that it is used by the organisation correctly.	**Policies should be in place to ensure that:** • Data held by the organisation is accurate and up-to-date, e.g. through the use of validation and verification procedures. Ensuring that data is up-to-date may involve regular contact with data subjects, asking them to verify currently held details. • Data use is consistent with the requirement that data must only be used for the originally designated purpose. • There are measures in place to protect the integrity and physical security of the data held. This will involve the employment of various security measures, including: physical access, system access, firewalls, back-ups, etc. • All staff are aware of data protection issues and of their personal responsibility for ensuring the terms of the act are complied with. • Data subjects are aware of their rights under the terms of the Act.
Computer Misuse Act This was designed to prevent computer crimes involving unlawful access to information systems/data. It is unlikely that a legitimate organisation would deliberately breach the terms of this Act, but individual employees may use company resources to hack into other systems. If it were shown that the organisation was negligent in taking steps to prevent this, it could be held partly liable for the actions of its employees.	**Policies should be in place to ensure that:** • Employees are aware of the terms of the Act and the consequence of being in breach of it, i.e. organisational disciplinary procedures. • Computer use by employees is audited and suspect access activity is fully investigated, i.e. by looking at what systems have been accessed by different employees at specified times. • Access to different areas of the system is tightly controlled – i.e. employees should have no more system access than is necessary for the completion of their work. • Controls are in place to prevent employees using the organisation's ICT resources for illegitimate activity, e.g. using communication links to 'hack' into other systems.
Health and Safety at Work Act Health and safety legislation is designed to protect employees in the work place. There are some specific concerns relating to the use of ICT, and organisations must have measures in place to ensure the welfare of their employees who work in this area. If an organisation is negligent in this area and an employee suffers injury as a consequence, the organisation can be deemed liable and may have to make compensation payments.	**Policies should be in place to ensure that:** • There is a Health and Safety Officer (or team, depending on the size of the organisation) with responsibility for monitoring the organisation's compliance with the terms of the Act. • Regular inspections of equipment and procedures are undertaken and potential problems are followed up. • All employees are trained in the correct use of ICT resources and are made aware of the health risks associated with them. • The procedures followed by employees are in keeping with health and safety requirements. • The design of work spaces and the purchase of resources should take into account health and safety factors.
Copyright Designs and Patents Act This legislation is designed to protect the ownership rights of the originators of intellectual property such as design, music and software. The greatest concern in the area of ICT is software piracy, i.e. the illegal copying of software. This may occur on an organisation-wide level (e.g. a small business trying to save money) or an individual level (an employee 'borrowing' software disks and copying them at home). Organisations have to ensure that they do not permit their resources to be used for this purpose. Failure to do so can result in legal action.	**Policies should be in place to ensure that:** • All employees are aware of the terms of the Act and the consequences of being in breach of it. • The organisation audits the software that it owns and monitors who has access to that software. • Licensing agreements are fully adhered to – i.e. if the company has a software licence for 100 users that's how many there should be. • Application files are kept secure and employees are not allowed access to them for personal use. • Employees are only allowed to have authorised programs on their PCs. Unauthorised software, perhaps brought from home or downloaded from the Internet, is not permitted. • There is a centralised mechanism for purchasing software. There should be a senior manager with technology expertise who authorises all software acquisition.

Legislation: 2

Ensuring that an organisation complies with legislation

For an organisation to comply with existing and new legislation, it must have a systematic approach to staying informed about legislative changes, interpreting their impact on the organisation, developing policies to ensure compliance, and monitoring the effectiveness of these policies. Legislation is too important to be managed in an *ad hoc* manner; set procedures must be employed.

Staying informed There are various law-making bodies that can pass legislation that will impact on an organisation. They include: local authorities, national government, and transnational bodies (e.g. the EU). Large multinational organisations have to be particularly attentive to changes in legislation as they may be affected by the laws of several countries. Organisations may choose to have an individual or a team of people dedicated to monitoring legislative changes. Additionally, many government bodies send regular updates to organisations informing them of changes that may affect them.

Developing policy Policies are documented guidelines that outline how things should be done in an organisation. When a piece of legislation is enacted, an individual or group will have to be responsible for interpreting the law as it relates to the organisation. A policy can then be developed that puts into everyday language the rules and procedures that will have to be followed in order to comply with the legislation. This policy is the first line of defence against the organisation being in breach of the law and suffering negative consequences.

Disseminating information In order to be effective, the policy must become embedded in the everyday practice of the organisation. The first step in this process is to ensure that all employees are aware of the policy. The usual channels of communication may be used for this (bulletins, memos, internal emails, meetings, etc). However, because of the legal repercussions of people not receiving the information, the communication must be formal, i.e. it should be documented (electronically or in hard copy format) with its source, destination and date of transmission noted.

Monitoring An individual or a team must take responsibility for ensuring that the legislation is being complied with on a day-to-day basis. It is rarely possible to do this constantly and so periodic check-ups need to be undertaken. For example, in order to comply with Health and Safety legislation, a Health and Safety Officer may be appointed who would then undertake regular checks of the working environment, examining whether or not all the requirements of the legislation are being met. Where the legislation is specifically concerned with ICT systems (e.g. Computer Misuse Act) audit trails may be used.

Enforcing In order for a policy to have any influence, there must be negative consequences for those employees who contravene it. Disciplinary actions can range from verbal and written warnings to dismissal. In some instances it would even be necessary to involve the police. These disciplinary measures must be seen to be fair and consistent – i.e. punishments are not just meted out in an ad hoc way, there being set punishments for specified breaches of policy. The channels of communication within the organisation must be used to ensure all employees are fully aware of the consequences of policy contravention.

Copyright legislation

The Copyright Designs and Patents Act of 1988 is designed to protect the property rights of those individuals and organisations that create and produce material based on original ideas. Material of this kind, sometimes referred to as 'intellectual property', includes books, articles, music, films, software, etc. In relation to ICT, there are three main areas where legislation may be needed:

- software piracy: the illegal copying or downloading of software;
- the 'theft' by one company of the ideas and methods of other ICT companies;
- the use of ICT to copy or download material such as music/video/text-based files, thus avoiding the price of purchase.

Software piracy is widespread. The US computer industry believes that the extent of illegal copying is impossible to quantify but must be measured in billions of dollars. One estimate that was made – in 1994 by the Software Publishers Association – placed the figure at $8.8 billion world-wide. Piracy takes two main forms:

- individual users borrowing CDs or using the Internet to copy a piece of software to their own computers;
- professional criminals making copies in bulk and selling them through illegal outlets.

The software industry believes that there are two negative effects of this piracy: first, it results in higher prices for those customers who are buying software legally; and, secondly, it discourages software houses from being innovative.

Licensing

Most organisations run their computers on networks. When they buy a piece of software, they also purchase a licence for a certain number of users. They are then legally permitted to distribute the software for a fixed number of users at any one time. If the organisation wants more users to access the program, then they have to pay for more licences. Some organisations, however, do not do this. They distribute the software over the network with no regard for how many licences they have or, indeed, whether they have a licence at all.

What can be done?

Technical solutions	Software companies have experimented with techniques to prevent illegal copying. The main approach is based on giving each instance of the software an electronic signature. It can then be determined whether the version on any one machine originated from a legal version or an illegal copy of the software.
Enforcement	Organisations and individuals can be and are taken to court for copyright violations. This might involve the arrest of individuals trading illegally copied CDs from market stalls or car boot sales, or spot checks on organisations where copying or breaches of licensing agreements are suspected.
Education	'Don't copy that floppy' was an advertising slogan run as part of a campaign by the Software Publishers Association. The aim of this campaign was to alert people to the indirect costs that resulted from software piracy. This organisation and others like it have also encouraged organisations to develop codes of practice that will discourage employees from using organisational resources to copy software.
Abandon copyright	A more radical solution has been suggested by some individuals and organisations. They believe that software should be seen as a 'public good' and that its distribution should be largely free. Given the commercial forces involved in this issue, and the money at stake, it is unlikely that this argument will become anything other than a minority view.

Difficulties in preventing illegal copying

There are three main difficulties in preventing the practice of software piracy:

- Many people do not view small-scale copying as a crime at all, or at least not a serious one. They weigh up their resources against the wealth of the software companies and consider it justified to copy a borrowed edition.
- Privacy laws prevent investigation into the contents of server files or hard drives unless there is reasonable suspicion that a crime has been committed.
- A significant amount of copying takes places in countries that are less regulated in this regard and jurisdiction then becomes a problem.

The Computer Misuse Act (1990)

How the Computer Misuse Act came about

As general computer use grew during the 1970s and 1980s, so did the incidence of people using computers for criminal purposes, e.g. accessing and amending data in bank accounts. Additionally, a new crime emerged: 'hacking'. Hacking may be defined as intentionally gaining access to an ICT system without the owner's consent. Hacking might have a 'mischievous' intent, e.g. the hacker proving that they can beat a security system, or a more malicious one, e.g. to damage a system or compromise data integrity.

In the late 1980s individuals were taken to court for such activities and tried using existing legislation relating to theft, criminal damage or the interception of telecommunications. These cases were rarely successful and, in the case of Crown v. Gold, the House of Lords ruled that, in effect, hacking was not a crime. This prompted a Private Member's Bill that became law as the Computer Misuse Act in 1990.

Offences under the Computer Misuse Act

1 Gaining unauthorised access to data or programs on a computer

Individuals can be prosecuted under this section of the Act if:

- *they have caused a computer to perform a function with the intent of allowing the user access to data and/or programs;*
- *they do not have authorisation to access the said program and/or data;*
- *they know and understand that they do not have authorisation.*

This offence would be handled by magistrates and could result in a £2000 fine or up to six months in jail.

2 Gaining unauthorised access with intent to commit a further serious offence (even if that offence is not committed)

Individuals can be prosecuted under this section of the Act if:

- *they have gained unauthorised access to a computer system in order to use that system to commit a serious crime. Serious, in this case, is defined as an offence for which the maximum sentence is not less than five years (e.g. theft, blackmail, obtaining property or services by deception).*

This offence is punishable by up to five years' imprisonment.

3 Intentional unauthorised modification to impair operation

Individuals can be prosecuted under this section of the Act if:

- *they have modified the content of any computer without authorisation with the intention of impairing the operations of programs or the reliability of data. This would include the deliberate introduction of a virus.*

This offence is punishable by up to five years' imprisonment and a fine.

Difficulties with the Computer Misuse Act

The intention behind the Computer Misuse Act was to prevent both the use of ICT systems to commit crimes and deliberate attacks on those systems. The act is not, however, without its critics and some legal experts believe that it is too full of loopholes to function as an effective deterrent. These are some of the difficulties:

- Organisations are often unwilling to acknowledge publicly that they have a problem with their security. To do so, they believe, will result in a decline in public confidence. The consequence of this is that organisations sometimes choose to manage their security problems internally and without reference to law enforcement agencies.

- The global nature of ICT communication means that offences on the ICT systems of one country are often committed by a citizen of another country. This is particularly the case where viruses are concerned. This leads to problems with jurisdiction: which country's laws should be invoked against the perpetrator?

- The complex nature of ICT systems can mean that it is difficult to prove intent. A defendant could argue that unauthorised access was gained accidentally and that there was no intent to cause damage or commit an offence.

The Data Protection Act (1984, 1998)

The Data Protection Act (DPA) first became law in 1984. The Act was the consequence of increasing concern about the number of computer-based systems that stored data. People were concerned about how secure this data was, how accurately it was recorded, and the purposes to which it was being put. The DPA aimed to allay some of these concerns. In 1995 the European Union published its Data Protection Directive. The aim of this was to bring into line the data protection legislation of member states. This required the UK to update its DPA. The consequence of this was the amended DPA of 1998.

The eight principles

The Act sets out legal guidelines for the way that personal data should be obtained, processed, stored and maintained. These guidelines are set out as eight key principles:

1. Personal data shall be processed fairly and lawfully. This principle also sets out the criteria that should be met for processing to be lawful, e.g. the data subject has given their consent.
2. Personal data shall be obtained for only one or more specified purposes and shall not be processed any further for purposes incompatible with the original purpose.
3. Personal data shall be adequate, relevant and not excessive in relation to the purpose for which it is being processed.
4. Personal data shall be accurate and up to date.
5. Personal data shall not be kept for longer than is necessary to fulfil the original purpose.
6. Personal data shall be processed in accordance with the rights of the data subject.
7. Personal data shall be held securely and appropriate technical and organisational measures shall be taken to prevent unauthorised access and/or processing.
8. Personal data shall not be transferred outside the EU without appropriate safeguards being put in place.

Exemptions from the Act

All data users (i.e. any organisation or individual that holds personal data on individuals) have to register with and pay a fee to the office of the Data Protection Registrar unless they are covered by one or more of a number of exemptions, including data that is:

- for personal, family or recreational purposes;
- for the processing of information relating to wages, pensions, accounts, etc.;
- being held in the interests of national security or for the prevention of a crime;
- being used for statistical or research purposes;
- being used for the processing of mail-merged documents.

The registration process involves data users registering their name and address, a description of the data that they hold, the purposes to which it is being put, how and where the data is being held, etc.

The role of the Data Protection Registrar

The office of the Data Protection Registrar is responsible for:

- maintaining a register of data users and making that register publicly available;
- ensuring that the terms of the Act are widely known and that detailed information is freely available to the public;
- promoting compliance with the terms of the Act and prosecuting individuals/organisations who breach it;
- encouraging organisations to develop codes of practice that will help them comply with the terms of the Act.

The rights of the data subject

The data subject is the individual on whom a data user holds information. Under the terms of the Act the data subject:

- has the right to access data that is held on them (they may choose to pay a fee to the data user in order to have it made available to them more quickly);
- has the right to be compensated if the data held on them is inaccurate and they can show that the inaccuracy has caused them damage;
- has the right to be compensated if data held on them has been accessed by unauthorised users;
- has the right to insist on the modification of data held on them that is inaccurate.

Health and safety

Complying with health and safety legislation

Health and Safety regulations provide legal guidelines for what constitutes a safe working environment while using desk screen equipment. All organisations are legally required to comply with the requirements of such legislation. Failure to do so can lead to prosecution and/or legal action by employees who suffer from injuries or illnesses as a result of factors within their working environment. Most large organisations have a Health and Safety Officer who is responsible for monitoring working conditions and ensuring that anything that might be injurious to the well-being of employees is corrected. Organisations can also keep within the law by designing **ergonomic** work places. Ergonomics refers to the study of the relationship between people and their working environment. When an environment is described as being ergonomically effective, it means that it has been designed with the needs of people in mind.

The ergonomic office

General environmental factors There are various environmental factors which, if left unchecked, can lead to problems. Air quality should be monitored and adequate ventilation provided. The temperature should be comfortable to work in: the recommended temperature is 20–23.5 °C in the winter and 23–26 °C in the summer. Noise levels should be monitored: an excess of loud, distracting noise can lead to stress.

Light Poor-quality lighting in an office environment can lead to eyestrain. Ideally there should be a good balance of natural and artificial light. The light should be strong enough for people to read documents but not too strong for working with a computer screen. There should not be direct sunlight on the screen.

Hardware and software Employee stress is a consequence of working with hardware and software that does not perform as it should. The hardware should be of a sufficient specification to do the job required of it, and minor technical problems should not be allowed to develop into major ones. Software should be designed to be user-friendly: the user should feel comfortable with the application and should not find themselves constantly encountering error messages and 'crashes'.

Monitors VDUs should be positioned at a suitable height (eyesight naturally falls 20% below the horizon). They should be adjusted so that the user's neck is straight when they look at the screen. The monitor settings (e.g. brightness) should be at a level that is comfortable for the eyes. Anti-glare screen filters may be necessary.

Timed breaks In order to avoid both stress and some forms of repetitive strain injury (RSI), it is necessary to take regular breaks. It is generally recommended that employees working at a computer screen should take 5–10 minute breaks every hour. They should ideally do something that involves standing up and moving around. This will give tired muscles a 'break'.

Eye tests Employees who regularly use desk screen equipment can request that their employer pay for eye tests and, if needed, further eye tests at the request of the optometrist or doctor. Should the employee require special glasses (for example, prescribed for the distance at which the screen is viewed) to assist with their work, the employer must oblige and fund the purchase.

Keyboard and mouse The keyboard and mouse should ideally be slightly below elbow level and close to the body. The keyboard should be angled so that the user's wrists remain naturally straight. There are some ergonomically designed keyboards and mouse devices that have been designed to avoid problems associated with RSI. When the mouse is used for any length of time, the lower arms should be supported.

Chair and posture If an employee is seated for much of their working day, it is essential that their posture is good. Incorrect posture can lead to severe back problems. Chairs should be easily adjustable by the user whilst they are sitting in the chair. The backrest should be curved to fit the shape of the back and there should be padding for the lower back area. The user should be able to fit their legs comfortably under the desk. Angled footrests can also be used to improve the seating position.

Computer networks

What is a network?

A computer network describes any situation in which two or more computers are linked together via some form of communications medium for the purpose of exchanging data or sharing resources. Almost all organisational computing now takes place in a networked environment. Non-networked use of computers – i.e. a stand-alone environment – is still the norm in domestic situations, although one could argue that the Internet connection used by most domestic users transforms them into network users. Very small businesses and businesses where independent working is the norm, e.g. some design studios, may operate on a stand-alone basis.

Two categories of network

One way of categorising networks is by considering their scale. Using this approach two major categories have emerged:

Local Area Networks (LANs)   An LAN is a network that is confined to a small geographical area, usually one building or closely connected group of buildings, e.g. a university campus. The predominant mode of communication is physical cabling, usually a combination of fibre optic and copper cabling, although there is growing use of wireless devices in LAN environments. Another defining feature of a LAN is that all of the network resources are owned and managed by the organisation that uses them.

Wide Area Networks (WANs)   A WAN is a network that spreads across a large geographical area, connecting LANs via a wide range of communications media. In addition to physical cabling, wireless and satellite technologies may be used to complete a network that may be literally world-wide. Working in a WAN environment will involve using network resources owned and managed by a wide range of organisations. WANs can be further sub-divided into public WANs (the Internet is, in effect, a public WAN) and private WANs, i.e. a secure network owned and managed by one organisation. The aim of those who control WANs is to increase the range so that they can be accessed in places such as the Channel Tunnel without the need for cross-channel commuters to hardwire their laptops.

Advantages and disadvantages of networked environments

Advantages	Disadvantages
• Data can be pooled and therefore accessed by a wide range of users. This is especially valuable when access to a shared database is necessary. Instead of each user having a copy of the database on their machine, they can use client–server software to read-from and write-to the centrally stored database. This helps to ensure data integrity. • Hardware resources such as printers and scanners can be shared. This is a more cost-effective solution than providing each user with their own set of peripheral devices. • Software resources can be shared. Instead of buying a copy of the software for each user, one version can be bought and accessed by each user in the network. It will be necessary to purchase licences to ensure that the shared use of the software is legitimate. • Security is centralised and so improved. The network manager can control access by setting access rights and user permissions and by auditing computer use. Centrally located virus-checking software can be used to check all files on the network. It is easier to control access to Internet sites and to determine users' abilities to download files. • Back-up procedures are easier to complete if centrally located and managed. Instead of each user being responsible for backing up their data, the network manager will take responsibility for running regular back-ups and recoveries.	• Setting up a network is more costly than running a group of stand-alone computers. In addition to the workstations, a central server – usually a more powerful computer – is required, as is communication media (e.g. cabling) and devices such as hubs, connectors, repeaters, bridges, etc. • Networks are particularly vulnerable to viruses. If one machine is 'infected', it is easier for this infection to spread than would be the case in a stand-alone environment. • Network management requires a degree of specialist knowledge and this will mean employing a network manager for this purpose. • Networks are vulnerable to crashes. If a stand-alone computer 'goes down', only that machine is affected, whereas when a network crashes the whole system can be put out of commission. • Networks require more maintenance. Put simply, there are more things that can go wrong with a network: cables can break, network files can become corrupted, the system can become 'jammed' due to excess data traffic. This often means employing people to complete this maintenance. • The users of the network may be ignorant of the damage they can cause by bringing in media from home or recklessly downloading files from websites that may harbour viruses or other malicious software which could make the network vulnerable to outside attack.

Hardware elements of a network: 1

Physical cabling

	Twisted pair copper cabling As the name suggests this cabling consists of a pair of braided copper cables. They are braided to help protect them from electromagnetic interference. They can be either shielded or unshielded; the shielded version has an extra layer of insulation to prevent interference. Unshielded twisted pair cabling is the cheapest cabling option and is relatively easy to install. It has a lower capacity than fibre optic or coaxial cabling and has a maximum distance of 100 metres between network points.
	Fibre optic cabling A fibre optic cable consists of three elements: a core (a glass or plastic fibre); cladding (glass or plastic coating with a different composition to that of the core); the jacket (the outer protective layers, usually made of a plastic material, designed to protect the core and the cladding). Fibre optic cabling is expensive to buy and complicated to install. It is, however, the fastest physical medium and can send data across vast distances without the need for intermittent connections.
	Coaxial cabling Coaxial cabling has a single copper wire at its core. This is surrounded by a plastic insulation casing and a further layer of braided copper insulation. Finally, there is a plastic jacket to offer further protection. Coaxial cable is priced between twisted pair and fibre optic cabling. It offers faster data communication than twisted pair but is slower than fibre optic. It can be difficult to install in a building as the cable is rather rigid and inflexible. It is suitable for medium distances, typically 500 m.

Connection devices

	Hub A hub is a device for connecting a number of terminals to a network connection in a 'star' configuration. For example, one network line comes into an eight-point hub. Each of the eight sockets in the hub can then be used to connect a terminal (or a peripheral device such as a printer) to the network. Hubs can be used in connection with each other: an output from one hub can lead to another hub which, in turn, can connect a further set of terminals.
	Bridge A bridge is a device that connects two different LANs. The incoming data from one LAN is stored in a buffer memory and then, when the second LAN is ready to receive it, the data is communicated. For a bridge to work effectively, the two LANs must run on the same platform but the buffer memory means that they can be running at different speeds.
	Gateway A gateway is a device that enables LANs to communicate with WANs. LANs may be operating on different, incompatible platforms. Gateways use conversion software to ensure that data transmission protocols are compatible and that dissimilar LANs can connect to WANs. Gateway devices have been critical in ensuring the success of the Internet.
	Router A router is a device which helps to determine the optimum route for a packet of data across a network. It has been especially valuable in the development of the Internet, preventing 'traffic jams' of data communication. Routers can be dynamic or non-dynamic. A non-dynamic router sets an optimum route through a section of network and sends the data packet in that direction. A dynamic router monitors data traffic and can redefine the optimum route in response to that traffic.
	Connector The RJ-45 connector is used with twisted pair cabling and connects to the back of the network card through the back of the computer. It will be familiar as a standard telephone connection. The BNC T-connector is a metal connector that is used with coaxial cable. One end plugs into the external end of a network card and the other two sockets provide a connection for other elements of the network.
	Modem Modem is short for modulator/demodulator. A modem is designed to translate analogue signals to digital signals. Although there is a general trend towards all data communication being digital, there are still many occasions when data needs to be converted from analogue to digital format. Some Internet connections, for example, use a standard telephone line (i.e. analogue) connection. In order for a computer to process the incoming data traffic, the signal must be converted from analogue to digital.

Hardware elements of a network: 2

Network interface card

The network interface card (NIC) is a printed circuit board that plugs into one of the expansion slots of the computer's motherboard. It converts the data that is stored in the computer into a form that is suitable for transmission along the network. The type of NIC that is needed will vary according to what type of network is in operation. The most common type is the Ethernet card.

Uninterruptible power supply

An uninterruptible power supply (UPS) is not an essential part of a network but is certainly a highly desirable one. If a power failure occurs when the main server is in the middle of a critical job, it may lead to a disastrous loss of data. A UPS helps to protect against this. A UPS consists of four essential components: a device that monitors the incoming electrical supply, checking for fluctuations in voltage; a back-up source of power, usually a battery of some kind; a means of switching from mains supply to battery supply if there is a power failure; a means of communicating to the server – and thus the network administrator – that there is a problem.

Firewalls

Any network that connects to the outside world, e.g. via the Internet, needs to protect itself against unwarranted intrusion. 'Firewall' is a generic term that describes a combination of hardware devices and software programs that act as a network filter, monitoring all incoming messages and determining whether the originator of the message should have access to the network they are protecting. They are, in effect, computerised security guards, authenticating and validating the credentials of visitors. Where security is critical, firewalls are often established in their own small network. This mini-network – sometimes referred to as a sandbox or DMZ (demilitarised zone) – lies between the internal network and external connections.

Servers

Strictly speaking, a server is any computer that runs server software. In practice, because computers acting as servers have to perform tasks that client computers don't, they are designed specifically to fulfil a server role. Servers, then, are powerful computers that are designed to fulfil a specific purpose, i.e. to share their resources in a networked environment. The key features of a server are set out below:

Powerful processing capabilities

CPUs found in servers run faster than those in PCs. This is because they have more data to process, specifically more data to locate on the hard drive and transfer to the network connection. In many servers more than one CPU is provided, thus enhancing processing capabilities.

Built-in network cards and hubs

Unlike most PCs, servers have their own built-in network cards, allowing them to connect to other network components. Many also have a built-in hub. This is a switching device that helps to manage the flow of data traffic around the network.

Redundant hard drives

Hard-drive redundancy refers to the practice of automatically backing up data on to more than one hard drive. This type of set up (referred to as RAID: Redundant Arrays of Inexpensive Discs) operates in different ways. One method (referred to as RAID 1) entails disc mirroring or duplexing. All data is written identically to two different drives. If one drive fails – or the connection to the drive is lost – the other drive kicks in, allowing continuous data access.

Fault tolerance

If an individual network workstation crashes, it is a problem for the user but is unlikely to lead to massive loss of data or significant computer 'downtime'. This is not the case with the server. Therefore, servers have more built-in 'fault tolerant systems' to protect them against crashes. These may include 'redundant' data storage, back-up power supply and even back-up motherboards.

Software elements of a network

Network operating systems

A network operating system (OS) provides many of the same functions for a network as an operating system does for a stand-alone PC. It manages resources, allocates memory, communicates with input and output devices, schedules tasks and provides a user interface. The key differences are in terms of scale (there is far more of this work to do on a network) and priority (a desktop OS is designed to optimise the performance of whatever application a user is using; a network OS is designed to balance the needs of all those users who are logged on to the network at any one time).

As with desktop OSs, there are different proprietary brands to choose from. Some of the best known are: Windows server 2008, Cisco IOS and Inferno. They all have their strengths and weaknesses, and often the decision to choose any one of them will depend on compatibility with existing systems, and the preference and experience of the network administrator.

Network management software

The network administrator will routinely need to perform network maintenance tasks and application software can make these tasks more manageable. In some cases, the software required to perform the task will have been 'bundled' with the network OS; in other cases, it will need to be acquired and installed as an add-in. Below are the some of the tasks that a network administrator would use software to perform:

SETTING UP ACCOUNTS

The network administrator has to ensure that each user has their own network account. The account will specify which applications they can access, what levels of access they have to different data, how much disc space they have to store files, etc. The network account system will also define user names, passwords and user permissions. In some cases users of a similar kind are categorised into workgroups, e.g. 'student' and 'teacher' on a school network.

ACCOUNTING LOG

Network software can automatically maintain an accounting log that records various details about the use of the network. Details recorded by such a system will include: user name, workstation used, log-on and log-off times, applications used, files opened/amended/deleted, errors and crashes, etc. This information can be used for a variety of purposes including security checks and analysis of errors/crashes.

REMOTE MANAGEMENT

Remote management is a valuable tool for supporting users working on a network. In the event of a significant problem or recurring error, it allows the network administrator to take control temporarily of a user's workstation. Once in control the problem can be identified and (hopefully) solved. The user can also be advised on what to do to avoid similar problems in the future. It is especially valuable when the network is spread across a number of remote sites.

NETWORK MANAGEMENT SOFTWARE

HARDWARE/SOFTWARE INSTALLATION

It is the task of the network administrator to ensure that all new software and hardware installed on the system is compatible with existing systems. Installation-enabling software speeds up this process, facilitating the distribution of software to local hard drives where necessary. Software-metering programs can be used to monitor software usage, checking for illicit installation and ensuring the organisation is not in breach of any licensing agreements.

CONFIGURATION MANAGEMENT

One of the challenges of network management is to maintain a balance between the need for centralisation and the needs and preferences of individual users. Configuration management programs enable the network administrator to monitor the way in which individual workstations are configured (i.e. what applications are available, the appearance of the desk-top, etc). This can help prevent users downloading potentially harmful software for personal use.

AUDITING

Auditing, i.e. the systematic examination of resource usage, may be undertaken for a number of reasons, e.g. concern about the downloading of illicit material, monitoring of network performance, unusual patterns of data access, etc. An automated accounting log may well provide the base data for such an audit, but software will also be needed to interrogate this data meaningfully and present information in a form that is useful for the person conducting the audit.

Network topologies

A topology is a way of describing the <u>physical</u> layout of a group of networked computers. It describes the various elements of the network (server, PCs printers, etc.) and the connections between them. The three main topologies are described below:

Star network

There is a central computer – called a hub – that connects all the nodes of the network. All data communications between workstations/servers/printers go through this central hub.

Advantages	Disadvantages
• Because each computer is independent of the others, if one breaks down, the others can continue to function. • Different workstations may need to send different volumes of data across the network. The Star set-up allows for different capacity communication links to be established, related to the different needs of the workstations.	• There is a good deal of dependency on the hub working effectively. If this component fails, the whole system may be put out of action. • Both the hardware and software required for the effective running of a Star network are expensive to set up.

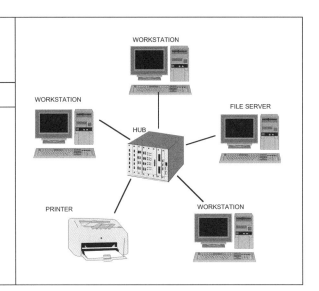

Bus network

In a bus topology, the different nodes are all connected to a single communication path. Data is transmitted in any direction along a central cable. Using this system workstations can communicate with each other, with servers and with peripheral devices.

Advantages	Disadvantages
• Compared to other topologies, a bus network is the least expensive and the easiest to set up. • If one workstation malfunctions, it does not affect the rest of the network. • It is easy to install additional devices.	• The system is dependent on the correct functioning of the main cabling. If this malfunctions, the whole network will go down. • If the cable does fail, the point of failure is difficult to isolate. • The performance of the network will be detrimentally affected by heavy data traffic.

Ring network

This topology usually consists of a collection of workstations and peripheral devices linked together in a circular configuration. There is no central host computer in a ring network, though one node may control overall access to the network.

Advantages	Disadvantages
• The system is not dependent on a central computer. • Using fibre optic links, good transmission speeds can be achieved over a wide area. • This system works effectively when processing is distributed across a number of remote sites.	• The effective running of the system is dependent on one communication link. If this malfunctions, the whole system goes down. • If one node malfunctions, it can have a negative effect on the whole system.

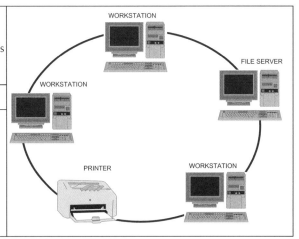

Logical topologies

The physical topologies (layouts) of networks are described on page 102. In addition, one can define a network in terms of its logical topology. Whereas the physical topology defines the physical arrangement of servers, workstations, cabling, printers, etc. the logical topology defines the way in which data is transmitted around the network. There are two predominant logical topologies: ethernet and token ring.

Ethernet

Networks transmit data using a packet-switching system. A block of data – a word-processed file, for example – is divided into standard-sized chunks (i.e. packets). These packets are then given a destination address, a sender's address, a means of checking whether the transmission has been error-free (e.g. a check sum) and instructions for the reassembly of the original file (since these packets may not arrive in the order in which they were sent).

Ethernet is an approach to packet-switching data transmission that was first developed in 1973 by Robert Metcalfe. It is based on a protocol called 'Carrier Sense Multiple Access/Collision Detection' (CSMA/CD). According to this protocol, all computers logged on to a network share a segment of the network called a 'collision domain'. Each computer monitors this 'collision domain' and determines whether there is 'free run' available to transmit data. If there is, that computer sends its packet(s) of data. If another computer sends its packet(s) at the same time, a 'collision' occurs. The computers on the network acknowledge the collision and wait a random time before sending their packets of data again. Even in a small network segment, collisions are inevitable. This is not as damaging as it sounds. The time that a computer has to wait for a free run can often be measured in nanoseconds, although it is true that the more network traffic there is, the slower the network will run. There are different varieties of ethernet, each being suitable for different physical topologies and cabling media.

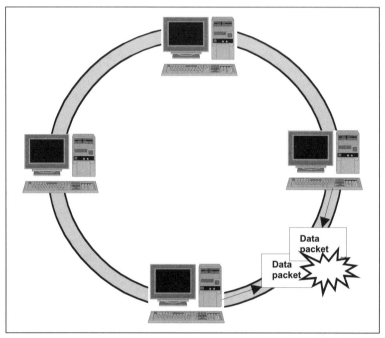

Token ring

The token ring system also operates on packet-switching principles. When the network is switched on, a special data packet – called a 'token' – circulates the network. When an individual workstation has a data packet to transmit it waits until the token is available. It then takes control of the token, and transmits its data. When it has finished transmitting, it releases the token, thus making it available to any other workstation on the network that is waiting to transmit. A token ring system is a robust system that works well with both twisted pair and fibre optic cabling. It is a lot more costly than ethernet, more difficult to set up and harder to troubleshoot. Consequently, it is not suitable for all organisational set-ups.

Creating a networked system

A network is a collection of ICT components linked together in order to facilitate the sharing of resources and/or transmission of data. Part of the work of an ICT department is the creation of new network systems or the expansion/development of existing systems. In undertaking this process, a number of key decisions will have to be made about what software, hardware, and communication technologies will be employed, and in what configuration. The main decision areas involved are described below. These decisions will be informed by several factors that must be taken into account. These are described on the following page.

Decisions that have to be made

TOPOLOGIES

There are three main topologies to choose from: ring, bus and star. Each of these has strengths and weaknesses and will be more suited to some contexts than others. Most networks are not restricted to one of these topologies but are rather a combination of different topologies. These are known as 'hybrid networks'.

SERVERS

There are several different servers that might be used in a network, including: file servers, database servers, web servers, application servers, etc. One or more of these servers may be combined in one machine held in one location or they may be distributed on different machines around the system.

DISTRIBUTION

Increasingly organisations distribute processing and/or databases around their network. Decisions will have to be made as to where the processing will take place, i.e. whether it will be centrally located or distributed to remote locations. There are also different approaches to distribution (e.g. duplication, partition, etc.).

NETWORK STRATEGY

There are three main network strategies: terminal (i.e. mainframe plus dumb terminals), peer-to-peer, and client–server. The decision will be based largely on a consideration of network size and primary usage. If a client–server strategy is chosen, a decision will have to be made about whether 'thin' or 'fat' clients are used, i.e. whether or not the workstations require a stand-alone capacity.

DECISIONS

SHARED RESOURCES

In addition to workstations and servers, a network will also allow access to resources that can be shared by network users. Printers are the most obvious example of a resource of this kind. Decisions will have to be made about which resources are required, where they will be located, which users will have access to them, how the 'queuing' system will operate, etc.

COMMUNICATION MEDIA

There are decisions that will have to be made about whether to use cable-based or wireless communication media. If cabling is chosen, there will be further decisions to be made about what type of cabling to be used where, e.g. UTP, coaxial, fibre optic, etc. This decision is constrained by both cost and the physical layout of the area being networked.

NETWORK OPERATING SYSTEM

Network operating systems (NOS) control and centrally manage the activities of computer resources on a network. This work includes the management of user access, data transmission, file sharing, network accounting, etc. There are various proprietary systems that are available, including Windows NT and Novell.

STORAGE NEEDS

Decisions will have to be made about the storage capacity of the system, considering questions such as:
- What data will need to be stored and for how long?
- How many applications will need to be stored and who will need access to them?
- What back-up/duplication facilities are required?
- What will happen to data that needs to be archived, etc?

Creating a network architecture

Factors informing the decisions

COST

Whether developing a computer network from scratch or developing an existing system, the individual(s) responsible will have a limited budget to work within, i.e. budgetary constraints will determine what can and cannot be purchased. Fibre optic cabling, for example, offers faster transmission times than other media, but costs significantly more. It is important to take into account not only the initial capital outlay but also the ongoing maintenance costs, e.g. wireless systems can offer greater flexibility but are more costly to maintain than a conventionally wired system.

SCALE

The size of a network can vary in scale from a small room, containing half a dozen PCs and a printer, to a global network, consisting of a huge number of network elements. The network may be a small, self-contained LAN, connecting the users on one site, or a combination of LANs based in different geographical locations connected in a WAN. Even where a small-scale network is being developed, the physical geography of the area being covered by the network will need to be factored into any decisions, e.g. some communications media are limited by the distance they can cover.

USAGE

A key question to ask is: How will this system be used? Are users going to require access to a wide range of applications? Are they going to store a large number of data files? Where will the majority of processing be done? The nature of the usage will determine the nature of the network in a number of different ways. For example, if users are required to complete a significant amount of processing, their workstations will need to be sufficiently equipped, whereas if the majority of processing is completed by a central mainframe, individual workstations will require fewer resources.

FACTORS

EXISTING SYSTEMS

Although there are occasions when networks are set up from scratch, it is more often the case that networks have to be built as extensions of existing systems. For example, a company may open a new office and establish a network system for that office. That network will have to connect to the rest of the company's network. The platform that this existing network uses will have certain defining features, including: the communications media it uses, its geographical location, the network operating system it employs, etc. These all constitute constraints that the new system will have to work within.

PERFORMANCE

There are various ways in which a network's performance may be measured: speed of processing, reliability, user friendliness, capacity, etc. Different organisations – and, indeed, different functional areas within an organisation – will prioritise different performance criteria. For example, a company whose core operation involves real-time processing may be primarily concerned with speed of processing, whereas an organisation with a large multi-user environment and a small maintenance team may be more concerned with robustness.

SECURITY

There are a number of security issues that need to be taken into account when setting up a network and these will vary according to the organisation concerned. For example, a business organisation may be primarily concerned with outsiders accessing and compromising their business critical systems, whereas a college may be more concerned with students downloading illicit material from the Internet. Different security emphases will lead to different decisions being made about how the system should be set up to minimise areas of vulnerability.

Approaches to organisational computing: 1

Client–server computing

PCs connected in a network allowed small- to medium-sized business to access the type of processing power they needed to support their core business activities. There were, however, problems with such an approach, mainly associated with the absence of centralised control. A system was needed that combined the centralised control of a mainframe system with the usability and distributed processing of a PC-based network. This led to the development of client–server systems.

A client–server system consists of a combination of computer devices that act as either clients or servers. A server will act as a host device, providing a centralised resource that other devices – clients – can make requests to. A typical client–server system consists of one powerful computer that acts as a server and is connected, via a network, to a number of workstations that act as clients. When a user makes a request for a service via a workstation – e.g. access to a software application, a query to a database, a printer request – the server provides the service required. In addition to providing the functionality necessary for the storage and processing of data, servers manage background functions such as file management, user permissions and access rights, back-up facilities, etc.

Although 'clients' and 'servers' are often used to refer to devices, in fact it is the 'client software' and 'server software' that handle the necessary processing. It is therefore possible to run different types of client–server software on one machine.

How a client–server system works

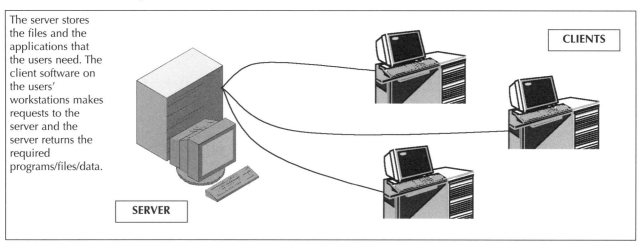

The server stores the files and the applications that the users need. The client software on the users' workstations makes requests to the server and the server returns the required programs/files/data.

CLIENTS

SERVER

Different types of client

Workstations used in client–server systems fall into two broad categories, usually referred to as fat clients and thin clients.

Thin clients   The workstation consists of a network computer that is designed to work only as part of a network, i.e. it does not have any stand-alone capacity. It does not have a built-in hard drive or expansion slots and only has such processing capacity as would be needed to run applications and output to a monitor.

Fat clients   The workstation is a PC with stand-alone capacity. It has its own secondary storage components and CPU. This means that it is less economical than a 'thin client' because there is an unnecessary duplication of storage and processing facilities – i.e. the PC has the capacity to do work that is in fact performed by the server.

Different types of server

Servers fall into different categories. These categories are related to the service they provide and include:

File server   provides clients with access to data files and software
Database server   provides access to databases and handles queries
Web server   stores and handles requests for individual web pages
Application server   handles high speed processing for applications
Email server   manages the sending, receipt and temporary storage of emails
Print server   manages requests to the printer, controlling job queues, print quotas, etc.

Different types of server software may be located in one machine.

Approaches to organisational computing: 2

Three-tiered client–server architecture

One popular set-up involving different servers comprises a network of clients, an application server and a database server. In this arrangement the user – working through client software installed on a networked PC or network computer – makes a request for data to the application server. The application server determines what data is needed and queries the database accordingly. The database server returns the required data to the application server which, in turn, processes the data into a suitably user-friendly format before returning it to the client. This is referred to as three-tiered architecture.

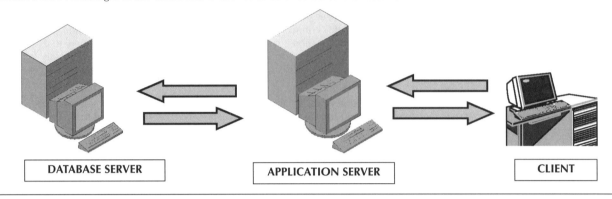

| DATABASE SERVER | APPLICATION SERVER | CLIENT |

Peer-to-peer systems

An alternative to client–server set-ups that may be employed by small organisations is a peer-to-peer system. A peer-to-peer system comprises a group of workstations that are joined together in a network. Each workstation acts as both client and server, sharing resources and communicating data to each other. One computer can both request data held on another file and provide data for another user.

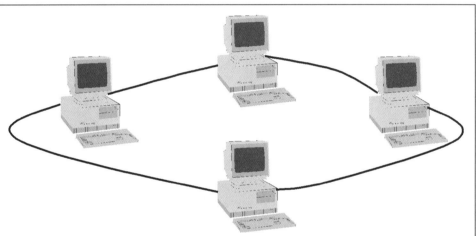

Peer-to-peer system versus client–server

Peer-to-peer system	Client–server
✓ Initial start-up costs are lower because an expensive server isn't required. The network operating system is also less sophisticated and therefore cheaper.	✓ There is efficient centralised management of security, back-up and file management systems.
✓ There is less reliance on one central computer and therefore less vulnerability to crashes.	✓ It offers users easy access to a central pool of data.
✓ It is simpler to set up and maintain than a client–server system.	✓ The system will perform processing tasks more quickly than a peer-to-peer system.
✗ The system only works well when the number of nodes (network connections) is small, i.e. below 15.	✓ Users do not have to worry about performing network management tasks as the server does this work.
✗ Security and back-up are not centralised and so are more difficult to manage.	✗ The initial start-up cost can be high: dedicated servers are more expensive than PCs and the network software required also costs more.
✗ Data can be more difficult to find because it is not centrally stored and organised.	✗ Client–server systems often require specialist personnel – network managers – to run them. This incurs cost.
✗ Users need more technical knowledge because they are required to perform jobs that would otherwise be taken care of by a server.	✗ Reliance on one central server can cause problems – i.e. if the server crashes the whole system is out of commission.

Wireless networking

The need for wireless networks

Traditional wired networks make an assumption about the way that people work: that they will only need to access network resources from static locations. There are, however, many areas of work where people need to be mobile *and* access a network. Some doctors, for example, visit their patients in a wide range of locations. Data on these patients may well be held on a networked database. It would clearly be advantageous for the doctor to access this information at the point of contact with the patient and to be able to update the same database following the examination. There are workers in other environments who would benefit from the same technology: sales staff who travel around the country, emergency and breakdown personnel, delivery drivers, etc. The advent of wireless networks offers a solution to this problem.

Wireless networking may be used as part of a LAN, e.g. a mobile bar code reader being used in a warehouse stock control system, or as part of a WAN or Virtual Private Network, e.g. a delivery driver using a hand-held device to confirm deliveries and update a central database.

What wireless networking entails

Wireless systems transmit data by using radio waves or infrared light. They consist of devices with radio transmission capabilities and radio receivers able to capture the signals from such devices. The receivers are attached (usually via cable, thus ensuring that wireless networks are not wholly wire-less) to individual computers or network servers. A simple model of wireless data transmission is shown below.

The wireless keyboard has a built-in transmission component, able to transmit a radio signal over short distances. When a key is pressed a digital signal that represents the chosen typographical character is sent for transmission. The transmitter sends out the digital signal as radio waves (typically) in a predetermined frequency band.

A radio receiver constantly scans the airwaves for incoming signals. When it detects a signal it recognises it captures it and converts it back into a digital signal.

The digital signal is transmitted via a cable from the receiver to the computer. It arrives in the same format as it would have done had it been transmitted through a cabled network. It can now be processed in the usual way.

Problems with wireless networking

Wireless networking technologies are still in early stages of development and there are at the moment a number of problems associated with their implementation.

- There is a gradual move towards standardisation of wireless devices, with two standards, Bluetooth and IEEE 802.11, currently dominant. In order for wireless networking to develop fully, manufacturers of input/output devices, computers, transmitters, and receivers need to agree on a broadly implemented, common standard. There is a trend towards this but it has not, as yet, been achieved.
- The cost of wireless networking use to be prohibitive, but as with all technology these costs have fallen and the benefits gained from allowing the workforce greater mobility in the work place have been recognised.
- Transmission speeds are slower than cabled networks and there can be problems if there is too much competing radio traffic in one building.
- There are new security issues that need to be dealt with. Viruses can be spread through wireless networks and the technology exists for radio frequencies to be monitored and the data transmitted across these networks to be captured by unauthorised individuals. There are encryption technologies available – e.g. Wired Equivalent Privacy – but these have been shown to be vulnerable to intrusion.

Standards and protocols

During the period when computers were first being developed for the mass market, manufacturers gave little thought to the need for compatibility between different systems. The new computer industry did not have a regulatory body imposing authoritative standards on it, and so each company operated according to its own rules. Before long, however, it became clear that some form of standardisation would be necessary. Organisations did not necessarily buy all of their hardware and software from one manufacturer but they did need all the different components of their systems to work together. Standards therefore began to emerge in two distinct ways: *de facto* standards and *de jure* standards.

DE FACTO STANDARDS

De facto means 'in effect' and describes the way that some standards have emerged gradually through the market domination of a particular product or set of products. The clearest example of this in the world of ICT is the domination of the PC operating systems market by Microsoft's Windows products. The Windows standard is so dominant that other companies coming into the market are obliged to adhere to it or risk rendering their products unsaleable. *De facto* standards are not laid down in law but companies have to take them into account when developing new products.

DE JURE STANDARDS

De jure means 'by law' and describes the way in which some standards are imposed by a group that has some form of authority. *De jure* standards can be defined by groups such as the International Standards Organisation (ISO), the International Electrotechnical Commission (IEC) and the American National Standards Institute (ANSI). National and transnational government organisations may also become involved in determining standards. In computing, the majority of standards are voluntary. Manufacturers tend to comply with them rather than risk producing incompatible products.

Standards – good or bad?

It may seem, at first sight, that standards in ICT are eminently desirable. Users, after all, want to be able to transfer data and connect devices without worrying all the time about compatibility. On the other hand, the existence of standards can be seen as a conservative force that limits innovation. It is a balancing act that manufacturers and consumers need to be aware of.

Standards ensure that users can connect devices to each other, transfer data easily, purchase software from different vendors, etc. They make possible the development of public Wide Area Networks like the Internet.

Standards stifle innovation. The dominance of the market by one manufacturer, and the creation of standards that perpetuate this dominance, prevents new businesses producing innovative products.

Protocols

Protocols are sets of rules that are agreed to by a group of people involved in a co-operative enterprise. In ICT terms it refers to agreements made by manufacturers to abide by a set of rules that have been defined by industry bodies such as the International Standards Organisation. Many of the key protocols in ICT relate to the way in which data is transmitted across networks. They include:

OSI   Open System Interconnection. OSI is not strictly speaking a protocol. Rather, it is a model for how data should move around a network. It effectively operates like a protocol, i.e. by providing an agreed approach to network architecture that is adopted by manufacturers.

FTP   File Transfer Protocol. FTP defines the way in which files can be downloaded from the Internet. If a user wants to download graphics, audio files, software, etc. from an Internet site, FTP facilitates this.

Internet protocols

Why does the Internet need protocols?

The Internet is a complex 'network of networks'. It consists of many systems located all over the world, all unified by a series of communication links. These systems will vary in many ways. For example, they will not all use the same operating system: some may be operating on a Windows platform, others on a Linux platform. In order for Internet traffic to move smoothly through this network, there needs to be an agreed set of rules – or protocols – for the transmission of data. All data traffic must conform to these protocols if the system is to work effectively. The most important of these protocols is TCP/IP

What is TCP/IP?

TCP stands for Transmission Control Protocol and IP stands for Internet Protocol. The two terms almost always appear together because they form two complimentary halves of a system that ensures consistency in the transmission of data across the Internet.

The Internet is a packet-switching network. This means that when a piece of data is sent across the Internet it is first divided into 'packets', i.e. blocks of data comprising no more than 128 kb of data. These packets are then sent across the network, being directed on their journey by routers which determine the optimum path to their destination. At the destination machine the packets are reassembled in the correct order. TCP/IP ensure that this process is conducted according to set rules:

TCP   creates the packets, adding a 'header' that contains information about how the data packets should be reassembled at the destination. A checksum is also added as a validation device.

IP   labels each packet with a correct destination address. This address is the one used by routers to direct the packet to its destination.

How does TCP/IP work?

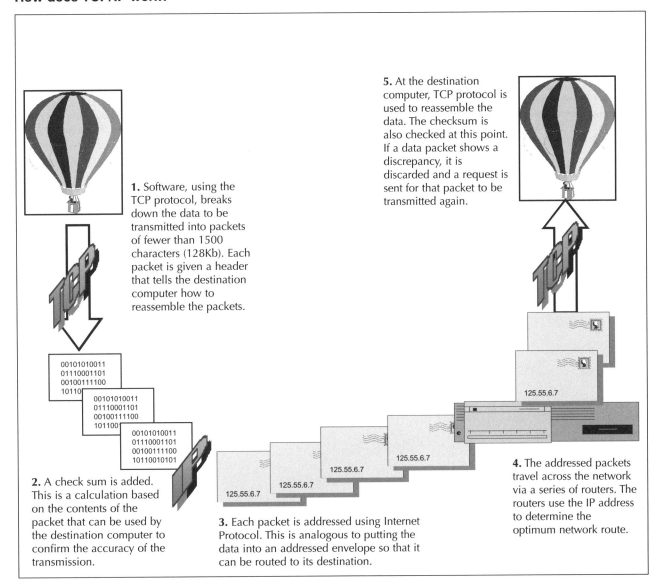

5. At the destination computer, TCP protocol is used to reassemble the data. The checksum is also checked at this point. If a data packet shows a discrepancy, it is discarded and a request is sent for that packet to be transmitted again.

1. Software, using the TCP protocol, breaks down the data to be transmitted into packets of fewer than 1500 characters (128Kb). Each packet is given a header that tells the destination computer how to reassemble the packets.

2. A check sum is added. This is a calculation based on the contents of the packet that can be used by the destination computer to confirm the accuracy of the transmission.

3. Each packet is addressed using Internet Protocol. This is analogous to putting the data into an addressed envelope so that it can be routed to its destination.

4. The addressed packets travel across the network via a series of routers. The routers use the IP address to determine the optimum network route.

The Internet: introduction

What is the Internet?

The Internet is, in effect, a very large network of computers. It might better be described as a network of networks. It works by allowing individuals to connect to a worldwide network so that they can communicate with any other computer user in the world who has the same facility. This essentially simple concept, which has developed during the past few decades, has had a revolutionary impact in many areas of human interaction.

- People are able to communicate more easily with people who live far away from them. The Internet has made such communication cheaper, more instantaneous and more flexible, allowing the user to send not just text but also still images, video images and sound.
- Virtual communities have been created whereby people sharing areas of interest can exchange opinions and information. This has had an enormously beneficial effect on those working in specialised fields whose colleagues may be based in locations on the other side of the world.
- Individuals who, because they live in remote locations or because they suffer from a disability that renders them house-bound, can feel more connected to the rest of the world and can avail themselves of services that were previously unavailable to them.
- Business organisations that have branches in different locations can improve the level of communication, collaboration and sharing of information between branches.
- At the moment the Internet is (relatively) unregulated. This has led to it being a place where individuals and organisations can express opinions and publish materials that are not usually granted expression in the mainstream media or are explicitly banned, e.g. under a repressive regime that forbids anti-government views. This has had both beneficial effects (allowing people living under dictatorships to communicate with the outside world) and more problematic effects (the availability of previously banned hard-core pornography).
- It has facilitated the creation of new businesses and has transformed the way in which established organisations conduct their business. As with any change in business methods, this has created losers as well as winners.

Hypertext

The term hypertext is usually associated with the World Wide Web and is taken to refer to the way in which clicking on a specially demarcated piece of text or image will link the user to another piece of information. On a typical web page there will be several hypertext links. These are usually in the form of words or short phrases that can be identified by the fact that they have a different colour typeface and because of the way the mouse cursor changes shape when it moves across them. Activating such a link may open a dialogue box with further information in, open a picture file or take the user to a new web page. The links are not necessarily between two pieces of text-based information: sound/graphics/video files may also be involved. Consequently, the term 'hypermedia' may also be used to describe this process.

In fact, the concept of hypertext predates the World Wide Web by over 40 years and has its own history. In 1945 Dr V. Bush outlined the idea of a mechanical store for different forms of information based on microfilm. He termed this idea Memex. The central principle was that the reader would be able to create their own pathways through the mass of information, linking ideas in an individualised way. Bush argued that such an approach is more consistent with the way our minds work than the strictly sequential approach of a book or a lecture. Our minds do not generally investigate ideas in a linear fashion. Rather, they jump around from topic to topic, going off at tangents and spending time exploring off-shoots of the central idea.

This idea was further elaborated on in the 1960s by Ted Nelson (who coined the term 'hypertext') and Douglas Englebart (the inventor of the mouse), but didn't really take off until Apple Computers devised the Graphical User Interface and the HyperCard system, that operated on the hypertext principle. Those working on the development of the World Wide Web used the concept of hypertext as an organising principle for their new creation.

Different ways of connecting to the Internet

MEDIA	HOW IT WORKS	EVALUATION
Dial-up	The user's standard telephone line is used in combination with a modem. The modem, which may be located internally or externally, converts the analogue telephone signal into a digital signal that can be processed by the computer.	This was the most commonly used approach to domestic Internet connection in both the UK and the USA, although it was not generally considered suitable for business organisations. It had the advantage of using existing telephone connections and was relatively cheap. The main disadvantages are its slow transmission speeds, its inability to manage broadband access and the fact that, unless you have a dedicated second line, you cannot make telephone calls when on the Internet.
ISDN	ISDN stands for Integrated Services Digital Network. ISDN connections use existing telephone cables but require both the telecom provider and the user to have digital switching equipment installed. These terminal adaptors facilitate the transmission of digital data across existing connections.	ISDN is an improvement on dial-up, allowing both faster transmission speeds and greater bandwidth. Many versions also allow simultaneous transmissions over the same line, making it particularly useful for video conferencing. It is more expensive than dial-up, the telecom companies charging both an installation fee and a regular (usually monthly) tariff.
DSL	DSL stands for Digital Subscriber Line. Like ISDN this system uses existing telephone lines for transmission but sends and receives all data in a digital format. It requires the telecom provider to have digital switching equipment installed and the user to have a DSL modem. This modem enables end-to-end digital transmission. DSL comes in many flavours including ADSL (Asymmetric DSL) and HDSL (Higher-speed DSL).	DSL is faster than ISDN and many times faster than dial-up. It is an 'always-on' broadband connection that can be used simultaneously with normal telephone communications. Unlike cable, each user has a dedicated line. This means that (a) the connection is more secure and (b) transmission speeds are not affected by the number of subscribers using the service. One disadvantage is that the distance between the user and the telecom office will significantly affect the quality of the connection. For this reason, DSL is not viable in some remote locations.
Cable	The coaxial connection that is used in some areas to pipe television services into the home, coaxial cable, has broadband capacity and so is capable of simultaneously delivering television signals and data. The cable provider needs to have a high-speed connection to the Internet and communication devices to service all the connected homes in one neighbourhood. The user has to have a cable modem to convert the incoming signal.	Cable is a broadband connection that can provide very high transmission rates. There are costs involved but the consumer may have already absorbed those costs as part of their TV access package. Cable does not tie up any other domestic communication services, i.e. one can surf the net, watch TV and be on the phone at the same time. The main disadvantage is that cable access has to be in place before the connection can take place. This will depend on the geographical area: some locations have well-developed cable infrastructures, others have little or no cable access. Because each neighbourhood – a neighbourhood may consist of up to 500 homes – has one dedicated node, an excess of traffic can cause the system to slow down significantly.
Wireless	Radio frequencies are used to transmit data from a local network station to a receiver on one's device.	The main growth in the use of wireless access is likely to be on mobile devices, in particular the 3G (third-generation) mobile phones and hand-held devices currently being developed. The promise is of fast, always-on Internet access, with users being able to download large files quickly and view/listen to them on their portable devices. This has proved to be the major ICT development over the past five years.

Initially when the opportunity to benefit from broadband was delivered to the market the take up was not very encouraging. However, when the potential of speedy downloading became apparent; familiar use of broadband within homes and business became the norm. The rise of more complex and heavily animated websites and broadband went hand in hand. The MP3 revolution also prompted the need for faster web access, so that songs, podcasts, and movies could be downloaded without a long, drawn-out wait. Although broadband is not available everywhere in the UK, the majority is covered. The cost to access broadband is on a similar scale to that of the original dial-up connection, and because the speed is so fast it is now possible to watch live sporting events and concerts. Broadband works well with wireless technology, and many homes now have routers which generate a fast connection to equipment in other rooms with little loss in quality of data transfer. The drive by the market and demand for broadband has enabled suppliers to offer various deals at different prices depending on the needs of the user.

Accessing a website: 1

Step 1: Requesting a website using a URL

One way of accessing a particular location on the Internet is to type the address of the site that you wish to visit into the address box of the web browser. This address is known as a Unique Resource Locator (URL) and is made up of different elements:

| http: indicates that the site is located on the World Wide Web and that it uses hypertext markup language. Some URLs have the prefix 'ftp', indicating that the site is on a File Transfer Protocol server. | www: originally this was used to distinguish between sites that were on the World Wide Web and Internet files. It is now almost redundant and can be omitted from most addresses. | org: this part of the URL is called the Top Level Domain. .org is a generic TLD and refers to the type of organisation that the site belongs to. Other generic TLDs include .net, .com and .gov. There are also ccTLDs (country code TLDs). These indicate the country of origin of the site. ccTLDs include .uk (United Kingdom).de (Germany), and .es (Spain) |

ADDRESS   http://www.suttonlea.org/welcome.html

| :// is a signal to the browser that what follows is the domain name. The rest of the domain name will be separated by full stops and, where necessary, slash marks. | suttonlea: this is the domain name, a unique combination of letters, numbers; and punctuation marks that has been registered with an Internet registration company. It usually describes the owners or nature of the site. This domain name is that of Sutton Local Education Authority. | welcome.html: this refers to a specific page, in this case the welcome page, of the site. html (hypertext markup language) indicates that the page, in common with most files on the web, has been coded using this language and so requires this file extension. |

Step 2: Accessing the Internet Protocol address

When the enter key is pressed or the 'Go' icon clicked, the address (**1**) is sent to the Internet Service Provider (ISP) (**2**) or Local Area Network (LAN) that is being used to connect to the Internet. The ISP or LAN connects to a device called a Domain Name Server (DNS) (**3**). The DNS is a collection of databases that stores all registered domain names. It contains the data to match the URL to an Internet Protocol (IP) address. Unlike the URL, the IP address is expressed wholly in numerical terms. So the IP for the above URL would be 23.45.168.98. This change is required because computers find it easier to use numerical identifiers whereas humans prefer text-based names. The DNS returns the IP, and this is used to direct the request through a series of routers (**4**) to the server where the website resides (**5**).

Accessing a website: 2

Step 3: Retrieving the web page from the web server

The server where the website is located receives the request (**1**). The server can tell where the request originated by looking at information contained in the request header. The server (**2**) sends a message back indicating: 'Website found. Waiting for reply.' Somewhere on the server the web page itself will be stored as an HTML text file (**3**). The code contained in this text file will define the content and appearance of the web page. It may contain references to URLs where graphics, video or sound files are stored. (**4**) The server will put the request in a queue. When it is in a position to respond, the server sends the HTML file to the requester's browser. (**5**) It also sends a message to those locations where other files (e.g. graphics) are stored to send the appropriate files to the same browser.

Step 4: Opening the web page

As the different parts of the web page arrive (**1**) at the requester's PC or server, they have to be stored before being reassembled. They are therefore held in the computer's cache memory (**2**), a particular type of memory that temporarily holds required data. As the data is being collected, the browser begins putting the page together. It uses the HTML code as a guideline for this process (**3**). The different elements of the website arrive at different times – larger graphics/animation files arriving later than simple text. This is why the website visibly 'constructs' itself on the screen in stages. When the page is complete, the user is generally given a message to this effect, e.g. 'Done' (**4**).

Using search engines

Search engines are used to locate websites or find information when a URL is not known. Search engines are big business and the most popular are Google, Yahoo and Ask. With so many web users relying on search engines it is imperative that they return search results quickly. Results are presented in list form and it is no surprise that well-established big companies usually appear at the top. Search engines are natural language interfaces driven by key words that are entered by the searcher in the hope of finding a close match. If the user enters a shop name, the URL is likely to be given, but when a general product name is entered it is sometimes hard to find what is wanted from a list of millions.

How a search engine works

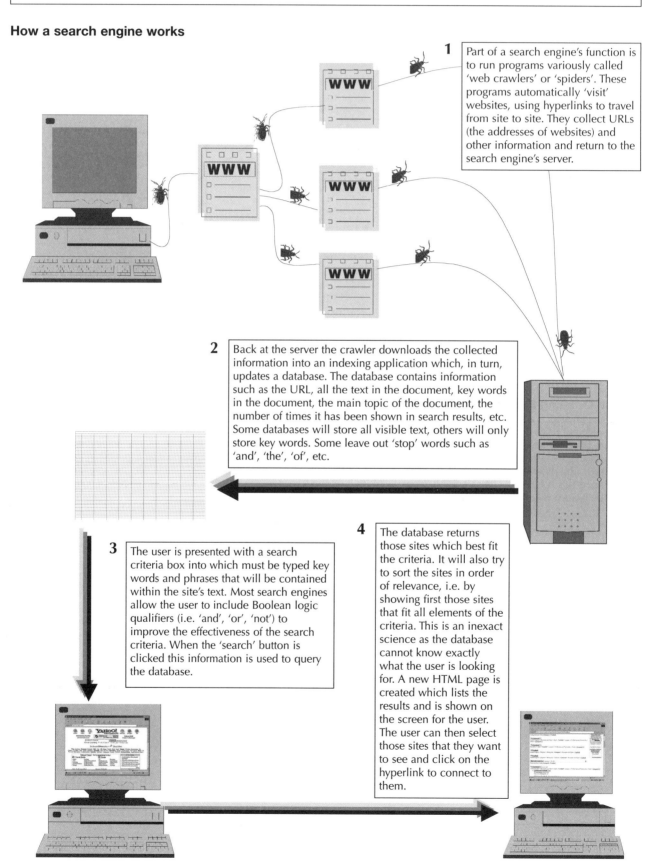

1 Part of a search engine's function is to run programs variously called 'web crawlers' or 'spiders'. These programs automatically 'visit' websites, using hyperlinks to travel from site to site. They collect URLs (the addresses of websites) and other information and return to the search engine's server.

2 Back at the server the crawler downloads the collected information into an indexing application which, in turn, updates a database. The database contains information such as the URL, all the text in the document, key words in the document, the main topic of the document, the number of times it has been shown in search results, etc. Some databases will store all visible text, others will only store key words. Some leave out 'stop' words such as 'and', 'the', 'of', etc.

3 The user is presented with a search criteria box into which must be typed key words and phrases that will be contained within the site's text. Most search engines allow the user to include Boolean logic qualifiers (i.e. 'and', 'or', 'not') to improve the effectiveness of the search criteria. When the 'search' button is clicked this information is used to query the database.

4 The database returns those sites which best fit the criteria. It will also try to sort the sites in order of relevance, i.e. by showing first those sites that fit all elements of the criteria. This is an inexact science as the database cannot know exactly what the user is looking for. A new HTML page is created which lists the results and is shown on the screen for the user. The user can then select those sites that they want to see and click on the hyperlink to connect to them.

Emails

Electronic mail (email) has been an extremely popular and successful aspect of the Internet. It is a means of sending written messages via the network of networks that comprises the Internet. Email is now an essential communication tool, used extensively for business and personal purposes.

How email works

Using email client software the sender composes a message, addresses it to the recipient (using their email address), and sends it. The sender may also choose to attach a document. Email software allows for the attachment of files in a variety of formats: images, spreadsheets, etc.

When the 'send' command is given, the software connects with the Internet Service Provider. The ISP has a mail server and, using a protocol called Simple Mail Transfer Protocol (SMTP), the message is transferred to this server. The server confirms to the sender that the message has been received.

The email server communicates with another piece of software – the domain name server – and this determines what path the message will take to reach its destination. The domain server looks at the destination part of the address and works out the most effective route through the Internet.

The message travels through a series of routers. Routers are devices which decide upon the optimum electronic route for the message to take, i.e. to reach its destination in the shortest time. To take account of different operating systems, the message may have to pass through gateways – i.e. devices that translate data when necessary.

When the message arrives at the destination server, it passes the message to another server, called a Post Office Protocol (POP) server. The POP server is like a set of electronic pigeon holes. It stores messages in designated locations until they are ready to be collected.

When the recipient wants to check their mail, their email client software communicates with the ISP and checks the contents of their POP server 'pigeon hole'. If there are messages there, they are transmitted to the recipient's client software. They can then be opened and read.

Advantages and disadvantages of email

Advantages	Disadvantages
• Messages can be sent across the world for the price of a local phone call. • You can send not only simple text messages but also attached files in a variety of formats. • You can use an address book to send the same message to several different people. • The message will arrive much more quickly than conventional mail (though it is less instantaneous than a telephone message).	• You are reliant on the recipient having suitable hardware and software. Though email is increasingly popular, it is still not universal. • There are security and privacy issues. Confidential mail is travelling across a very public network. • Email attachments have proved to be a security 'Achilles' heel', providing an entry point for destructive viruses.

Uses of the Internet

Communication

Electronic mail is a widely used mode of communication. Its relative immediacy makes it more popular than conventional mail for communicating urgent messages, it is cheaper than the telephone and more flexible than a fax (being able, for example, to carry file attachments such as photographs and even video clips). It is seen as a valuable business tool. Businesses value its ability to copy a piece of correspondence to any number of people selected from an electronic address book. For many people 'checking one's emails' has become an established part of office life. In fact, in some instances, this has proved counter-productive, with many hours being spent opening, reading and responding to emails. This has been exacerbated by the 'spam' phenomenon, i.e. where people receive unsolicited email, usually from companies trying to sell them something. Growing in popularity is VoIP, which allows callers to use the Internet to talk to each other as if they were using the telephone. The calls are free and the software to facilitate the process can be downloaded for free. Many organisations are colluding with other businesses to encourage them to use VoIP and help reduce business costs. VoIP software can show when other users are online and also provides a chat facility if the other users do not have a microphone or speaker to hand.

Making files available

Organisations sometimes need to make document files, data or software available to other parties. The Internet is a simple way of achieving this. The file in question is stored on a special server called a file transfer protocol (FTP) server. Specified users can then contact this server and download the files that they need. Some of FTP sites are private and require an ID and password before they can be accessed, others (anonymous FTP sites) are freely accessible. FTP is often used by software companies who want to distribute their products online. They may wish to make free trial products available or distribute upgrades or anti-virus 'patches'.

Sharing ideas

The 'Newsgroups' Internet application is perhaps the element of the Internet that is most consistent in its purpose with the ideals of the Internet's originators. These are sites where people who share a common area of interest or expertise can exchange views, ideas and information. Newsgroups are organised into a hierarchical tree structure to make searching for the site of your choice easier. If, for example, you wanted to enter into an online discussion about a recent film, you could go first to the heading 'rec' (for recreation), from there you would go to the subgroup 'arts.cinema.name of film'. A newsgroup user can make comments of their own, respond to comments made by others and even create their own newsgroups. Some businesses have found that there are newsgroups about their products that are not always complimentary or accurate. In some cases the business has monitored the newsgroup so that it can effectively counter any negative publicity.

Accessing information

The World Wide Web is a vast repository of information. Organisations and individuals have created websites containing information on just about every subject imaginable. Some now argue that there is too much information on the Internet and that it is virtually impossible to isolate what you need from all the irrelevant material that is offered. This difficulty notwithstanding, the Internet continues to be the first port of call for many in their search for information. It can provide reasonably up-to-date information on the weather, travel conditions, the stock market, and breaking news stories. It can also be searched for archive information on recent news events, advice on everything from DIY to snake handling, current research in all major academic disciplines, the latest bargains from online stores, etc. Some commentators feel that this free access to information cannot last for ever. As has already been noted, information has value and the practice of charging for access to valued information has already begun on the Internet. For example, some financial research papers are only available to those users who pay a subscription to a commercial company.

Publishing information

One of the most noteworthy benefits of the Internet has been the way it has provided opportunities for individuals and small organisations to create their own websites. In recent years the software and hardware required to create a website has become widely accessible and relatively easy to use. Individuals with relatively little experience of computers have found themselves able to create websites that have proved more popular than those of large, commercial concerns. This has meant that people with minority interests have been able to publish information about those interests and so make contact with people around the world. In this sense, the Internet has been a democratising force. It is a space which, at the moment, is not dominated by controlling interests, and so offers a platform to groups and individuals who might otherwise be denied a voice. There is, however, a negative consequence of this openness: the presence of sites run by paedophile groups, race-hate organisations, terrorist sympathisers, etc.

Moral and ethical issues in ICT: 1

What are ethics?

Ethics are moral principles that help to inform the decisions that individuals make. There are a number of professions where complex and far-reaching ethical decisions have to be made on a regular basis. The most obvious case is the medical profession: doctors have to decide whether to undertake a course of treatment that might mean the difference between life and death for the patient. In making this decision the doctor will be able to refer to her own set of moral principles, e.g. on whether euthanasia is morally justified. Additionally there are codified ethics that may be drawn upon, including:

The law	Law-making often starts with a moral principle (e.g. 'stealing is wrong') and codifies it as a law, the breaking of which incurs negative consequences.
Codes of practice	Many organisations develop codes of practice which, while not carrying the force of law, provide guidelines for employees to work within.
Professional ethics	Some professional bodies develop ethical principles that are relevant to the members of that profession. Although they do not carry the force of law, a breach of them may lead to expulsion from the professional body. The British Computer Society, for example, has developed a Code of Conduct for ICT professionals. It covers such areas as: The Public Interest, Duty to Employers and Clients, Duty to the Profession and Professional Competence, and Integrity.

ICT is not usually identified as an area where ethical issues are a priority. However, professionals working in ICT may well face a number of ethical issues related to the impact of their work, both on individuals and on society as a whole. ICT developments have had – and will continue to have – an enormous impact on society. Ethically speaking, ICT professionals have a responsibility to consider the consequences – positive and negative – of the technologies that they work to develop and the data they have access to.

Some ethical issues in ICT

PRIVACY

ICT systems have enabled a wide range of private and public organisations to hold electronic data on vast numbers of individuals. Data subjects are not always aware of their rights under data protection legislation and not all organisations act ethically in regard to their use of data. Information that individuals may wish to keep private is not always securely held and can therefore be accessed by organisations and individuals who should not have access to it. Electronic monitoring systems, such as those that track emails, can be used – sometimes legitimately, sometimes not – to view individuals' personal messages.

EMPLOYMENT PATTERNS

ICT has had an enormous impact on employment patterns and working practices. It would not be an exaggeration to state that ICT has transformed the workplace over the past 30 years. Some of this change has been beneficial to organisations and individuals but, while there have been obvious winners, there have been losers too. Some people have been de-skilled by the arrival of ICT and have found themselves out of work as a consequence. In other cases the nature of ICT-based work has created its own problems. Call centres, for example, which use computerised communication technology, have been referred to as 'the sweat shops of the 21st century'.

EQUITY

It has been argued that the introduction of ICT has led to a divide both within and between societies. This divide has been characterised as one between 'information rich' and 'information poor'. As societies rely more and more on ICT, ownership of and access to the appropriate technologies increasingly determine which individuals/organisations/ societies succeed or fail. Since these technologies incur financial costs, those individuals/organisations/societies who already possess material wealth are in a stronger position to take advantage of them and, in so doing, increase their wealth, power and status still further. The materially less well off are excluded from the technological loop and thus the divide between the two groups widens.

PROPERTY RIGHTS

The capabilities of ICT, and of the Internet in particular, have led to a number of problems associated with what is generally referred to as 'intellectual property'. The Internet was, in part, developed to facilitate the free exchange of ideas and research. Problems emerged, however, when the 'free access' principles of the World Wide Web were applied to such things as published text, music, video, software, etc. This has led to battles between those individuals and organisations who have ownership rights and those users who believe the Internet should not become another space that is owned and run by large corporations. This conflict of values is exemplified by the legal battles that have taken place between music publishers and file-sharing systems such as Napster.

The British Computer Society (BCS) and the Association for Computing Machinery (ACM) both publish codes of conducts which outline the expectations of those who work with computers. Those companies who take the ownership and treatment of data seriously tend to use the codes as templates which they alter to suit the needs of their own business. With access to personal data and sensitive information it is crucial that some form of internal standards are applied to adhere to legislation and create a trusting working environment.

Moral and ethical issues in ICT: 2

Moral, social and ethical issues associated with the Internet

Censorship

The Internet is transnational in its scope and not centrally owned or controlled, making it virtually impossible to police. Consequently, material which would be illegal if published in 'hard copy' format, is easily accessible on the Internet. The clearest example of this is hard-core pornography. This leads some people to argue that the Internet should be censored. While many agree with the need to prevent the publication of offensive material, e.g. paedophiliac imagery, others argue that the introduction of censorship will undermine the freedom of expression that, at the moment, the Internet facilitates. There are also issues about who does the censoring and what form of centralised control might be needed to impose censorship.

Accuracy of information

Many people use the Internet as a source of information. There is no guarantee, however, that the information that they find is accurate. An example of this can be found among the many websites that offer medical advice. The advice given on some sites has been shown to be erroneous and there is a danger that some people will accept this advice at face value. It could be argued, of course, that this is equally true of other media, e.g. newspapers and magazines, but the unregulated nature of the Internet can make the publication of inaccurate information a particular issue.

THE INTERNET

The effects on community

Some argue that the Internet has increased valuable interactions between individuals as a result of its new modes of communication. Additionally, it is argued that communities previously separated by geographical location are now able to form connections and this has led to a greater awareness of other cultures. There is, however, a counter-argument. Some have suggested that computer usage is essentially a solitary activity and that valuable forms of social interaction are declining as a result of its increase. An example of this would be shopping on the Internet. If people increasingly shop from home using the Internet, local shops will go out of business and their capacity to act as a site of interaction for a local community will be lost.

Privacy

The technology involved in the Internet means that it is a fairly straightforward matter to intercept and view Internet communications. This leads some to argue that communication on the Internet should be protected by privacy laws and that one's emails should be as confidential as one's conventional mail. Others argue that, because the Internet has been used to assist in the commission of criminal acts, industrial espionage; and terrorist attacks, law enforcement agencies should have the power to intercept and view electronic correspondence. This issue has come to the fore in the debate over encryption: should individuals/organisations have the right to encrypt their data without providing the security services with the key?

Ownership and control

The ideal of many of those involved in creating the Internet was that it would be a virtual location for the free exchange of knowledge, opinions and ideas. While this still holds true to some extent, the Internet has also become a profoundly commercialised space where different corporations struggle to increase their market share. There are people who fear that the Internet will go the way of other media, i.e. it will become dominated by a small number of organisations who will effectively determine its content. Others argue that the Internet is big enough to allow both large-scale commercial and small-scale independent concerns to coexist. They further argue that without commercial investment the Internet will not be able to sustain itself.

Ownership, control and consequences (effects to society and communities)

Debates rage over the control of information and how it should be used. Businesses spend millions of pounds collecting, storing and processing data as part of their daily operations. It would be unrealistic to expect them to relinquish this data for nothing. Some firms solely trade in the sale of information, which is bought with the intention of generating further income.

Controversy over data begins when it is withheld but could be used to do good. Those holding the data may have incurred a huge financial undertaking in its collection and may be unwilling to let it go for free. Examples include the details relating to a medical breakthrough. Such information could save millions of lives – but only after a royalty fee has been agreed.

Fortunately, there are many people in the world who believe that all information should be available to everybody at no cost. An example of this includes those who write software free and host websites where like-minded people publish research for all to access. The Linux community gives away its operating system and software, which are frequently enhanced and released at no charge to anyone with a link to the Internet. This type of action makes it possible for developing nations to access the Internet and benefit from faster communication, better and more up-to-date information about market prices, weather forecasts, and assistance with journey planning. Such information is useful to farmers trying to sell their cattle or crops at a price which is competitive and helps limit their exploitation at the hands of those with access to similar types of information. By withholding information a competitive edge can be achieved, but by opening up the world's information resources children in deprived areas can be better educated, orders for emergency supplies can be placed in a more timely way, and modern construction methods can be shared with those who need them. The limitation of electricity and access to the Internet still prohibits widespread global access, but over time mobile equipment reaches deprived areas and could make a difference.

Moral and ethical issues in ICT: 3

An approach to ethical decision-making

IDENTIFY THE FACTS

An ethical dilemma may be initiated when an individual is required to act in response to an event or an instruction. There is a dilemma because the individual feels uncomfortable with the required action if it conflicts with their principles of right and wrong. For example, an ICT professional may be asked to work on an application designed to help an organisation monitor employees' personal email, and may feel that this conflicts with his notion that individuals have a right to privacy. In order to make an ethically sound decision, the individual first needs to apprise himself of all the relevant facts. In the example given, there would be a need to know who would be using the application, what purpose it would be put to, whether employees would know of its existence, etc. The individual must be in full possession of the facts before they can make an informed decision.

DEFINE THE ETHICAL CONFLICT

Typically, an ethical conflict involves a choice between mutually exclusive courses of action, each of which is informed by a different set of values. Defining the ethical conflict requires the individual to identify the moral values that are in conflict. In the example given, the employees' right to privacy is in conflict with the organisation's right to protect itself from the damage caused by (for example) the circulation of false rumours. It may be, at this stage, that the ethical dilemma can be resolved by the emergence of a compromise solution that respects both sets of values. If for, example, the employees were aware that their emails were being monitored, they could choose a different means of communication for personal messages. Some ethical dilemmas, however, are not amenable to compromise solutions.

TEST THE REQUIRED ACT AGAINST PERSONAL AND CODIFIED ETHICS

The law If the required act is against the law, the dilemma may be solved. The ICT professional can, in this instance, justifiably claim an unwillingness to step outside the law. The law does not always provide a simple answer to ethical dilemmas: in some circumstances – i.e. where laws are unjust, an act that goes against the law may be the most ethical thing to do.

Codes of practice Organisational or professional codes of practice may provide guidelines for action. The British Computer Society's Code of Conduct states that 'members shall avoid any actions that adversely affect (basic human) rights'. It could be argued that, in this case, the right to privacy in one's personal communications is a basic human right. Codes of practice do not, however, carry the weight of law and may be interpreted in different ways.

Personal ethics Individuals live their lives according to a set of ethical principles. Those principles may be more or less flexible and more or less consistent with the general moral principles of a society. They provide individuals with guidelines for action. Some individuals have a relatively rigid moral code – inspired, for example, by religious precepts – and this will make ethical dilemmas easier to resolve: the action is either acceptable to them or it is not.

DEFINE POSSIBLE COURSES OF ACTION AND THEIR CONSEQUENCES

If, after the required act has been tested against the above ethical codes, the dilemma still remains, the next stage is for the individual to set out the courses of action available. Each option will involve a different set of consequences. These positive/negative consequences can then be weighed against each other. In this example, the ICT professional can see that one option is to refuse to work on the system. The consequence of this may be that his contract is terminated and someone else is hired. This negative consequence has to be weighed against the consequences of a developing a system that diminishes the ICT professional's colleagues' right to privacy.

APPLY ESTABLISHED ETHICAL PRINCIPLES

The Golden Rule This can be stated as 'do unto others as you would have them do unto you'. The individual should put himself in the position of those likely to be affected by his actions. How would he feel were he in their position?

Kant's Categorical Imperative Immanuel Kant was a philosopher who proposed that one should, when making an ethical choice, ask oneself: 'If everyone in society acted in this way, could society survive?' In other words, if an act is right for one person it should be right for all persons.

The Utilitarian Principle This principle states that one should weigh all the consequences of different possible actions and select the one that results in the greatest good for the greatest number of people.

DECISION

Privacy

Privacy issues

A distinction should be made between privacy and security. Security is primarily a concern for the organisation: How can it ensure that data and systems are protected from both internal and external infringements? Privacy is more a matter for individual users: how they can ensure that their personal information remains private? The coming of the Information Age has brought in its wake a number of new threats to personal privacy:

- The Internet is by no means a secure medium of communication, and yet individuals choose to divulge personal details on it, including financial information such as credit card numbers. There are many ways in which motivated individuals can gain access to insecure Internet transactions. At the criminal end of the spectrum, this includes individuals and (criminal) organisations who wish to steal credit card details and, in some cases, people's identities. At a less nefarious level, commercial companies may use 'cookies' to identify web-surfing behaviour.
- An inevitable consequence of the trend for commercial companies and public institutions to store personal records electronically is that one's personal details are likely to be held on a number of databases. The level of security applied to these databases varies widely, leaving open the possibility that such personal details may be accessed by individuals who should have no authority to do so.
- The use of the Internet, and email facilities in particular, is widespread in places of work. In office environments employees are likely to spend a good deal of the time at a computer and research suggests that a significant proportion of that time will be spent sending personal emails and conducting personal business over the Internet. An increasing number of organisations use specialist applications to monitor both the web-surfing activities and the email traffic of their employees. They can claim that they are justified in so doing because (a) time spent on personal business necessarily results in a loss of productivity and (b) they wish to protect themselves against the legally actionable offences of their employees, e.g. harassment suits that might result from the transmission of pornographic images. Employees, on the other hand, may feel that their privacy is under threat from such monitoring.
- National security organisations and law enforcement agencies have successfully argued that they are justified in monitoring electronic communications, including emails, because they are used in the commission of criminal acts and terrorist atrocities. There are a number of systems in operation that perform such monitoring, the best known of which are Carnivore, a monitoring system run by the FBI that filters Internet traffic looking for key words such as 'bomb', and Echelon, an internal data communications monitoring system run by a consortium of English-speaking countries. While most people would support measures taken against criminal and terrorist activity, there are many individuals and groups who believe that the individual's right to privacy is being undermined by the technological sophistication and secretive nature of such systems.

Ways in which the individual user can preserve privacy

ENCRYPTION

Encryption programs convert one's text into (hopefully) indecipherable code. There is a wide variety of encryption programs available. The latest version of Windows has a simple encryption facility and programs such as Pretty Good Privacy (PGP) can be downloaded free from the Internet. Simple encryption systems are, of course, easily broken, but they do offer a measure of protection against unsophisticated 'data snoopers'.

WEB BROWSERS

All web-browsing software allows the user to define security settings. It is advisable to maintain the latest version of browser software, as security is an area that has improved with each successive version. The user should not just accept the default settings, but establish what each security level involves and define settings that are appropriate for the level of security they require.

ANTI-VIRUS SOFTWARE

Apart from the obvious threat that viruses pose to programs and data, they can also be used to invade privacy and capture data. The 'invader' deploys a 'worm' or 'Trojan Horse' to install a program called a 'keystroke logger' on the target computer. This program will remain hidden from the user and log every keystroke they make. The resulting data can be retrieved by the hacker who can then 'read' everything that has been written via the keyboard.

AWARENESS

Being aware of threats to privacy will help one make informed decisions about what details to reveal via which medium. For example, if one is aware that employers have both the technological means and, in certain circumstances, the legal right to monitor one's personal emails, one may choose to be careful about how much one reveals during such communications.

BASIC SECURITY

Following some basic security procedures can help maintain privacy. One should avoid, for example, leaving a computer logged-on whilst one is away from it. Passwords should be used to protect sensitive material and the password should not be one that can be easily predicted, e.g. a date of birth or name of pet. If one is working on a network one should be aware of who else has access to shared areas.

FIREWALLS

Firewall is a generic name for software/hardware that is designed to protect systems from intrusion. While most commercial organisations deploy expensive and sophisticated systems, there are simple and relatively cheap versions available for the individual user. The latest version of Windows has a built-in Internet Connection Firewall that provides some protection for the individual user.

Organisation structure

An organisation is a collection of human and non-human resources brought together in order to fulfil a designated purpose. An organisation may be a large, commercial enterprise such as IBM, or a small, informally structured, non-commercial group, e.g. a local charity. All organisations have structures. In some instances these structures are clearly defined and fairly inflexible; in other instances, the structure is looser and less formally defined.

The hierarchical model

This used to be the standard model for large, commercial organisations. Recently, other models have grown in popularity, but hierarchical models still dominate the business world. Many hierarchical models are based on a division of personnel on the basis of the role that they play within the organisation. This is known as functional specialisation.

The above diagram represents the basic structure of the hierarchical model. If this were a real organisation, the diagram would be more extensive and would include further levels. For example, the Head of Regional Sales might be responsible for a number of heads of specific regions who, in turn, would have responsibility for sales representatives. Some further points to note about this model:
- **The chain of command** is the path through which instructions are given and decisions are requested. Instructions move from the top downwards, following the line of authority; problems requiring decisions follow similar paths but move from the bottom upwards.
- **The span of control** refers to how many people a manager is responsible for. Too wide a span of control can lead to inadequate control; too narrow a span can lead to unnecessary layers of management.

Problems associated with a 'tall' hierarchical structure

- The organisation may become inflexible, unable to change quickly because decisions have to travel a long way 'down the line' and so take time to implement.
- Communications which have to travel through a number of levels may become lost or distorted in the process.
- Upper echelons of management can become remote from what is happening 'on the shop floor'. This can lead to opportunities being missed and problems going unnoticed.
- Junior employees can feel that they have no stake in the organisation because they are not required to make any decisions.

The flat structure

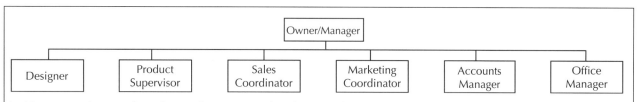

In this structure there are fewer layers of management but the span of control is much wider. Such organisations can be more flexible as the implementation of decisions can happen more quickly. Greater independence is given to different departments and there is more delegation of responsibility. However, specialisation of departments may lead to inadequate communication between departments.

Factors which determine organisational structure

- The size and complexity of the organisation: the larger and more complex the organisation, the more likely it is to formalise clear lines of authority.
- The nature of the organisational goals: some organisational goals (e.g. a multinational business trying to establish markets in different countries) require the establishment of separate areas of specialisation.
- The beliefs and values of the head(s) of the organisation: some executives prefer looser, more flexible structures, believing that they make better business sense.
- The geographical spread of the organisation: organisations spread across a number of regions often develop structures that reflect this, i.e. regionally based departments.

Corporate information systems strategy

Why is a corporate information systems strategy necessary?

A corporate information systems strategy is a coordinated approach to the planning, resourcing, development and implementation of ICT systems in an organisation. The aim of such a strategy is to ensure that ICT systems add value to the organisation by contributing to organisational goals (e.g. maximising profit, reducing hospital waiting lists, etc.) in an efficient, reliable and cost-effective manner. It is important to have a strategy to achieve this aim, i.e. as opposed to an *ad hoc* approach, for several reasons, including:

- Information systems may be found in the different functional divisions of an organisation. They fulfil different functions in these divisions but there is still a necessity for the divisions, and therefore the systems, to be able to 'talk' to each other. Systems must therefore be compatible and allow for the free exchange of data.
- ICT is fast-changing and influenced by external events. There needs to be a planned and coordinated response to these changes and events or the organisation will suffer by being unprepared.
- ICT incurs cost and often this cost is a significant proportion of the organisation's budget. An unplanned, unstructured approach to ICT resourcing is likely to lead to poor decision-making and financial loss.
- ICT systems are increasingly likely to be 'business-critical' – i.e. without them the business cannot operate successfully (in some cases it can't operate at all).

What factors will influence the development of an ICT systems strategy?

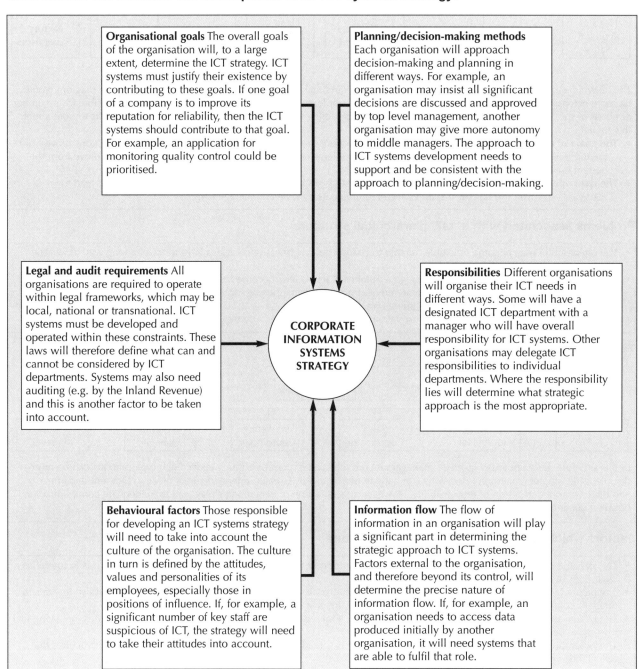

Organisational goals The overall goals of the organisation will, to a large extent, determine the ICT strategy. ICT systems must justify their existence by contributing to these goals. If one goal of a company is to improve its reputation for reliability, then the ICT systems should contribute to that goal. For example, an application for monitoring quality control could be prioritised.

Planning/decision-making methods Each organisation will approach decision-making and planning in different ways. For example, an organisation may insist all significant decisions are discussed and approved by top level management, another organisation may give more autonomy to middle managers. The approach to ICT systems development needs to support and be consistent with the approach to planning/decision-making.

Legal and audit requirements All organisations are required to operate within legal frameworks, which may be local, national or transnational. ICT systems must be developed and operated within these constraints. These laws will therefore define what can and cannot be considered by ICT departments. Systems may also need auditing (e.g. by the Inland Revenue) and this is another factor to be taken into account.

CORPORATE INFORMATION SYSTEMS STRATEGY

Responsibilities Different organisations will organise their ICT needs in different ways. Some will have a designated ICT department with a manager who will have overall responsibility for ICT systems. Other organisations may delegate ICT responsibilities to individual departments. Where the responsibility lies will determine what strategic approach is the most appropriate.

Behavioural factors Those responsible for developing an ICT systems strategy will need to take into account the culture of the organisation. The culture in turn is defined by the attitudes, values and personalities of its employees, especially those in positions of influence. If, for example, a significant number of key staff are suspicious of ICT, the strategy will need to take their attitudes into account.

Information flow The flow of information in an organisation will play a significant part in determining the strategic approach to ICT systems. Factors external to the organisation, and therefore beyond its control, will determine the precise nature of information flow. If, for example, an organisation needs to access data produced initially by another organisation, it will need systems that are able to fulfil that role.

ICT and the organisation

The position of ICT in the organisation

When ICT was first introduced into organisations its main function was to improve efficiency, i.e. by performing repetitive data processing more quickly and more accurately than humans were able to. Information systems serviced the needs of the different functional divisions of the organisation, e.g. processing invoices for the accounts department. Different divisions ran different systems and there was only a partial attempt to coordinate these systems. As information systems grew in complexity, a greater degree of coordination was required. Systems had to be able to 'talk' both to each other and to other systems beyond the organisation. Additionally, the functionality offered by advanced information systems meant that it was no longer appropriate to position ICT as a mere service. Increasingly ICT came to be at the heart of the organisational structure, not only fulfilling the requirements of different functional divisions but determining the strategic decisions of the organisation.

Information management policy

Centralised versus decentralised model

Organisations regularly have to make decisions about how their ICT systems should develop. These decisions may cover many different aspects of ICT, including hardware, software, networking capabilities, communication systems, etc. In many organisations these decisions are business-critical, i.e. they impact directly on the ability of the business to function effectively. It is therefore inadvisable for organisations to make such decisions in an *ad hoc* manner. Rather, they should develop a strategic ICT policy. Such a policy would place ICT-oriented decisions in the overall context of organisational needs and goals.

There are, broadly speaking, two models for developing an ICT policy: the centralised and decentralised models.

Centralised   In this model an Information Systems Department takes responsibility for the development of all ICT systems in the organisation, regardless of which functional area is being served. All decisions about purchasing, development, training, etc. go through this centralised department. It therefore determines the overall ICT policy of the organisation.

Decentralised   In a decentralised model, each functional area makes its own decisions about what systems to develop and/or acquire. If accounting, for example, needed a new application, it would evaluate what was on the market and make a decision based on its own criteria.

The decentralised model is rarely found these days. The need for interconnectedness between systems based in different functional areas makes the centralised model much more desirable. The decentralised model had one main advantage: it allowed individual departments/functional areas the autonomy to make ICT-based decisions using criteria that related primarily to their own functional needs. This one advantage is, however, outweighed by the advantages of a centralised approach. These include:

- increased ability to maintain compatibility between the different elements of an organisation's ICT infrastructure;
- improved discounts as a consequence of high volume purchasing;
- better deals on service level contracts;
- easier for employees to move from department to department if systems are similar;
- greater control over security issues.

Factors in ICT policy development

Developing an integrated system An organisation's ICT systems must be able to communicate with each other. Users must be able to integrate data held in different systems and transfer files without encountering problems. Systems must also communicate with external systems, especially if such systems are integral to the organisation's operations, e.g. the Internet. Each ICT development must therefore be consistent with this overall aim.

Budget Organisations often have to dedicate large proportions of their budget to ICT systems. It is therefore important that all ICT-based decisions are cost-effective. If a development is going to take place, it must be costed thoroughly, taking into account both open and hidden costs, e.g. the cost of retraining users. The cost must then be justified in terms of what value will be added to the organisation by the new development.

ICT POLICY

User impact Decisions regarding ICT developments often have significant impact on an organisation's employees. This impact might be minor, e.g. the need for retraining, or more dramatic, e.g. loss of job or relocation. An organisation's workforce is often its single most valuable asset. An ICT policy must therefore ensure that policy decisions do not have an unnecessarily detrimental effect on the day-to-day lives of employees.

Consistency with organisational goals ICT policy decisions must be justified in terms of the overall strategic goals of the organisation. If, for example, an organisation has, as a key strategic goal, the development of new markets for existing products, new ICT developments and acquisitions should be able to contribute to that process. If this factor is not taken into consideration, new technologies might be developed/acquired unnecessarily.

Future-proofing

Ideally an ICT policy will 'future proof' its systems. That is, it will predict future needs and build in functionality and system capacity to deal with these needs. In practice, future proofing is all but impossible. There are too many unknowns, including events in the business environment of the organisation, changes in key personnel, developments in technology, unexpected budget constraints, etc. Nevertheless, ICT policy decisions will have to <u>try</u> to take into account possible future developments that might impact on the organisation and its ICT systems.

Information flow

What is information flow?
Information flow refers to the procedures whereby information is communicated to various parties both within an organisation and between the organisation and the outside world. Effective information flow is essential for an organisation as it enables the efficient maintenance of key processes. These processes include:

- informing employees of organisational changes;
- issuing management instructions to subordinates;
- receiving communication from clients, customers, suppliers, etc.;
- maintaining awareness of 'environmental' changes that might impact upon the organisation.

Formal methods

FORMAL METHODS	COMMENT
Meetings	Formal meetings may be scheduled or called as a response to a particular issue/incident. A formal meeting will be chaired, have an agenda and have minutes taken. A meeting may be between two people or many hundreds (e.g. a shareholders' meeting). It may be held 'live' or using videoconferencing technology. The participants may be based entirely within the organisation or be a mixture of organisational members and outside agencies. Meetings allow for a two-way flow of information, with ideas being exchanged and different opinions being aired.
Memos	Memos convey information from one individual to another, or a group of individuals. They were printed or handwritten on paper and distributed by hand. It is now likely that email or intranet links are used to distribute the messages electronically. Memos generally convey information within the organisation. It is usually the case that memos convey 'top-down' information, i.e. where a manager wishes to convey information to subordinates.
Documents/manuals	Organisations often maintain policy documents both in hard copy and electronic format. These are used as a repository of organisation-specific information, policy statements that everybody in the organisation needs to be aware of, and instructions for Standard Operating Procedures. The document is then made available to everybody that needs access to the information.

The restraints of organisational structures

Many formal communication methods use the layers and connections of the organisational structure to guide the flow of information. For example, an executive-level manager will send a memo to Heads of Department instructing them to advise their subordinates of changes that will affect the organisation. This relationship between channels of communication and organisational structure can lead to problems, for example:

- If an organisation has many levels of communication, the information can become lost or distorted during its 'journey'.
- There may not be clear, well-established lines of communication between different functional areas. This can lead to business-critical information not finding its way to the right person at the right time.
- A wide, geographical distribution of organisational elements can lead to problems with maintaining information flow. This has been made easier with the advent of electronic communications.
- The flow of information can become too unidirectional. The information flows down from managers to subordinates, but there is no equivalent mechanism for managers at higher levels to receive information from below. This can lead to them becoming remote from shop-floor operations.

Informal flow of information

The above procedures are formal, i.e. they involve planned, officially sanctioned events with an agreed format. Formal modes of communication also tend to be documented, i.e. there is a stored record of whatever communication took place. This may be important if, at some future date, the content of the communication is disputed.

Information also flows in an organisation via informal mechanisms such as casual conversations, personal emails, telephone conversations, etc.

Informal methods have their value. For example, a casual conversation between a senior manager and a production worker can enable a flow of information that a rigid hierarchical structure might otherwise inhibit. However, informal methods are, by their very nature, unreliable. They cannot be counted on to deliver critical information to the right person at the right time.

Levels and uses of information

Roles and functions	Information needs	Decision authority	Planning orientation	Nature of information
STRATEGIC — **Chief executives, directors, leadership teams, etc.** • To define objectives and policies for the whole organisation. • To establish long-term goals. • To make decisions on resourcing and large-scale investment. • To decide upon plans for expansion/contraction/changes in direction. • To respond to significant external events which may impact upon the organisation (e.g. new legislation).	• Reports showing overall performance of the organisation, relative to past performance and to that of competitors. • Modelled information showing the possible effects of different decisions. • Accounting information showing overall financial performance. • Information about external developments that might impact upon the organisation. • Summary reports on the performance of different departments.	HIGH	LONG-TERM	SUMMARY
TACTICAL — **Heads of large departments, functional supervisors, project coordinators, etc.** • Managing budgets and allocating resources. • Monitoring progress and ensuring quality of outcome. • Appointing, supervising and assessing staff. • Developing operational policies and ensuring their implementation. • Providing information to line managers.	• Reports showing available resources and budget allocations. • Summary reports on departmental performance. • Information and performance data on subordinate staff. • Reports on availability of products and services. • Information on requirements of senior management.	↕	↕	↕
OPERATIONAL — **Heads of small departments, individuals with specific areas of responsibility** • To ensure efficient practice on a day-to-day basis. • Making effective use of existing resources. • Ensuring effective contribution to the overall objectives of the organisation.	• Instructions from supervisors regarding operational requirements. • Information that can be used to monitor the effectiveness of operations. • Day-to-day task information, e.g. what needs to be done by when?	LOW	DAY-TO-DAY	DETAILED

Functional areas: MARKETING · ACCOUNTING · PRODUCTION · OTHER FUNCTIONAL AREAS

Decision-making

Different levels of decision-making

Decision-making is one of the key functions of managers at all levels. The nature of the process will vary according to the level of management involved:

- **Strategic decision-making** involves making decisions that will determine the overall direction of the organisation and the establishment of organisation-wide policies and goals.
- **Tactical management control** involves making decisions that will ensure the optimum utilisation of human and non-human resources. It is the interface between strategically established goals ('what we want to achieve') and how, operationally, those goals will be achieved ('how we will achieve it').
- **Knowledge level decision-making** deals with the management of information within the organisation and the evaluation of new ideas and products.
- **Operational control** determines how exactly the decisions made at a strategic and tactical level are put into practice in day-to-day operations.

Structured versus unstructured decision-making

Structured decisions are routine decisions that are made on a regular basis. When a decision of this kind is to be made there is a defined procedure to follow. These are decisions that organisations expect to have to make and so they establish 'rules' for dealing with them. For example, a decision may be needed about when to re-stock a certain product. The organisation will decide that once stock falls below a certain level then re-stocking will take place. Once the manager has information about current stock levels, the decision can be made quickly and without having to consider other possibilities.

Unstructured decisions are not routine and therefore contain unexpected elements. They require managers to consider the existing situation and evaluate possible courses of action. Decisions of this kind are not predictable and so procedures cannot be laid down for dealing with them. Rather, managers have to use the available information and apply their knowledge and insight in order to come to a decision.

The process of decision-making – how information helps

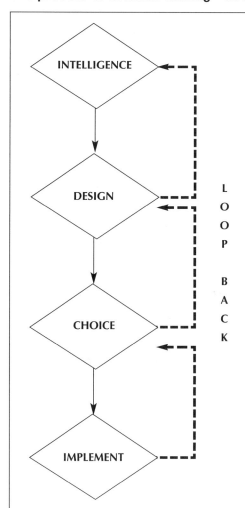

Intelligence This involves identifying a problem/opportunity that requires a decision and gathering together all the information that may be needed to make that decision. Management Information Systems are designed to support this process.

Design Different possible solutions are developed and formulated. Each different scenario is researched and the possible costs and benefits established. This then provides a fixed number of options for the decision-maker(s) to select from.

Choice The designs are evaluated and the consequences for the organisation of implementing any one of them are considered. Modelling software can be used to support this process. One designed solution is selected as being the optimum one.

Implementation The chosen solution is put in place and its effect is monitored and evaluated. Regular reports will be needed in order to establish whether the solution was indeed the best one.

Loop back Decision-making rarely follows a simple, linear pattern. It is often necessary, having reached one stage, to loop back to a previous stage, either to gather more information or to reconsider a choice.

Upgrading hardware and software: 1

Upgrading a piece of computer hardware/software entails acquiring a newer, enhanced version of the existing component. There are a number of reasons why an individual or organisation may wish to upgrade components. These can be categorised as 'push' and 'pull' factors.

- The current component is functioning inadequately and needs replacing.
- There is a new business requirement that cannot be met by current resources.
- The acquisition of another resource requires associated components to be upgraded, e.g. a new software package requires enhanced memory resources.

PUSH → **UPGRADE** → **PULL**

- New products come on to the market that offer functionality that will be beneficial to the individual/organisation.
- There is a financial incentive associated with upgrading, e.g. a company offers free upgrades if other items are purchased.
- A resource, available on the market, offers the facilities needed to undertake a new venture, e.g. creating a website.

Different types of upgrading

HARDWARE

The processing speed and memory capacity of computers has increased steadily over the past few years. At the same time their cost in real terms has declined. This has encouraged users to upgrade regularly, purchasing new machines with faster processors and increased memory capacity. This trend is driven by the 'need for speed', i.e. impatience with the time taken by an existing computer to perform simple actions. This works in tandem with the development of new software, which is often heavily coded: new programs become available with enhanced functionality, users acquire these programs and then realise that they need higher specification machines for the programs to run properly.

In some cases the individual/organisation may choose to replace old computers with new ones. Equally, they may install additional resources (e.g. adding more RAM) or replace one particular element of a system, e.g. network cabling.

Some types of hardware, e.g. printers, will wear with age and use and need replacing.

SOFTWARE

Software manufacturers are constantly upgrading their merchandise and offering it to consumers. In their drive to increase their market share, they improve the functionality of existing software and try to tie the consumer in to their products.

The Microsoft products are a good example of this. A new version of a generic package, e.g. MS Word, is released every few years. It offers enhanced facilities and the consumer is encouraged to accept it as the new standard.

Other software may need upgrading because changes in the organisation's requirements mean that it can no longer perform adequately. For example, business users may have to upgrade their software in order to process transactions involving the euro, or changes come about to enhance connectivity between various portable devices.

Some issues associated with upgrading

Compatibility	The upgraded component will need to be compatible with existing systems. In the case of software this will mean that files created in an earlier version can still be opened and edited. This is referred to as backward compatibility.
Scale	There is often an issue about the extent to which an organisation should upgrade at any one time. For example, if part of an organisation upgrades their software, should the rest of the organisation do likewise? If they do not, there is the risk of compatibility problems when files are transferred from one user to another. Likewise, upgrading one element of a system (e.g. software) often creates a demand for upgrading in other parts of the system (e.g. memory resources).
Need	It is easy for organisations and individuals to be drawn into a constant cycle of upgrading, but this might not be in their best interests. A question must be asked of an upgraded component: how will it justify the cost and disruption associated with its implementation?
Training	Upgraded software, with new functionality and a changed user interface, may mean that users have to be trained in its use. There may also be a need for additional user support resources.

Upgrading hardware and software: 2

Reasons to upgrade

Organisational ethos	New developments	New requirements	Maintenance issues
The image an organisation presents to potential clients/ customers is very important. One aspect of this image is the extent to which the organisation appears technologically advanced. Both in regard to the hardware/software on show and the material that is produced as a consequence, a successful organisation will want to present itself as current with the latest ICT developments.	New software and hardware technologies are emerging constantly and an organisation will be regularly presented with new products. Some of these products will not add anything of significance to the organisation but some will. Such products may help to perform existing procedures in a new way (perhaps a more cost-effective way) and are therefore attractive because they have the potential to 'add value'.	Organisations – and the environment they operate in – are constantly changing. Consequently, new needs and requirements regularly emerge. This may occur as the result of: • a change in legislation – e.g. new data protection laws; • a change in business practice – e.g. the development of a new product; • a change in scale – e.g. a growth in the volume of business.	A piece of hardware or software can become a liability by constantly breaking down or failing to perform as it should. This might occur as the result of an inherent weakness – i.e. a badly designed product – or as the consequence of wear and tear. Organisations often have (sometimes costly) maintenance contracts in order to manage such eventualities, but sometimes the answer will be to acquire a new piece of software/hardware.

Make the decision to upgrade Whatever the reason for the upgrade, someone must make a decision to go ahead. This decision will usually be based on a cost-benefit analysis, i.e. what will the upgrade cost (in terms of time, money, disruption, etc.) and what will be gained from it (in terms of increased efficiency, greater reliability, an improved product, etc.). Clearly the benefits will need to outweigh the costs.

Evaluation and choice An individual or team must now take responsibility for choosing the product. First, they must find out what products are available; secondly, they must establish criteria for making a judgement; and thirdly, they must measure possible acquisitions against the criteria they have established. This last part of the process may involve using benchmark tests or running trials with demonstration copies in their own environment.

Analysis of consequences Due to the interconnectedness of ICT systems, even a minor change is likely to have consequences for other aspects of the system. For example, if a new version of software is to be introduced there will be consequences for any user who still has to run an earlier version, i.e. they may not be able to transfer data. A decision will then be needed as to whether the whole organisation should upgrade at the same time or whether it should be done in phases.

Preparing the ground Once the choice has been made and the consequences analysed, the systems must be prepared for the upgrade. Depending on the likely impact of the product, it may be necessary to perform a 'dry run' in a test environment to discover any problems that might emerge. If the change is a significant one, users will need to be prepared for its implementation. This may involve dissemination of documents, training, etc.

Implementation and monitoring The implementation itself may be a complex process: some upgrades require the server to be 'downed' for a period of time. If this is the case, the down-time will need to be planned for, especially if it involves business-critical systems. One the upgrade has been completed it will require close monitoring. If compatibility problems do occur, they are likely to emerge in the period immediately after implementation.

Back-up: 1

The importance of backing-up data

Regardless of how many security measures an organisation has in place, systems are still vulnerable to a number of threats. Consequently, in addition to standard security procedures, an organisation should have a clear, well-organised back-up and recovery system. A back-up strategy is similar to an insurance policy: it will allow an organisation to recover data even if the loss is disastrously widespread. The back-up policy should be set out in a formal document, and all personnel involved should be aware of procedures and responsibilities, both for backing-up and recovering data. In developing such a policy a number of different factors will need to be taken into account. These are set out below.

Factors to be considered when developing a back-up strategy

Medium

A decision must be made about which storage medium will be used. The most commonly used options are:

- DAT tape was a popular method for storing back-up data but the increased capacity and physical size of external hard drives means that DAT tape is slowly being replaced and the back-up process is becoming faster as a result.
- Zip drives can be used where there is a relatively small amount of data. These devices can store around 250Mb of data, are fairly cheap and can facilitate speedy access of individual files. They are, however, only suitable for small organisations or individual users.
- CD ROM may be used when the data need to be backed-up once and then kept, e.g. a piece of applications software. Rewritable optical discs, capable of storing up to 10Gb, are increasingly being used.

Which medium is used will depend on factors such as cost, capacity required, speed of recovery, how long the data needs to be kept, etc.

Volume

The availability of back-up media, importance of the data and how often certain data changes will dictate how much data is backed-up each time the process takes place. Ideally ever single item of data would be backed up all the time but this is not practical and can slow down business operations.

Schedule frequency

The back-up procedure will need to be completed at regular intervals and according to a fixed schedule. This schedule may be different for different parts of the system. For example, some transaction data may need to be backed up more or less at the same time it is processed. Other data – i.e. data which changes less often – may only require backing-up once a week. The policy will also need to specify how long backed-up data should be kept for. In some cases, backed-up data will be overwritten as soon as a new back-up file is created, in other cases it may be necessary to keep an archive file for a set period of time. The schedule will need to take these factors into account and establish set times for the backing-up of each part of the system.

Location

The policy will need to specify where the data should be kept. Those responsible for back-up procedures should always consider the worst case scenario – e.g. the main site, together with all hardware, software and data, being destroyed. Even small to medium-sized organisations should consider provision of a secure, fireproof safe in a secondary location for storing backed-up data. Larger organisations, especially those that rely on ICT systems for day-to-day operations, should consider backing-up to various locations, including a secondary server based on another site.

Testing that it works

The effectiveness of the back-up system should be regularly tested by undertaking recovery of backed-up data. In its simplest form this might mean accessing specified pieces of data at set intervals. Some large organisations may choose to undertake full-scale rehearsals of disaster recovery scenarios, i.e. where there has been a disastrous loss of data which needs to be recovered.

Personnel

The responsibility for organising, running and monitoring the back-up procedures cannot be left to chance. Various people in the organisation have to be given distinct responsibilities in regard to different aspects of the procedure. Account should also be taken of what happens if personnel are absent. There therefore needs to be a clearly established rota which also includes reference to 'cover for absence'.

Back-up: 2

Different back-up strategies

Standard data back-up procedure

This involves periodically copying data files on to a separate storage device. Typically, this would be performed at scheduled intervals, often overnight when servers are not in use, with data being copied on to the selected media. In the morning, the network manager would check a printout to ensure that the back-up had been successfully performed. The resulting tape is then stored off-site in a secure, fireproof safe.

The organisation can choose whether to complete a full back-up where all files are copied. This will make recovery easier but may take a long time if copied on to tape. Alternatively, it may perform an incremental back-up, i.e. all files are copied, for example, once a week. Then, each night, only those files that have been created or updated will be backed-up. This is a less time-consuming process but it makes recovery more complex.

One limitation of this strategy is that the back-up is never fully up to date. If, for example, there is a system crash in the late afternoon all the changes made during that day will be lost. This is because the back-up tape will only contain changes made up until the end of the previous day's business. This back-up strategy is therefore suitable only for small- to medium-sized organisations in which day-to-day transactions are not critical.

RAID system

RAID stands for 'Redundant Array of Inexpensive Discs'. There are various RAID systems but they all involve writing data to a series of magnetic discs. In one system, called 'disc mirroring', whatever data is written on to one hard drive is copied on to another at the same time. This means that if one hard drive is corrupted the user can switch straight to the mirrored version without any loss of data. In order to protect such a system from disaster scenarios (e.g. a fire), one of the disks to which the data is being written may be located in a different site.

Data is written simultaneously to two discs. If one device fails the other can take over

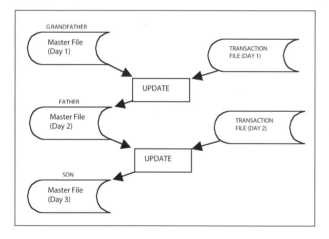

Grandfather–father–son

This approach involves 'generations' of master files. In the example shown, the 'grandfather' master file is merged with another file, the transaction file, which contains all the changes that need to be made to the master file. This results in a new master file, called the 'father' file. This, in turn, is merged with the next transaction file to create a new master file, the 'son' file. By keeping the master files and transaction files of three generations, the organisation will always be able to recover a lost or missing master file. This strategy is most appropriate for a batch processing system, i.e. where there is a regular updating of a master file using new transactions.

Backing-up program files

It is sometimes necessary to restore program files. If a system has been bought 'off the shelf' this might be achieved by using the CD ROM(s) on which the original program was stored (or a copy of the same). There are circumstances, however, where this not an appropriate strategy, e.g. where a program will need to be configured in a particular way before it can be installed on a system. If it is critical to restore such a program quickly, it will not be sufficient to rely on an original copy of the (unconfigured) version. Also, programs have changes made to them, e.g. an anti-virus security patch might be added on to the original version. For these reasons, it might be necessary to maintain an up-to-date copy of all program files so that they can quickly be restored. A grandfather–father–son strategy may be suitable for this task.

ICT and the organisation

Outsourcing

Sometimes it makes sense for an organisation to pay another company to take responsibility for providing one of its services or taking care of some of its day-to-day maintenance requirements. For example, many organisations do not employ their own security guards; instead, they pay a specialist security firm to provide that service. This is called 'outsourcing'. Some organisations choose to outsource some or all of their ICT provision. Such organisations argue that their core business is not ICT and they do not, therefore, possess sufficient expertise in this field. It therefore makes sound business sense to outsource the maintenance of a large, expensive and (possibly) troublesome ICT infrastructure to a specialist ICT company. The degree of outsourcing will vary from company to company: some may choose to outsource all of their ICT needs, from specialist application provision to basic maintenance; other companies may outsource only one aspect of their ICT provision, e.g. network security. When a significant amount of outsourcing is undertaken, the function of an ICT manager changes: instead of being primarily responsible for maintaining and developing systems within the organisation, their main function becomes one of liaison, i.e. finding and communicating with various third party providers. This is shown in the diagram below.

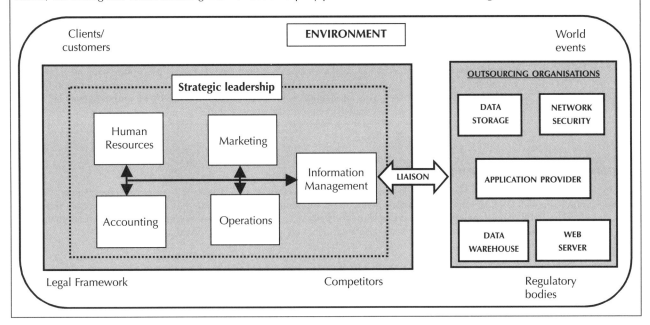

Application Service Providers

Application Service Providers (ASPs) are companies that deliver software via a networked connection (usually the Internet). There are various types of ASP: some simply sell downloadable software via the net, others allow users to 'lease' the applications, paying a fee according to how much use they make of the ASP. It has been argued that such an arrangement offers a model for distributing software to consumers. Businesses would only need to use those applications that suited them for as long as they needed them and they wouldn't have to worry about upgrades, as the applications would be kept up-to-date by the ASP. Some of the disadvantages of such a system are similar to the general disadvantages of outsourcing (see below) but, additionally, companies have to have robust broadband capabilities if they are going to run their business-critical applications online. The ASP's main concern is that their software might be 'stolen', i.e. downloaded on to the hard drive of the user during the time when it is being leased.

Advantages and disadvantages of outsourcing

ADVANTAGES	DISADVANTAGES
• The company can focus on its core business and not have to worry about acquiring and developing expertise in an area (i.e. ICT) that is not its main concern. This is particularly true of those companies whose core activities are not intrinsically wrapped up with ICT, e.g. manufacturing. • Space, and therefore money, can be saved by locating servers and mainframes off site. • If a company does not have sufficient in-house expertise, there is a strong possibility that it will make errors in the development of systems and the acquisition of ICT resources. These problems can be avoided if all ICT services are outsourced.	• There may be a concern about lack of control. The organisation has to rely on the expertise of the provider. This can be limiting if the provider doesn't understand the specific needs of the core business. • Security can be an issue. Although providers will promise robust security procedures they are still out of the hands of the organisation. This may make some organisations feel vulnerable. • The provision has to be reliable. Some businesses can fold if they lose their ICT capability, even temporarily. Providers will offer Service Level Agreements to guarantee service but these cannot always be counted on.

Standardisation

Organisations need to consider whether or not – or rather to what degree – they should impose defined standards on the ICT systems that are used. These standards can apply to platforms, versions, user interfaces, reports, file types, etc.

Typically an organisation will be divided into different functional areas. These areas will fulfil different functions in relation to the organisation's core activity. For example, a school will have a teaching staff, an administrative team, a catering staff, an examinations officer, a site supervision team, etc. A commercial organisation will be similarly divided, some of the typical functional specialisations being: Accounts, Marketing, Sales, Administration, Production, Human Resources, Legal, etc.

Each of these areas may use three different types of applications:

Shared	Some applications need to be shared because they are required for access to the organisation's resources. These might include front-end programs for a Database Management System or browsing software for the organisation's intranet. Such applications are therefore standardised across the organisation.
Common	Examples of common applications are generic off-the-shelf solutions such as the 'office suites' that give the user access to word-processing, spreadsheet and simple database facilities. Such applications are not necessarily standardised. For example, two departments may be running different versions of the same software.
Functionally specific	There are a number of applications that are designed to perform a specific task. Such applications may have been produced according to a user specification by a software provider or may have been bought 'off the shelf' and customised. The Marketing Department, for example, may have an application that analyses customer responses. This application will be unique to this department and may even be incompatible with systems running elsewhere in the organisation.

To standardise or not to standardise?

Actually, the question should really be: to what degree should an organisation standardise its ICT systems? Some degree of standardisation is inevitable: most large organisations need access to commonly held data and this requires a common 'front-end' access application. Should an organisation extend this standardisation to all its applications, enforcing the requirement that all users operate on the same platforms and run the same applications where possible and compatible ones where not?

The need for standardisation	The problems with standardisation
• The most obvious need for standardisation is where it enables the straightforward transfer of data. People within organisations need to share data and if this process is made more difficult by the use of different proprietary systems, there will be a corresponding loss of efficiency. That said, the problem can be overcome through the use of common file formats, e.g. .txt files.	• Depending on the nature of the organisation, different functional areas will have more or less autonomy. An autonomous department may wish to make its own choices about the applications it runs and the way it configures and customises them. Enforcing standardisation can create resentment at what will be seen as a challenge to autonomy.
• Standardisation can prevent compatibility problems when two applications have to interact with each other. In fact, the applications don't even have to interact with each other to cause problems. Sometimes, just the fact that they are open on the desktop at the same time can cause problems.	• Standardisation may force an organisation to sacrifice quality for conformity. For example, it may acquire an application not because it is the best for the task, but because it provides the best fit with the rest of the organisation's resources.
• Users sometimes have to transfer between departments and use different systems. Standardisation of user interfaces assists the familiarisation process, thus aiding efficiency.	• There can be all manner of logistical problems caused by enforcing widespread standardisation. For example, an organisation may be running an early version of an application on some of its machines and a later version on others. It wants to update all machines so that they are running the later version. But it is not just a matter of upgrading the software. The later version may require more memory resources and this may entail upgrading hardware as well as software.
• Standardisation of report formats can help to create a corporate identity and make the presentation of information more accessible, i.e. because it is in a format that the reader is used to.	

Employee code of conduct

What is a code of conduct?

An employee code of conduct is an undertaking that an employee makes to abide by certain rules and legislation, and work within specified guidelines. The code of conduct will explicitly set out what is expected of an employee, what will constitute an infringement of the policy and what the consequences of such an infringement will be. In relation to ICT, the code of conduct will focus on the manner in which the employee uses the organisation's information system resources. Depending on the nature of the organisation, the employee may be required formally to sign the code of conduct and accept it as part of their contractual obligation.

Problems a code of conduct is designed to prevent

A significant number of problems that beset information systems have as their root cause the accidental or deliberate misuse of resources by employees. By obliging employees to abide by a code of conduct it is hoped that some of these problems can be avoided. These problems include:

- Introduction of viruses into the system – for example, by downloading illicit software from the Internet or carelessly opening an email attachment.
- Distribution of material that is sexually offensive or likely to incite racial hatred. Infringements of this kind can leave the organisation vulnerable to legal action by employees who have been offended by the material.
- Extraction of data for illicit purposes. Activities such as this can make the organisation liable to prosecution under the terms of the Data Protection Act.
- Copying software for personal use or illicit sale, thus violating the terms of copyright laws and software licensing agreements.

Contents of a code of conduct

RESPONSIBILITIES

This section will set out what responsibilities the employee has to the organisation. This may include: respecting the rights of other users; abiding by current legislation – e.g. Data Protection Act, compliance with current licensing agreements, protecting systems from damage, etc.

PENALTIES FOR MISUSE

This section will define what the penalties are for various infringements of the code of conduct. It is important that each employee knows what the consequences of violating the code will be. Penalties may range from an informal warning by a line manager to dismissal and prosecution.

RESPECT OF RIGHTS

People have the right not to have details of their personal data discussed, and it should be stored in compliance with the Data Protection Act. Employees within a firm may wish to have details of salary, holiday entitlement and bonus kept confidential.

LEGISLATION

Details of the Data Protection Act, Computer Misuse Act, Health and Safety and Copyright laws will all be detailed and employees will be told what they must do to comply with them.

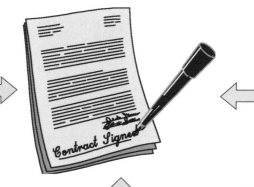

AUTHORISATION

This section will define the employee's authority to access different parts of the information systems. It will also identify what authority is required for different actions – e.g. if the employee wishes to change a database structure. If actions are performed without authority, the code will have been infringed.

ACCESS TO DATA

Employees should only have access to data they require. This means access levels are usually set up on the network to restrict what can be viewed, according to what the employee's job description specifies. This often varies according to seniority within a company.

SECURITY

This section will set out the terms of the security policy as it applies to each employee. It might include the definition of rules concerning: use and disclosure of passwords, personal use of email facilities, logging-on and logging-off procedures, routines for the transfer of information, use of storage devices from home, etc.

Corporate information security policy

Why is a policy required?

- All organisations that store data have a legal obligation under the terms of the Data Protection Act to ensure that their data is secure and its integrity is protected. In addition to this statutory obligation, most organisations rely on their information systems to function effectively, and cannot afford for those systems to be damaged, either accidentally or deliberately. In some instances, security of information is critical for a business and can mean the difference between success and bankruptcy.

- It is therefore important to ensure that all possible measures are taken to protect information systems from the threats to which they are vulnerable to. These threats, and some of the protective measures that can be employed against them, are set out on pages 000–00.

- It is not, however, sufficient to employ these measures in a haphazard manner. Organisations that rely on their information systems must develop policies that define all aspects of corporate security. This policy should have the support of senior management and be clearly understood by all organisational members.

- If a security policy is to be successful, it must have high status within the organisation. All organisational members should be aware of its requirements and of the consequences of breaching it. One way of ensuring that the policy has the requisite importance is to make it the responsibility of a senior manager who has an organisation-wide remit to ensure its successful implementation.

Factors to take into account when setting up a corporate security policy

Prevention of misuse

The essential purpose of a security policy is to prevent the misuse of information systems. This means accounting for both accidental misuse (caused by incompetence, poorly designed systems, etc.) and deliberate misuse (caused by criminal activity, malicious damage, etc.)

Detection

Computer systems are designed to hide their processes, so misuse can easily go undetected. One of the most powerful aids to a systematic approach to detection is the use of audit trails. Sophisticated software can be used to search file activities for irregularities.

Investigation

Once an irregularity has been identified, it must be investigated thoroughly. The security manager will need to discover the cause of the breach and, if necessary, invoke disciplinary procedures. It will also be necessary to review security in the wake of any such breach.

Procedures

Set procedures for accessing information should take into account the potential threats to systems. If followed, these procedures can contribute to system security. Systems can be designed so as to oblige users to follow set procedures, e.g. log-on procedures.

Staff responsibilities

All staff should be aware of what their individual responsibilities are with regard to security. Managers should be aware of their responsibilities within the area that they manage. Senior managers should take an overview of security arrangements.

Disciplinary procedures

If the policy is to have any force, there must be disciplinary consequences for breaches of security. All staff should be aware of these consequences. Disciplinary procedures should be clearly set out and should be in keeping with existing employment legislation.

Creating an awareness of a security policy

It is not sufficient for a security policy to exist in documentary form. Its prescriptions must be embedded within the everyday practice of the organisation. The best defence an organisation has against threats to its information systems is a workforce that is security conscious. There are various ways of encouraging security awareness in employees, including:

Induction programmes	When staff first join an organisation they are informed about all the security procedures that exist and what their own responsibilities will be.
Security bulletins	Employees are kept informed about changes to policy and specific security threats (e.g. a new virus) through printed and/or electronic bulletins.
Training programmes	Employees with specific areas of responsibility, e.g. department heads, may be sent on training courses to improve their awareness of security issues within their own area.
Visible reminders	Posters, on-screen messages, screen savers, etc. can all be used to reinforce the message that corporate security is important.
Contractual obligation	An element of an employee's contract of employment can be an undertaking to abide by the company's security policy.

The content of a corporate ICT security policy

General aspects

- A security policy is a formal and official document that sets down the rules, procedures and responsibilities associated with the protection of information systems, the hardware and software used to run them, and the data they contain.

- A typical policy would begin by setting out its aims, establishing its scope (i.e. who and what is covered by it) and defining the various responsibilities people within the organisation have.

- The rest of the document would cover in detail how different aspects of the policy should be implemented. Below are some of the areas that might be covered under different headings.

Specific areas of implementation

Personnel administration

The policy would:
- Set out procedures to be followed when new employees join the organisation: i.e. screening during the interview process, follow-up of references, checking police records, induction programmes, etc.
- Establish routines for the separation of duties and role rotation, thus avoiding a situation where one employee has sole access to certain parts of the system.
- Set out clearly established disciplinary procedures for breaches of security policy.
- Establish training programmes for employees in security procedures.
- Establish routines for distributing updated information on security issues to all employees, e.g. virus alerts.

Operational procedures

The policy would:
- Define procedures and responsibilities for the systematic backing-up of data and software. Where necessary, this would include the supervision of off-site storage.
- Define and establish responsibilities for the Disaster Recovery Programme, i.e. procedures to be followed in the case of a catastrophic system failure.
- Establish routines for auditing employee use of systems, including setting up software to run audit trails.
- Establish responsibility for maintaining awareness of current virus threats. Included in this would be the maintenance of virus protection software and rule definition regarding computer use, e.g. downloading files from the Internet.

Security policy

Physical security

The policy would:
- Outline procedures for controlling access to the building, including the use of security guards, locked doors, signing in procedures, alarms, etc.
- Outline procedures for controlling access to specific rooms within the building, e.g. through swipe cards, iris recognition, etc.
- Define security status and physical access rights for different employees.
- Outline procedures for protecting hardware, e.g. through the use of locking devices, alarms, etc.
- Define and monitor a stock control system that would ensure that all items of equipment were accounted for.
- Establish procedures for maintaining document security, e.g. secure filing, document access restrictions, etc.

System access

The policy would specify:
- Logging-on procedures, including use of passwords, different user access levels, call-back systems for remote access, etc.
- Define different access rights and user permissions for all employees, ensuring that access to critical information is restricted.
- Establish routines and responsibilities for maintaining network security, including procedures for remote access and the establishment of 'firewalls'.
- Define rules for personal use of systems, downloading information from the Internet, installing software, transferring data and use of storage devices.
- Establish procedures for encrypting data, including the use of private/public keys.

Protecting a network

Threats to systems

There is another critical aspect of networks that needs managing, and that is security. The strength of networks, their ability to allow easy communication between remotely located users, is also their weakness: i.e. they allow access to the 'wrong' people. A good example of network vulnerability is virus spreading. If an individual user infects a stand-alone machine with a virus, the problem remains isolated. In a network environment, the virus uses the existing connections to spread itself to all connected machines.

It is the paradox of networks that their greatest virtue is also their chief weakness. They allow users to connect to each other and beyond that, via the Internet, to an unbounded global network. This confers enormous benefits in terms of the sharing of resources, the efficient transfer of files and data, and access to remote sources of data. The same connectedness, however, also creates a point of vulnerability. The network is, to a determined hacker, the equivalent of a window to a burglar: a possible point of entry. Whether the network is the equivalent of a cracked window in a rotten frame or triple-glazed security glass in a fixed metal frame will depend on the security measures that the organisation employs.

The security threats that network administrators need to be aware of fall into three broad categories:

Non-malicious attacks The aim of the intruder is simply to break through the network's defences just to prove that they can. It is, as far as the hacker is concerned, a type of game where their skill is pitted against the security resources of the system. These attacks can, none the less, create a great deal of damage.

Malicious attacks For whatever reason, the intruder wishes the organisation ill. They want to cause as much damage as they can to the ICT systems. They may achieve this by causing crashes, introducing viruses or corrupting data.

Criminal activity The prime aim of the intruder is not to cause damage but to commit a criminal act, e.g. by altering data for financial gain or by stealing information that has commercial value.

Defending the network

FIREWALLS

A firewall is a security device designed to protect a network from intrusion via the Internet connection. It may consist of a dedicated computer running firewall software or a specific piece of hardware that looks very much like a router. Whatever form it takes, its primary function is to authenticate incoming messages and verify the legitimacy of users trying to enter the network via an Internet connection.

A typical firewall set-up comprises a separate network (sometimes referred to as a 'sandbox') that sits between the internal network and the connection to the Internet. The firewall then checks incoming packets of data against rules of authentication (which can be determined by the network administrator). Any data packet that fails the authentication test can then be discarded. Firewalls allow the network administrator to determine what data should and should not be let through.

PROXY SERVERS

A proxy server is a device that stops potential intruders from identifying the Internet Protocol (IP) address of an individual user making an Internet request. All requests go first to a proxy server, the server notes the IP address of the user making the request, then sends the request out to the Internet. When the file is returned, it goes first to the proxy server. The proxy server then sends it to the user that made the request. This means that the only IP address that has been made accessible is that of the proxy server. The IP address of the proxy server is not much use to a hacker, whereas an individual's IP address is.

Threats to data security

Why is data security important?

As organisations become increasingly dependent on their information systems, it becomes more important for the organisation to protect those systems and the integrity of the data they contain. There are serious consequences of failing to do this adequately, including:

Financial loss   This results from having to replace systems, compensate customers, restore missing or compromised data, etc.

Loss of reputation   Businesses who fail to protect adequately clients' details, or their own confidential business information, will lose the trust of those who might have dealings with them.

Legal consequences   The Data Protection Act requires organisations to ensure that the data they store on individuals is securely held. Failure to do so can result in legal action by the Data Protection Commissioner or compensation claims by data subjects.

Threats to data security

Internal source – non-deliberate

An organisation's employees may accidentally compromise data security or integrity:

- simple clerical errors made during the inputting/processing stages may affect the accuracy of the data;
- files may be accidentally erased or corrupted through misuse;
- internally produced software applications may be flawed, and may consequently damage data;
- email attachments containing viruses may be accidentally opened and the virus thus activated.
- Staff are inadequately trained to use the systems

Internal source – deliberate

Those responsible for ICT security need to be aware of the 'enemy within', i.e. employees with access to information systems who decide to act against the organisation. There are two main threats of this type:

- The disgruntled employee with a grudge against the company who may decide to use knowledge of the systems to cause damage.
- The employee who decides to defraud the organisation for financial gain, e.g. by creating non-existent orders and channelling the payments to themselves.

External source – non-deliberate

The main threats of this type are 'disasters'. These may be natural (floods, extreme weather conditions, earthquakes, volcanoes, etc.) or human/mechanical (plane crashes, power cuts/surges, fires, building collapse, etc.). Incidents like this have the potential to wipe out an organisation's information systems, destroying hardware and software and eradicating data. A less dramatic external, non-deliberate threat can occur when an organisation acquires software that has undiscovered 'bugs' in it. Such software can lead to data corruption or loss.

External source – deliberate

Threats of this type can take many forms, including:

- criminals wishing to defraud the organisation by accessing and amending financial data;
- viruses with the potential to corrupt or wipe out data;
- industrial espionage, i.e. rival organisations accessing confidential information in order to gain competitive advantage;
- actual theft of hardware/software, i.e. through breaking in;
- terrorist attack, e.g. bombing, arson, systems attack.

Risk analysis

The value of data to an organisation is only realised when it is lost. Many businesses who experience severe data loss fail to kick-start themselves and are unable to continue to trade. The organisation that plans for disaster and is ready for it is likely to stand more chance of recovery than those who don't. By carrying out a risk assessment, companies are showing that they appreciate the value of their data, and the ICT and personnel involved in maintaining its value.

Some examples of digital data that companies may find hard to replace if lost include:

- Customer account and contact details
- Supplier account and contact details
- Internal prices and discount values applied to products for various customers
- Staff details, i.e. payroll number, salary details and tax contributions paid
- Current turnover figures.

Identify each element of an information system

Someone needs to be responsible for documenting the detail about data that is held, hardware and software that is used for processing, and the personnel involved in using the ICT systems. The scope of documentation will vary from company to company, but from this point value can be placed on each element identified.

Place a value to the business on each element

A company must decide how valuable each element is to the organisation. It may decide that data comes first as very valuable, with hardware coming in last as less valuable. From this point priorities for protection can be budgeted.

Identify any potential threats to that element

The organisation must think about the threats that can affect its data, e.g. hackers, what could affect its hardware, e.g. natural disasters, what could affect its personnel, e.g. terrorist attack, and what can affect its software, e.g. viruses. When threats have been identified protective measures can be ascertained.

Make contingency/disaster recovery plan based on the result

This will outline what to do should disaster strike. Personnel will be charged with various tasks and actions in order to get data and systems back online and working as if the disaster never occurred.

Calculate an overall risk figure

This is where the values of all the elements are added together and used to demonstrate how important the security and protection of data is to those who provide the funding.

Put a value against each threat

A company needs to know how much it would cost to replace staff, software, hardware and data. Again, by working out a financial cost the priorities for protection can be more focussed.

Identify the likelihood of the threat occurring

How likely are staff to corrupt the data? What is the chance of a flood or fire, what is the chance or a hacker gaining access. These all need to be evaluated against the current protection in place. If a threat is very likely to happen and the data is very valuable, serious measures need to be in place to ensure it safety.

Disaster recovery management: 1

Organisations that rely heavily on their information systems to conduct their business need to prepare themselves for the failure of those systems. While they may have a number of procedures and resources in place to protect their systems from expected threats and small-scale system failures, they also have to be prepared for unexpected, large-scale system failures. This is referred to as disaster recovery management and is, as the name implies, a set of resources and procedures to cope with the aftermath of a disastrous breakdown of systems/loss of data. The aim of such a program is to minimise negative consequences.

Threats and consequences

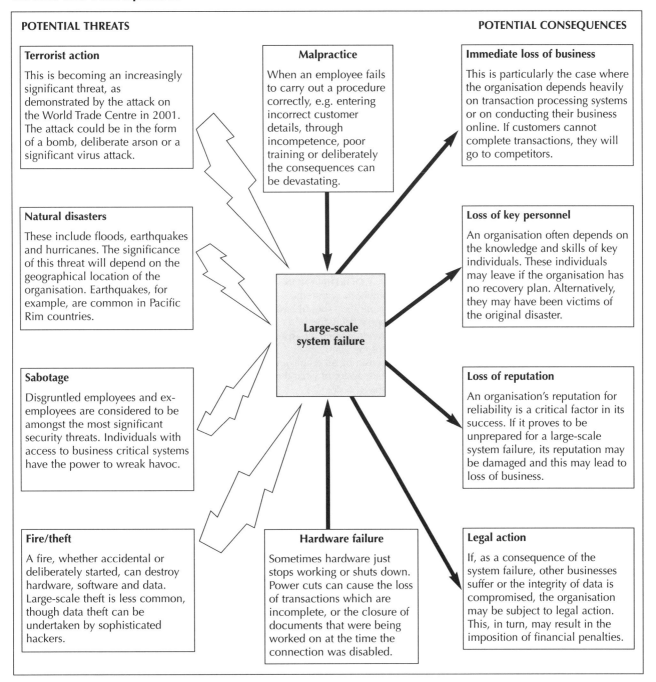

POTENTIAL THREATS

Terrorist action

This is becoming an increasingly significant threat, as demonstrated by the attack on the World Trade Centre in 2001. The attack could be in the form of a bomb, deliberate arson or a significant virus attack.

Natural disasters

These include floods, earthquakes and hurricanes. The significance of this threat will depend on the geographical location of the organisation. Earthquakes, for example, are common in Pacific Rim countries.

Sabotage

Disgruntled employees and ex-employees are considered to be amongst the most significant security threats. Individuals with access to business critical systems have the power to wreak havoc.

Fire/theft

A fire, whether accidental or deliberately started, can destroy hardware, software and data. Large-scale theft is less common, though data theft can be undertaken by sophisticated hackers.

Malpractice

When an employee fails to carry out a procedure correctly, e.g. entering incorrect customer details, through incompetence, poor training or deliberately the consequences can be devastating.

Hardware failure

Sometimes hardware just stops working or shuts down. Power cuts can cause the loss of transactions which are incomplete, or the closure of documents that were being worked on at the time the connection was disabled.

Large-scale system failure

POTENTIAL CONSEQUENCES

Immediate loss of business

This is particularly the case where the organisation depends heavily on transaction processing systems or on conducting their business online. If customers cannot complete transactions, they will go to competitors.

Loss of key personnel

An organisation often depends on the knowledge and skills of key individuals. These individuals may leave if the organisation has no recovery plan. Alternatively, they may have been victims of the original disaster.

Loss of reputation

An organisation's reputation for reliability is a critical factor in its success. If it proves to be unprepared for a large-scale system failure, its reputation may be damaged and this may lead to loss of business.

Legal action

If, as a consequence of the system failure, other businesses suffer or the integrity of data is compromised, the organisation may be subject to legal action. This, in turn, may result in the imposition of financial penalties.

Disaster recovery management: 2

Precautionary measures

- Some of the disasters described on page 140 are preventable. An awareness of potential threats combined with a comprehensive ICT security policy can minimise the risk of a disastrous system failure. For example, the threat of sabotage can be minimised by the implementation of strategies such as: secure password systems, clearly defined dismissal procedures, regular user audits, etc. In some cases the organisation must take precautionary measures that are specific to its geographical location. For example, organisations located in developing countries where power supplies are unreliable, must ensure that they have an uninterrupted power supply (UPS).

- Some disasters – fires, floods, terrorist outrages, etc. – are not preventable and may involve loss of software, hardware, data and even personnel. In order to be prepared for such instances it is necessary for an organisation to have a contingency plan, i.e. a well-established and organised routine that will enable the organisation to continue functioning following a disaster.

Elements of a contingency plan

PREMISES/FACILITIES

Some major disasters may involve extensive damage to or even destruction of the organisation's main premises. It may be necessary, therefore, to have a secondary site available for staff to move into. The site would be set up with all the facilities needed for the organisation to resume operations. A cheaper alternative option is to have a 'mutual lease' arrangement with another organisation.

PERSONNEL

Training Employees will need to know what their responsibilities are in the event of a disaster.
Counselling A disaster that involves loss of life may be traumatic for some employees and they may require support.
Role replacement Some employees may have been injured or even killed in a disaster. The plan will need to plan for all essential roles to be covered.

COORDINATION

Somebody within the organisation should have responsibility for:
- coordinating all aspects of the plan;
- ensuring all employees are aware of what they have to do;
- keeping the plan updated;
- testing the effectiveness of the plan using simulations or full-scale rehearsals.

DATA

Recovery of key data that may have been lost or damaged is a critical aspect of disaster recovery. Critical data should be backed-up and stored off site on a regular basis. If this has been managed successfully, restoration of data should be a straightforward matter. Even with back-ups, however, some data – e.g. that day's transactions – may have been lost and their source will need to be traced.

HARDWARE/SOFTWARE/COMMUNICATION

If a secondary site is part of the contingency plan, it must be equipped with sufficient hardware for the organisation to continue functioning. Communication links must be established and software must be available. It will help if an organisation doesn't locate all of its information systems in one place but distributes them across several locations, or outsources some of its processing or data storage.

Criteria for choosing a contingency plan

The scale and complexity of a contingency plan will depend in part on the results of a risk analysis such as that outlined on page 140. Additionally, the organisation will need to take into account the relative cost (in terms of time, money and personnel) involved in maintaining a contingency plan, and the relationship of that cost to the size of the organisation, the critical nature of its ICT systems, the likelihood of disaster, etc. For example, a multinational investment bank with many business critical systems may consider it cost-effective to maintain a secondary site; a small business with only a few systems may not be able to justify such a costly solution. There are organisations that offer a complete Disaster Recovery programme to businesses. Such a service may be expensive, but for a business that lacks the requisite expertise, it may be cost-effective.

Audit requirements

The process of auditing

- The purpose of an audit is to ensure that all procedures are being carried out effectively, accurately and lawfully. Traditionally, auditors would look through a company's account books and compare them to documentary evidence of transactions, e.g. invoices.
- If irregularities come to light, they are investigated. If it is discovered that they came about as a result of error, the auditor recommends changes to the system to improve accuracy. If they are the result of fraudulent activity, the auditor may pass evidence on to the police and recommend changes to the ICT security policy.
- Auditing may be an internal or external process. An internal audit may be commissioned by an organisation's management to ensure that their systems are working well and their resources are being well used. An external audit may be more concerned with whether or not the organisation's systems are operating within legal frameworks, e.g. the Data Protection Act. In some cases there are regulatory bodies that undertake this work. For example, some financial organisations have their systems audited by the Investment Management Regulatory Organisation (IMRO).

Auditing ICT systems

There are specific difficulties associated with auditing ICT-based systems:

- The auditor will not only need to be ICT literate but will have to understand the particularities of the organisation's ICT systems.
- ICT systems are designed to hide a lot of their processes and data is not always visible.
- Some systems do not, as a matter of course, maintain historical data.
- Transactions that are conducted electronically do not always produce a hard copy equivalent.
- Real-time and pseudo real-time systems pose particular problems: transactions are more difficult to trace and their accuracy more difficult to check.

Audit trails

In order to audit ICT systems it is usually necessary to utilise specifically designed software to run an audit trail. An audit trail is designed to track a particular aspect of the system in order to identify irregularities. There are different approaches to conducting audit trails, some or all of which may be used. These include:

- tracking a particular transaction from source to output;
- tracking changes to data, especially when applied to centralised data repositories;
- tracking when a system has been accessed and by whom;
- creating exception reports, i.e. looking for unusual instances of access to the system;
- using sampling techniques, e.g. randomly selecting transactions on a particular date.

Audit trail software is designed with the functionality to facilitate these and other auditing techniques.

Auditing a database

The diagram below illustrates one approach to auditing changes to a database:

Name	DOB	Position	Wage Rate
J Smith	12/03/74	Sales Man	10.75
K Brown	15/01/80	Sales Ast	5.60
M Tyler	23/08/78	Sales Ast	5.60

User Login	Date	Time	Field change	Old value	New value
BroK04	22/09/01	13.46	Wage Rate	5.60	6.70

The original database table, in this case a personnel file, contains some code that runs every time an action is performed on it. In this case a wage rate is updated.

The code updates another table with the time and date of the change, who made the change, and what change was made. The legitimacy of this change can then be checked.

Managing change

The consequences of change

The development of ICT systems in organisations often results in significant change. In fact, it has been argued that the introduction of ICT systems has, over the last 20 years, been the key change agent for many organisations. The speed of technological advancement in the field of ICT has meant that both the rate and extent of change has increased markedly over the last couple of decades. Change can take many different forms:

Skills required	New systems often require new skills. This is especially true of ICT systems, where employees may have to learn to navigate new on-screen forms, new keyed instructions, etc. This requires a continuous commitment to skills updating.
Organisational structure	New systems can create opportunities to change the structure of an organisation. For example, a more efficient method of communication may enable the dismantling of an unnecessary layer of management, thus making the organisation less top-heavy.
Work patterns	The introduction of new ICT systems can have an effect both on the hours that employees have to work and their work conditions. For example, a new system may require the monitoring of operations that take place 24 hours a day. Some work conditions may change for the better, e.g. by creating the possibility of teleworking. More dramatically, new systems can create a change both in the number and type of employees that are needed.
Internal procedures	A new system will involve changing the way that operations are carried out in an organisation. This will inevitably impact on employees: some may find that their work has been made easier (e.g. by being automated) whereas some may feel it has become more difficult (e.g. because they now have to perform tasks more quickly).

Fear of change

For many members of an organisation these changes can be a source of fear. They may fear that:

- they will lose their job because the new system will make their present role redundant;
- they will be relocated to another role, department or geographical location, thus causing upheaval and possible separation from friends and family;
- they will not be able to learn the skills required by the new system and they will be replaced by somebody that can;
- they will have to change their work patterns (their hours of work, for example) and this will have a negative impact on other aspects of their life;
- they will lose their current status and (possibly) the salary that goes with it as a consequence of organisational restructuring.

As a consequence of these fears some members of an organisation may be resistant to change. This resistance, if not taken seriously, can have a negative impact on an organisation's ability to change. Specifically in relation to ICT systems, it can determine the success/failure of the implementation process.

A model of successful change management

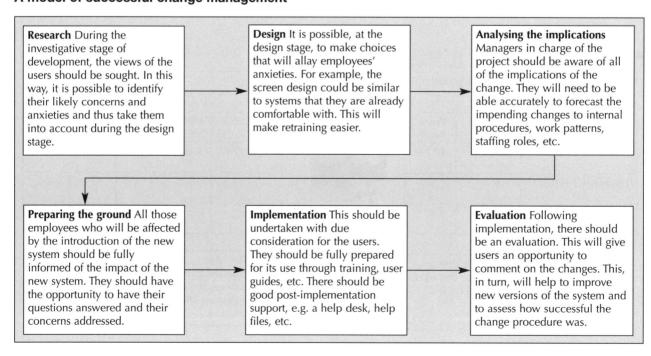

Research During the investigative stage of development, the views of the users should be sought. In this way, it is possible to identify their likely concerns and anxieties and thus take them into account during the design stage.

Design It is possible, at the design stage, to make choices that will allay employees' anxieties. For example, the screen design could be similar to systems that they are already comfortable with. This will make retraining easier.

Analysing the implications Managers in charge of the project should be aware of all of the implications of the change. They will need to be able accurately to forecast the impending changes to internal procedures, work patterns, staffing roles, etc.

Preparing the ground All those employees who will be affected by the introduction of the new system should be fully informed of the impact of the new system. They should have the opportunity to have their questions answered and their concerns addressed.

Implementation This should be undertaken with due consideration for the users. They should be fully prepared for its use through training, user guides, etc. There should be good post-implementation support, e.g. a help desk, help files, etc.

Evaluation Following implementation, there should be an evaluation. This will give users an opportunity to comment on the changes. This, in turn, will help to improve new versions of the system and to assess how successful the change procedure was.

Training: 1

The need for training

It is in an organisation's best interests to ensure that all of its employees are appropriately skilled for the jobs they have to do. This is partly achieved by employing people with the right skill set in the first place. However, job profiles change and new technologies are introduced, so these skill sets will need to be updated. Training in ICT is especially important because new technologies are emerging with increasing rapidity and an organisation cannot afford to be left behind. An organisation therefore needs to provide training for a number of reasons, including:

New staff The organisation will need to ensure that all new staff are proficient in the hardware and software they will be using. No matter how experienced new staff are, there will be specific features of an organisation's systems that they will need to be trained for.

New systems When a new system is implemented all users will need to be trained to use it and to understand its specific features. Inadequate training on a new system can lead to implementation failure.

Motivating staff Many employees see good training provision as characteristic of a good employer. Training develops an individual's skill set and this, in turn, enables them to seek promotion, either within the organisation or beyond it.

Improving efficiency A motivated, well-trained staff is an organisation's greatest asset. Effective, coordinated training provision will lead to improvements in efficiency as staff become more proficient in the tasks they perform and thus make fewer costly errors.

Different training for different levels

ICT training provision has to be effectively targeted. Employees operating at different levels within the organisation will have different training needs.

Senior managers Their contact is not likely to be at a user level. They are, however, required to understand how ICT contributes to the organisation's goals. They will also be making decisions about corporate information policy and allocation of resources to ICT. They are more likely to make effective decisions if they understand the latest developments in technology, and so their training should be in this area.

Middle managers Middle managers, such as Heads of Department, will play a significant role in the development of systems. They will have to define information needs, make tactical level decisions about resource allocation, plan the implementation of new systems, develop security policies, etc. They will therefore need to take an overview of how and why new systems are developed and how they impact on their specific area.

Users The form of training that end users need can be divided into two categories: skill-based and task-based. Skill-based training develops skills that can be applied in a variety of situations. For example, an employee may be trained in analysing figures using spreadsheets. This skill can then be employed in different contexts. Task-based training focuses on developing proficiency in an organisation-specific task. For example, a data entry clerk may require training in an organisation's procedures for batch processing.

Developing a corporate training policy

Many organisations view employee training as a key factor in their success. They therefore develop a corporate strategy for training, the elements of which are shown below.

Needs analysis The needs of users at different levels have to be identified. Account must be taken of users' current skills, their training history, their current job profile and their professional development (i.e. where their career is going).

Cost There are two main costs involved in training provision: the financial cost that may arise, e.g. from paying a training provider; and the time cost incurred when employees are not available for work because they are being trained.

Coordination

Availability Information related to training providers needs to be collated and the providers evaluated for cost and effectiveness. It may also be necessary to develop and/or evaluate in-house training provision.

Cost-benefit Training provision should be a good investment. For example, if the organisation pays for an employee to be trained, they want to be sure that the person's enhanced skill set will benefit the organisation and not just the employee.

Training: 2

Different approaches to training

Approach	Advantages	Weaknesses
Computer-based training This can take several forms. Some software packages provide step-through tutorials, showing the user how to work with the application. Some, more complex, online providers allow for some user interaction – e.g. the user can email specific questions that will then be answered.	• There are some cost implications, but provision of computer-based training is significantly cheaper than sending employees on training courses. • It can be undertaken at the employee's own pace; modules that are not understood can be re-visited when necessary. • It is flexible – i.e. it can be undertaken whenever the employee has spare time and without them having to leave the office. It can even be made available on a home PC. • The provision is standardised, so all the employees will learn the same material.	• Some people do not respond well to this method of learning. They need the human presence, peer support, and teacher–student interaction of a classroom environment. • There may not be a computer-based training program available for an organisation-specific application. If the organisation then has to develop its own software, this will incur additional costs.
Instructor-led courses These may be based in-house or with a training provider. They involve a trainer or trainers leading the class and providing computer and text-based materials.	• Many people learn best in a communal, interactive environment such as this. They have the chance to ask questions, to talk to fellow students and to ask for individual support. • The collaborative atmosphere of a classroom can enhance employees' team-working skills. • An effective teacher can respond flexibly to the needs of individual students. So, if one approach to explaining a topic is ineffective, the teacher can try another.	• Training courses run by providers are expensive and less prosperous organisations may not be able to afford them. An alternative approach is to develop an in-house facility, but this too can incur costs. • The quality of the training providers can vary considerably. Some have effective teachers as leaders, others are run by trainers who have the requisite technical knowledge, but do not know how to teach effectively. • Training courses are not flexible. They are run at fixed times and at fixed locations.
Self-taught using books, videos, etc. Some organisations do not have the resources and/or inclination to provide effective training for their employees. In such instances, employees may decide they want to develop their skill set by teaching themselves. There are books, CDs and videos on the market that can support this process.	• This approach is infinitely flexible. The individual can fit their learning time into their own schedule and can learn in the appropriate environment (at work in a lunch break, in a library, at home, etc.). • They are not reliant on or answerable to their employers in relation to what they learn. They can develop the skill set that will be of most use to them in terms of furthering their career.	• The individual can feel isolated. They are learning on their own, and though this may suit some people, many prefer to have interaction with other learners and people with more experience of the specific area. • They must bear the cost of resources themselves. Though these need not be excessive, some of the books can be expensive.

Boot camp

Boot camp training involves the employee leaving work for an intensive, specialised, rapid-fire, hands-on training which can run over several days. A specialist will lead the course and the learners will be immersed in whatever it is they are supposed to be studying. This method is often very expensive but regular courses are run and are used when new technology needs to be learnt and utilised in the very near future. The person sent on the training is likely to have some familiarity in the area the boot camp will be covering.

Cascade training

This is a very cost-effective method of training many people. An employee will have been instructed to learn something. In turn they will come back to the organisation and teach a smaller group what they have gained. This smaller group will go deeper into the organisation and teach more small groups until everybody who needs to be trained has had some form of contact with the new material. This method is potentially hazardous if people with minimal communication skills are initially sent on courses. They may not have the interpersonal skills to convey the message on their return.

In-house versus training provider

• Although training providers can be expensive, maintaining an in-house facility can be even more so. Trainers need to be employed, dedicated space has to be found and resources provided.
• The organisation can keep more control of the training process. They can ensure the quality of the trainers they use, organise schedules to suit their own needs, provide standardised resources so that all employees receive the same information, and develop courses that are tailored to their specific needs.
• Which approach an organisation takes will depend on what financial resources they have available for training and the extent and specific nature of their training needs. In-house provision is most appealing to organisations that have constant, year-round training needs that may not be provided for by commercial providers.

User support: 1

The need for user support

One of the key factors in the success or failure of information systems is the post-implementation user support. Users want to feel confident about using the system, but if they run into problems they want to be able to solve them quickly. User support can be provided in a number of ways. Large organisations may have their own help desk or they may buy in a help desk service from an outside provider. The way in which help desks work is discussed in more detail on page 000. However, help desks are not always an appropriate form of user support and smaller, less resourced firms may need to depend on alternative methods.

Different methods of user support

Existing user base

Experienced users can be a valuable source of information and advice. This can be accessed informally or through more formal training sessions. The support is free and based within the organisation. Some users, however, will be unable (or unwilling) to explain something clearly to a less experienced user. Also, this process may be impractical in a busy working environment.

Help files

Almost all applications, whether off the shelf or bespoke, provide help files that are accessible to the user. These provide a search engine or index so that pages covering different topics can be accessed. Some provide step-by-step multi-media tutorials. The quality of help files will vary from application to application and some fail to address the needs of the less experienced user.

Internet

There are a number of resources on the Internet that provide advice for the user. There are official websites run by software manufacturers with email access for users to send in their queries. Unofficial sites created by users can also provide the answers to FAQs (Frequently Asked Questions). There are also sites which store archived articles on different applications.

Support articles

There are many magazines that are aimed at users. Articles in these magazines will vary in their level of complexity. Some are aimed at very experienced users who may be considering customising generic applications. Other articles are aimed at the novice user and demonstrate simple procedures in a step-by-step format.

Documentation

Various user guides are available for most applications. These might be provided by the manufacturer or they may be produced by a commercial publisher. In the case of popular applications, there are many publications available. Users need to select the publication that is suited to their level of need: some documentation is aimed at developers, some at novice users.

Criteria for selecting user support

When an organisation is making decisions about what form of support is required, the following criteria should be taken into account.

COST — Some of the approaches cited above will cost little or nothing (e.g. help files), others will incur considerable cost to the organisation (e.g. a help desk).

USER EXPERIENCE — Users will require different types of support. The more experienced user will need access to material pitched at a sufficiently complex level; novice users will need to have things explained simply and clearly.

RESOURCES — Some of the approaches to user support will require resources. For example, dedicated websites will require good Internet access.

URGENCY — Users working on business-critical systems will need to have their problems answered more quickly than those working on less critical systems.

ENVIRONMENT — Some working environments lend themselves to the exchange of ideas between users. In other environments users may be isolated from one another.

User support: 2

What is a help desk?

In many large organisations user support is provided by a help desk. This can take two forms:

In-house The help desk is run by employees of the organisation, usually members of the technology department. This is especially the case where an organisation develops its own software. In this instance the team that developed the system is also likely to be responsible for post-implementation support.

Outsourced The organisation buys in the services of an organisation that specialises in supporting users. Alternatively, many organisations that develop software solutions also offer a user support service.

A help desk is a service that supports users by answering their questions and advising them on how to solve the problems they face with software, hardware, networks, etc. Users can phone or email the help desk with their enquiries and an operator will provide them with answers, solutions, advice, etc. When help desks work well, they provide an invaluable service. There are, however, some difficulties associated with running help desks. These include:

- Providing advice that is appropriate for different user levels. An experienced user may require some in-depth technical advice whereas a novice user will need a response at a more basic level.
- Ensuring the help desk has the expertise to answer the majority of questions they are asked. A help desk that is incapable of providing useful advice will soon lose the confidence of the users.
- Dealing with the anger and frustration of users whose work is being held up by inadequate or non-user-friendly applications.
- Managing the flow of requests. A telephone-based service, if swamped with requests, may be obliged to put users on hold, thus increasing their frustration.

There are software applications that are dedicated to supporting help desks. These applications typically contain a database with descriptions of problems and appropriate solutions. These can be queried by the help desk operator and relayed to the user. New problems, and solutions, can be added to the database as they occur. The system also allows the help desk to log details of the user so they can analyse problem 'histories'. Some help desk software allows the operator to view and even take control of a particular user's desktop in order to solve the problem.

Logging calls

Calls to help desks should be logged. A computerised system is used to log specified details about the call, including:

- a user identification code – this can be used to identify user, department, terminal, organisation, etc. and can also be used to establish the legitimacy of the call.
- the date and time of call.
- the software/hardware involved.
- the nature of the enquiry.
- the response of the help desk (i.e. whether the problem was sorted out immediately or dealt with in some other way).

This logged information can be stored in a database. It can then be used to analyse the frequency of particular problems, which, in turn, can help to improve the quality of service. The information can also be used by the help desk team to demonstrate its efficiency in solving problems or, conversely, its need for greater resources.

Evaluating help desk service

An organisation will need to evaluate the effectiveness of a help desk, whether it is one they are providing themselves or one they are paying for. The following criteria may be used:

Speed	How quickly the users' phone calls are answered or their emails responded to.
Helpfulness	How clearly the operator explains the solution, their general level of politeness, etc.
Frequency of requests	The number of requests for help received and the proportion of them where successful assistance was given.
User satisfaction	How happy the users are with the service, whether or not they would be willing to recommend the service to others, etc.

Global positioning systems (GPS)

What is GPS?

GPS is a system developed by the American military in the 1970s and the 1980s. It comprises 24 satellites positioned 11 000 miles above the Earth in geosynchronous orbit, which means that, relative to the Earth and each other, they maintain a constant position. They are distributed such that, at any one time, at least four are visible from any point on Earth. The satellites send out constant signals on predetermined frequencies. These signals can be captured by any GPS-enabled device and used to determine the exact location (in some cases with a precision level of a few centimetres) of the receiver. In recent years the military has made the technology commercially available and it has thus been used for a wide range of applications.

How does GPS work?

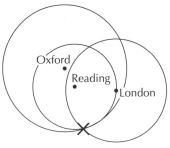

Using the principle of triangulation, GPS technology allows you to identify your precise geographical location if you know your distance from three different points. If, for example, you know that you are 50 miles from London, you also know that you must be at one point on the perimeter of a circle with a 50-mile radius.

If you know that you are also 60 miles from Oxford, you must be located at one of two points, i.e. the two points where the circles intersect.

Finally, if you know that you are 25 miles from Reading, you can identify exactly where you are, i.e. the point where all three circles intersect.

GPS uses satellite transmission to identify the three points required for triangulation, plus a fourth satellite to calculate altitude. The transmissions are picked up by a GPS device, which uses the data to calculate the longitude and latitude of its position and then applies that data to stored map data to display the result to the user.

WHAT APPLICATIONS ARE THERE FOR GPS?

GPS-enabled devices are found in a wide variety of applications:

- Travellers who are exploring remote areas can use them to identify their precise location and transmit this information to others if they find themselves in difficulty.
- Car manufacturers offer 'SatNav' facilities so that drivers can see where they are by combining GPS data with pre-loaded map-based information. The same system can be used as a security device to track stolen vehicles.
- Farmers in America have begun to use driverless tractors. These utilise GPS data in combination with pre-programmed route information and can be used to used to cover predefined areas.
- Delivery firms can use GPS to track the location and speed of any one driver.
- It has been suggested that GPS technology could be used to monitor drivers on British roads. The resulting data would then be used to determine what level of road tax an individual driver should pay.
- They are used to replace terrestrial systems for ships at sea. They can also calculate speed and distance covered.

Rapid Application Development

What is Rapid Application Development?

This is the act of producing software over a short period of time. Rapid Application Development (RAD) is a method which is suitable under certain conditions and far from ideal under others.

By deploying rapid application development the needs of the user can be met while they are still valid. The traditional structured route of the software development life cycle can be a long process and may result in the final program being obsolete before it has even been fully tested and ready for commercial use.

The following are the conditions likely to support RAD:

- When the business objectives are well defined and narrow.

- When the system requested is required to analyse data that already exists.

- When the decision-making process can be undertaken quickly in an ad-hoc fashion and is not hindered by layers of management.

- When the assigned personal numbers less than six.

- Much of the key hardware, software and technical network requirements are readily available.

RAD is not suitable under the following conditions:

- When the business objectives are confused, unclear and broad.

- When complex and multiple sets of data are to be collected, organised and structured.

- When many people are involved in various groups dealing with inter-related elements of a project.

- When decisions need to be taken and approved quickly.

- When the purchasing of new specialist hardware is required and technical alterations to the network are required.

The RAD method aims to demonstrate results as early as possible. User interface design, instruction manuals and lengthy testing are often not part of the process. Realistic data will be run through the system to ensure the application performs the task that has been requested but it will not be tested to the point of destruction. The process is made possible by using existing code and knowledge or by adding onto previously developed systems. Enhancements and more specialist maintenance is added to the prototype which provides more flexibility within the system and means that it can be quickly adapted to suit current business requirements.

Emerging technologies: 1

The next two pages considers some examples of emerging technologies through the use of ICT.

Touch screen
The act of using a screen or special sensory pad to select options and drive software is becoming more widespread. More imaginative uses of such applications are being introduced almost on a daily basis enabling users with minimal IT expertise, or experience, to use software to assist with learning, shopping, booking holidays or hiring cars. Touch screen applications limit input to accept few, or many pre-programmed operations, which has the advantage of reducing the entry of erroneous data and increasing the likelihood of accurate data being entered.

Uses of touch screen technology
Trigger cameras on rifles
Should a soldier lose his rifle during a conflict technology has been used to ensure that his, or her, own weapon cannot be turned against them. The trigger is specially configured to only allow the weapon to fire provided the user can activate the weapon with their finger print.
Such weapons can also be used to provide live video feed through a camera attached to the rifle site. This allows the soldier to hold the rifle around a corner and film, or see, what is there without putting their own body in the line of fire. The images are transferred to a secure location and details are passed to the soldier via a digital headset receiving audio. The video option is also switched on, or off, via the trigger which means soldiers need to take care when setting up their weapons to avoid filming rather than shooting or vice-versa.

Learning packages and communication devices
People learn in different ways and systems are being developed which allow learners to interact with software via the screen thereby eradicating the need for keyboards. Young children who are learning to spell can drag and drop images and icons using their hands rather than a mouse. Faced with such technology it is only a matter of time before laptops will be sold without keyboards and units will be folded away and carried around in pockets. The need to type could become a thing of the past. Most modern systems already include a screen keyboard operated by a mouse and it doesn't take a great leap of imagination to replace the mouse, upgrade the screen and utilise touch screen capabilities. The ability to input text quickly and accurately could speed up and enhance the quality of many business operations. Screens will be pulled up featuring images, perhaps of colleagues, which automatically display contact methods like phone or email address. By pushing the phone number the system will dial the number allowing communication through the required peripherals. Alternatively a simple tap on the email address could bring up the software to send emails and the on screen keyboard or voice recognition will be used to compose the message.
The number of uses for touch screen technology is endless. Systems are being simplified to allow more users access to them often for capital gain, security or because it could improve the quality of life for someone. Just about any process could benefit including school registration systems, online shopping, searching dynamic software like Google Earth, locating directions and instructions or simply downloading a recipe from the Internet. Potentially touch screen technology could infiltrate the automobile industry beyond the dashboard technology such as satellite navigation to actually being the medium for driving the car.
The impact of data is enhanced when it is combined with other types of data. The same is true with technology. Combining modern elements of technology, such as touch screen with voice recognition, will revolutionise the IT industry and further imbed itself into the lives of employees and home users. The way people work and pursue leisure activities will be governed by the available technology and its ability to appeal to the mass market and those who may have struggled with more cumbersome systems.

Emerging technologies: 2

Voice recognition

In some circles this technology was earmarked as the link between novice and expert users. The ability to verbally command computer systems has obvious attractions in that complex commands do not need to be learned and can be neatly packaged into one simple word or phrase. However, the ability for such technology to succeed is dependant on several key factors which often have to be present.

- The software has to be trained to respond to the voice which is giving the commands. This can take several hours which many users are not keen to sign over. Packages which have reduced the training time often yield poor input as phrases and words are incorrectly displayed or react to.

- A system which has been set up successfully and runs satisfactorily will still only respond to users who have entered verbal commands previously. Therefore, if a new user replaces an existing one the system will not respond as it should until the new user has had their verbal details accepted.

- It is crucial that the commands entered are clear and that background noise is reduced. Busy working environments, where many people work in close proximity, may be necessary for normal business functions but is not suitable, because of the noise pollution, for using voice driven technology. The same issue applies when such a system is to be used in a heavy manufacturing environment. The system will struggle to distinguish between the intended commands and the background noise and will produce garbage.

- The system will expect the data to be entered in the same format as that which was entered when the initial commands were programmed in. In some cases the tone, pitch and speed of the speaker must always be the same when using the system otherwise it will get confused. Changes to the voice (for example, stress or illness) will also cause the system to return incorrect responses.

- Computer systems are not able to distinguish the meaning of certain words which have two or three meanings. Words like 'their' and 'there', 'too', 'to' and 'two', 'cheap' and 'cheep', 'lion' and 'lying' are hard for systems to put into context or return the correct version of the desired word.

As a technology voice recognition is still developing to a reliable level but the issues detailed above will still remain. Some areas which have attempted, with some degree of success, to use voice driven technology include:

Call centers

Some call centers have installed systems, which ask questions of the caller with the intention of directing the call to the most appropriate operator, for example the caller may be asked to repeat a word from a list read out. The system will match the word to the most likely response which may lead to another request. Such systems are fine for one word answers but there can be problems with regional accents and longer commands like dates, account numbers or street names, especially if they are spoken very quickly.

Car manufacturers

In some cars efforts have been made to introduce voice technology to operate the controls on the radio and satellite navigation systems. It would take real confidence to solely rely on the system to take you to your destination but errors with radio tuning would be less drastic.

Dictation

Routine tasks can be undertaken quite well and dictating notes is a further use. Should the notes contain an error it is not a particular problem but anyone producing text for public viewing would be extremely brave to publish the work before undertaking some extensive editing and proof reading. The potential for verbally recorded diaries, the taking of course notes and those flashes of inspiration is a reality.

Total connectivity

More and more technology is being developed for personal, as well as commercial, use. With this in mind new system development must take into consideration compatibility issues. Currently audio players only play certain file types and the same limitations exist with motion picture media and other interactive products. The gap between what can be viewed, played or heard on a particular system will inevitably close. The alternative will be a reduction in competition and limited choice for consumers.

Systems that can talk to each other mean consumers need to buy less hardware and only upgrade when the technology becomes obsolete and superseded by better, more powerful, options. The increased development, deployment and use of wireless technology, such as blue tooth, allows (for example) commuters to access the Internet from locations often thought difficult to achieve. Faster connections between hardware means data and information can flow with less obstacles and allowing users to take advantage of systems via simplified user interfaces.

Radio frequency identification (RFID) is incredibly small technology which identifies whatever it is built into. Clothing with RFID tags can be read by washing machines with processors built in, which collect the garment details and then perform the most appropriate wash to ensure the garment is cleaned at the most appropriate time and temperature. Other household appliances can be labeled and processors around the home can read them at will. The potential for the use of RFID technology is not to be understated. Shopping trolleys loaded with groceries can be read and a bill produced in seconds; this would greatly reduce the time spent queuing. The payment method (debit card) could be read by processors at the shop exit and the correct deduction taken from the buyers account without even stopping.

Stolen vehicles could be tracked quickly as they travel past readers designED to read the RFID built into cars. More advanced technology will be able to read RFID tags, access a huge database and determine what they are looking at and, maybe, even how to operate it. By taking advantage of wireless technology a link to the Internet could be requested if its internal database didn't recognise a RFID.

It could be possible that the world would desire to enhance connectivity and bring the planets digital resources together so that they can be accessed by those who need it, and those who want it whenever and wherever they wish. Classrooms and offices would become wireless making most hardware portable. No lengthy set up and installations will be required other than opening the packaging and switching on. Systems would freely transfer data between each other and deliver crucial details in a timely fashion to those that would greatly benefit. For example satellites tracking tectonic plate movement or monitoring hazardous weather conditions should be able to send emergency notices to those likely to feel the full brunt of the damage to come. With good information escape and evacuation plans can be carried out with less panic.

The limitation of the use of ICT is in the hands of those who are prepared to think up new and creative uses for it, accept the dynamic nature of its capabilities and are willing to fund the next great advancement.

Practice questions

Systems

1 Using an example, explain what is meant by each of the following elements of an information technology system:
- input
- process
- output
- feedback

2 Describe three capabilities that computer-based systems have, that give them an advantage over non computer-based systems.

3 There are regular reports in the papers of critical, computer-based systems failing spectacularly. Describe three factors might lead to such a failure.

4 Identify three distinct ways in which medical health providers might benefit from deploying ICT systems.

5 Explain two of the benefits that have been expressed about the use of ICT systems in education.

6 ICT systems have transformed the way in which business is done, both at a national and a global level. Describe three ways in which ICT has supported this transformation.

7 List five different ways in which ICT has found its way into people's homes.

The nature of information

8 Using appropriate examples, explain clearly the difference between data, knowledge and information.

9 "Information adds value but incurs cost." Using appropriate examples, identify three ways in which information can add value to an organisation and three ways in which the production of that information incurs costs.

10 "Good-quality information is a prerequisite of good-quality decision-making." Identify five characteristics of good quality information.

11 Identify 2 negative consequences for an organisation of using poor quality information.

12 Using an appropriate example, explain what is meant by:
- internal and external information
- quantitative and qualitative information
- disaggregated and aggregated information.

Data: collection and processing

13 Using a appropriate examples, explain the difference between the direct and indirect collection of data.

14 Identify three different methods that may be used for inputting data into a computer system and describe one advantage and one disadvantage of each method.

15 "The quality of information is dependent on the data it is derived

from." Describe 2 problems that can occur at the data capture stage that might have a negative effect on the information produced.

16 Using an appropriate example, describe the stages involved in capturing and inputting data so that it is ready for processing.

17 Identify two reasons why it may be necessary and/or desirable to encode information before it is inputted.

18 Describe the issues associated with the encoding of value judgements.

19 Validation routines are used to improve the quality of data input. Identify three distinct types of validation routines that might be used and explain what type of errors they are designed to trap.

20 Using an appropriate example, explain the difference between validation and verification.

21 "Just because a piece of data has been accepted as valid does not mean that it is accurate." Explain, using an appropriate example, what is meant by this statement.

22 Explain fully two different methods that might be used to import an image into a document.

23 A user has created a file on their home PC but when they try to open their file on their office workstation it won't load. Explain (a) what the problem might be and (b) what might be done to solve the problem.

24 Identify two advantages and two disadvantages of using an integrated package.

25 Explain why there is an increasing need to develop effective file compression techniques. Describe one compression technique that can be used.

Computer hardware

26 For each of the following input devices: (a) describe how it works; (b)

identify one advantage and one disadvantage of using it and (c) identify an appropriate context for its use.
- bar code reader
- magnetic strip
- optical mark reader
- touch screen

27 What factors should an organisation/individual take into account when making a decision about acquiring a printer?

28 Describe two different types of printer that are currently available and explain the advantages and limitations of each.

29 Describe two different monitor types that are currently available and explain the advantages and limitations of each.

30 For each of the following secondary storage devices (a) describe its physical characteristics; (b) Describe what it is most likely to be used for and (c) comment on its general storage capacity :
- USB key
- digital tape
- external hard drive

31 Explain briefly the role of the CPU in a computer-based system.

32 Explain clearly the difference between Read Only Memory (ROM) and Random Access Memory (RAM).

Computer software

33 Explain clearly the difference between generic software, specific task software and bespoke software.

34 Describe five features that are desirable in any software package.

35 When an organisation wants to acquire a new software package it has a number of options it can take. Describe what is involved in any two of these options, identifying the strengths and weaknesses of each.

36 Describe the step-by-step process an organisation would undertake when choosing a software solution.

37 Identify four criteria that would be used to make a decision about which software solution to choose and explain the importance of each of these criteria.

38 Describe four features that you would expect to find in a standard word-processing package.

39 Explain how mail-merge works and in what context it might be used.

40 Identify four advantages of using a spreadsheet package over a 'paper and pen' system for processing accounts.

41 Identify three advantages of using presentation software over non-computer- based methods for giving presentations.

42 Identify three functions you would expect to find in a presentation software program.

43 Identify and explain three typical features of most graphics packages.

44 What are the advantages of using a CAD system over a non-computerised design system?

45 What additional resource demands do graphic programs make?

46 What is meant by computer modelling?

47 Explain how Global Positioning Systems work.

48 Describe the main function of web browsing software in helping the user access the World Wide Web.

49 What functionality would you expect to find in a program that helped users create their own websites?

50 Explain the difference between systems software and application software.

51 Identify, and explain the importance of, three key functions of a computer's operating system.

52 Apart from the operating system, identify three other types of systems software that might be found on a standard computer.

\

Databases

53 Identify two different types of organisation that might use databases, explaining how these might help to make those organisations more efficient.

54 What problems, relating to data redundancy and data integrity, tend to occur with flat-file databases?

55 Identify the key features of a relational database.

56 Identify three different data types that might be used in a database and, in each case, give an example of the type of data it might be used for.

57 The development of databases often involves two processes: entity relationship modelling and normalisation. Explain what is meant by each of these two processes and what important function they serve.

58 Explain what is meant by a database management system.

59 What are the relative advantages and disadvantages of a database management system for an organisation?

60 What are the advantages to the user of working with a client–server database?

61 Identify four key functions of a database administrator.

62 In addition to the usual security issues, what security concerns are particular to database management systems?

63 Explain what is meant by a distributed database system.

Networks and communication systems

64 The users in a company move from working in a stand-alone environment to a networked one. Identify two changes they would notice when they worked on their computers.

65 Identify two key differences between a Local Area Network and a Wide Area Network.

66 Identify four decisions that will have to be taken into account when setting up a network from scratch.

67 In relation to computer networks, describe the function of the following components:
  • network interface card
  • firewall
  • network operating system
  • hub
  • bridge
  • gateway

68 Explain the difference between a client–server and a peer-to-peer network strategy, stating the advantages of one system over the other.

69 Explain the difference between a Star and a Bus network.

70 Identify four functions that a network administrator would be expected to undertake.

71 Describe three security issues that affect networks and the protective measures that can be implemented by a network administrator.

72 Explain what is meant by a protocol and, by using examples, explain why they have been so important in the development of ICT.

73 Explain, with reference to examples, the difference between de facto and de jure standards.

74 The use of mobile wireless devices is on the increase. What are some of the issues associated with the introduction of such devices?

The Internet

75 The Internet has had a revolutionary impact in many areas of human life. Describe four ways in which the Internet has affected the way people live and work.

76 Outline the arguments surrounding the issue of censorship as it applies to the Internet.

77 Describe step-by-step the process involved when a computer accesses a website via the World Wide Web.

78 Identify three ways in which business has been able to utilise the facilities offered by the Internet.

79 What are the relative advantages and disadvantages of using e-mail over other forms of communication, i.e. letters, fax, telephone, etc?

80 Explain the process of using a search engines to help the user access information on the World Wide Web.

81 Identify three different ways that users can connect to the Internet. For each method, state the advantages to the user and the possible drawbacks.

82 Explain what is meant by the following terms:
  • hypertext
  • IP address
  • HTML
  • router
  • cookies

Human–computer interfaces

83 Describe four elements you would expect to find in a well-designed HCI.

84 Describe three of the psychological factors that designers should take into account when designing an HCI.

85 What are the advantages and disadvantages of a speech recognition system over other methods of data input?

86 Identify four ways in which a user might customise the user interface of an application.

ICT in the workplace

87 Describe two different roles that an ICT professional might take on.

88 Apart from their computer skills, what personal qualities is it advantageous for an ICT professional to possess? For each quality you describe, explain why it is useful.

89 What is the function of an employee code of conduct?

90 Not all types of employment are suitable for teleworking. Describe some of the conditions that are necessary for this method of working to take place.

91 Identify one advantage and one disadvantage of teleworking for (a) the organisation and (b) the individual worker.

92 Explain what is involved in video-conferencing and what resources an organisation needs to facilitate it.

93 Identify one advantage and one disadvantage of using video-conferencing as a way of facilitating meetings between members of an organisation.

94 Describe three health hazards that employees working with computers need to be aware of.

95 Describe four steps that an organisation can take to ensure that it complies with Health and Safety legislation.

96 Describe two moral/ethical problems that an ICT professional might face.

97 Faced with an ethical problem, what approach might an ICT professional take to deal with it?

Security, privacy and the law

98 "Computers have provided criminals with new tools to commit old crimes." Describe two forms of computer crime that support this statement.

99 Describe two ways in which law enforcement agencies have used ICT to combat various forms of criminal activity.

100 Explain how the following can be used to improve the security of ICT systems:
- encryption
- firewalls
- virus checkers
- staff training
- system access restrictions

101 Describe one threat to the security of ICT systems that might come from within an organisation and one that might come from outside it.

102 Describe four different aspects of security you would expect to find in a corporate information security policy.

103 Identify three measures an organisation can employ to ensure that its staff remain aware of security issues that might affect them.

104 Describe two issues relating to the privacy of the individual user that have arisen as a result of developments in ICT.

105 Identify three measures that an individual user can take to ensure the privacy of their communications.

106 Describe the step-by-step process involved in public key encryption.

107 Describe in detail four factors that should be taken into account when an organisation is developing a backup policy.

108 What are the particular issues associated with backing up program files?

109 Describe an appropriate back-up strategy for a medium-sized business that processes a large number of online transactions every day.

110 What processes are involved when an organisation undertakes 'risk analysis' in relation to its ICT systems?

111 Describe four elements you would expect to find in a large organisation's disaster recovery plan.

112 What steps should an organisation undertake to ensure that its employees comply with the Copyright Designs and Patents Act (1988), especially in regard to 'software piracy'?

113 The Computer Misuse Act identifies different categories of 'computer crime'. What difficulties have been encountered in enforcing the terms of this Act?

114 In relation to the Data Protection Act (1998), identify:
- four responsibilities of a data user
- two exemptions from the Act
- two functions of the Data Protection Registrar
- two rights of a data subject.

Management of information in an organisation

115 Many large organisations have 'tall' hierarchical structures. Identify some of the defining features of these structures.

116 Organisations have two choices regarding the management of information systems: a centralised model whereby all decisions have to pass through the ICT department and a decentralised model whereby different departments make ICT decisions more or less autonomously. What are the advantages of the centralised approach over the decentralised approach?

117 What are the advantages and disadvantages for an organisation of outsourcing some or all of its ICT functions?

118 Describe four factors that would need to be taken into consideration in the development of a corporate information systems strategy.

119 Explain fully how a client–server system works and how it can benefit the user and the organisation.

120 Peer-to-peer systems provide an alternative to a client–server strategy. Describe an organisation context where a peer-to-peer strategy might be preferred over a client–server strategy.

121 Describe what is meant by a Management Information System and explain how they are used by organisations to aid efficiency.

122 Explain the difference between batch processing and interactive processing. For each approach, describe an appropriate context for its use.

123 Explain what is meant by data warehousing and data mining and describe how an organisation might employ such facilities.

124 Explain how an expert system might help an organisation or individual in a work context.

125 Describe the different information needs of each of the following levels of management:
- strategic
- tactical
- operational

126 Explain the difference between formal and informal information flows within an organisation. Illustrate your answer with an example.

127 Sometimes a great deal of time and resources are put into the development of an information system which, often, fails. Explain some of the factors that are likely to lead to such a failure.

128 The introduction of new systems into organisations, especially those that entail a significant amount of change to working patterns, can create fear and anxiety amongst organisation members. Using appropriate examples outline some of these fears/anxieties.

129 What steps can an organisation take to manage successfully the change involved in the introduction of a new system?

130 Outline three reasons why an organisation might undertake an audit of its ICT systems.

131 Identify four reasons why an organisation may choose to upgrade a particular piece of hardware/software.

System development

132 In the context of the development of a new system, explain what is meant by the following:
- deliverable
- formal methods
- approval to proceed

133 Outline what you would expect to find discussed in a system feasibility report.

134 During the analysis phase, developers have to gather a great deal of information from parties both within and beyond the organisation. Outline three methods that might be used to gather this information.

135 Describe fully three tasks that would be undertaken during the design phase of the System Development Life Cycle.

136 In relation to the implementation of a new system, explain the difference between direct conversion, phased conversion and parallel conversion. Explain the advantages of each system.

137 Outline three methods that might be used to evaluate a new system after it has been implemented.

138 Despite rigorous testing, it is sometimes necessary for software developers to undertake maintenance on systems. Explain why this might happen and outline some of the different types of maintenance that might be undertaken.

139 Identify two different methods of training employees in the use of ICT systems. Describe what is involved in each approach and what its relative advantages and disadvantages are.

140 Why might an organisation choose to develop an in-house training facility rather than rely on external providers?

141 Explain, and illustrate with appropriate examples, three problems associated with running an in-house help desk.

142 Outline two different ways in which the effectiveness of a help desk can be evaluated.

143 Describe three tasks that would be undertaken by a project manager. Explain the importance of each task in relation to the successful development of the system.

144 Identify three attributes of an effective team. Explain, in the context of the development of ICT systems, the importance of each of these attributes.

145 Describe some of the different stages involved in testing a new system. Include in your answer a reference to Alpha and Beta testing.

146 State the purpose of entity relationship diagrams.

147 Explain the limitations and advantages of using questionnaires and observations in order to gather data.

Index